The politics of male friendship in contemporary American fiction

Manchester University Press

CONTEMPORARY AMERICAN AND CANADIAN WRITERS

series editors
Nahem Yousaf and Sharon Monteith

Also available

Crossing borders and queering citizenship: Civic reading practice in contemporary American and Canadian writing   ZALFA FEGHALI

The quiet contemporary American novel   RACHEL SYKES

Sara Paretsky: Detective fiction as trauma literature   CYNTHIA S. HAMILTON

Making home: Orphanhood, kinship, and cultural memory in contemporary American novels   MARIA HOLMGREN TROY, ELIZABETH KELLA, HELENA WAHLSTROM

Thomas Pynchon   SIMON MALPAS AND ANDREW TAYLOR

Jonathan Lethem   JAMES PEACOCK

Mark Z Danielewski   EDITED BY JOE BRAY AND ALISON GIBBONS

Louise Erdrich   DAVID STIRRUP

Passing into the present: Contemporary American fiction of racial and gender passing   SINÉAD MOYNIHAN

Paul Auster   MARK BROWN

Douglas Coupland   ANDREW TATE

Philip Roth   DAVID BRAUNER

The politics of male friendship in contemporary American fiction

Michael Kalisch

MANCHESTER UNIVERSITY PRESS

Copyright © Michael Kalisch 2021

The right of Michael Kalisch to be identified as the author of this work has been asserted by them in accordance with the Copyright, Designs and Patents Act 1988.

Published by Manchester University Press
Oxford Road, Manchester M13 9PL
www.manchesteruniversitypress.co.uk

British Library Cataloguing-in-Publication Data is available

ISBN 978 1 5261 5635 8 hardback
ISBN 978 1 5261 7204 4 paperback

First published by Manchester University Press in hardback 2021

This edition published 2023

The publisher has no responsibility for the persistence or accuracy of URLs for any external or third-party internet websites referred to in this book, and does not guarantee that any content on such websites is, or will remain, accurate or appropriate.

Typeset by Servis Filmsetting Ltd, Stockport, Cheshire

Contents

Series editors' preface	*page* vi
Acknowledgements	viii
Introduction	1
1 'The love alternative': Philip Roth's *I Married a Communist* (1998) and *The Human Stain* (2000)	29
2 The gift of friendship: Paul Auster's fiction and film	81
3 Broken utopias: Michael Chabon's *Telegraph Avenue* (2012) and Jonathan Lethem's *The Fortress of Solitude* (2003)	120
4 The borders of friendship: Dinaw Mengestu's *The Beautiful Things that Heaven Bears* (2007) and Teju Cole's *Open City* (2011)	175
Conclusion	202
Bibliography	213
Index	246

Series editors' preface

This innovative series reflects the breadth and diversity of writing over the last thirty years, and provides critical evaluations of established, emerging and critically neglected writers – mixing the canonical with the unexpected. It explores notions of the contemporary and analyses current and developing modes of representation with a focus on individual writers and their work. The series seeks to reflect both the growing body of academic research in the field, and the increasing prevalence of contemporary American and Canadian fiction on programmes of study in institutions of higher education around the world. Central to the series is a concern that each book should argue a stimulating thesis, rather than provide an introductory survey, and that each contemporary writer will be examined across the trajectory of their literary production. A variety of critical tools and literary and interdisciplinary approaches are encouraged to illuminate the ways in which a particular writer contributes to, and helps readers rethink, the North American literary and cultural landscape in a global context.

Central to debates about the field of contemporary fiction is its role in interrogating ideas of national exceptionalism and transnationalism. This series matches the multivocality of contemporary writing with wide-ranging and detailed analysis. Contributors examine the drama of the nation from the perspectives of writers who are members of established and new immigrant groups, writers who consider themselves on the nation's margins as well as those who chronicle middle America. National labels are the subject of vociferous debate and including American and Canadian writers in the same series is not to flatten the differences between them but to acknowledge that literary traditions and tensions are cross-cultural and that North American writers often explore and expose precisely these tensions. The series recognises that situating a writer in a cultural context involves a multiplicity of influences, social and geo-political, artistic and theoretical, and that contemporary fiction defies easy categorisation. For example, it examines writers who invigorate the genres in which they have made their mark alongside writers whose aesthetic goal is to subvert the idea of genre altogether. The challenge of defining the roles of writers and assessing their reception by reading communities is central to the aims of the series.

Overall, *Contemporary American and Canadian Writers* aims to begin to represent something of the diversity of contemporary writing and seeks to engage students and scholars in stimulating debates about the contemporary and about fiction.

Nahem Yousaf
Sharon Monteith

Acknowledgements

One of the great pleasures of working on this book has been the chance to talk shop (and football) with Kasia Boddy; I'm incredibly grateful for her guidance and kindness. My thanks also to David Brauner, for all his help along the way.

For financial support, I owe thanks to the School of Arts and Humanities at the University of Cambridge, and to the Trustees of the Henry Fund, who elected me to a Procter Fellowship at Princeton University, where the third chapter of the book was written. I'm also grateful to my editors, Sharon Monteith and Nahem Yousaf, for their advice and encouragement.

Harriet Baker made all the difference.

This book is dedicated with love to my parents.

Introduction

Set in 2003, with the Iraq invasion looming, Norman Rush's *Subtle Bodies* (2013) is the story of a group of male college friends reuniting in middle age to mourn the death of Douglas, the charismatic leader of their group.[1] At New York University together in the mid-1970s, the young men had thought of themselves as a clique of 'wits' who aspired to be 'social renovators of some unclear kind [...] by somehow generalizing their friendship' (*SB* 9, 11–12). In the intervening decades, however, both their friendship and their political commitment have waned: one friend owns 'an agency dedicated to creating public service announcements for television'; another is a stockbroker; a third, a cynical lawyer (41). Douglas became 'half-famous' in later life for debunking literary 'forgeries', but the friends begin to wonder whether he was in fact the real fake among them: were the politically tinged practical jokes they carried out together at college under Douglas's direction really incisively satirical, or just irritating (10)? And, given how they have all drifted apart, was their friendship genuine, or merely a kind of counterfeit?

Only Ned, the novel's protagonist, still seems to value the group's original idealism. Working for a Fair Trade co-operative, he devotes his spare time to organising a mass rally against the war and spends much of the novel trying to persuade his old friends to sign his petition opposing the invasion. Recalling his 1970s college days, Ned finds it 'embarrassing' how 'seriously he had taken the whole thing, the world remade, friendship at the core of everything' (48). But he remains invested in the idea that friendship might inform and inspire a broader kind of political engagement and solidarity. His wife, Nina, notes that Ned 'could still get solemn' talking about the group's hope for what they called 'molecular socialism' – a progressive politics grounded in their personal relationships that offers an alternative to normative family life (12, 48). As such, 'far from being spiritual as the title might imply, the question of friendship becomes a political one' in the novel.[2] Nicholas Dames suggests that *Subtle Bodies* mourns the political culture of the 1970s, a period marked by the 'decline of sixties radicalism', but in which a 'ramshackle', attenuated utopianism founded in collective action and community living still captivated the American New Left's imagination.[3] As well as an elegy for the counterculture, the novel is also a paean to an older ideal of male friendship. In his eulogy for Douglas, Ned reads from his friend's favourite book – a book partly about a male friendship: Boswell's *Life of Samuel Johnson*: 'We cannot tell the precise moment when friendship is formed' (234). If male friendship can seem utopian in the novel – capturing the promise of a 'world remade' – then *Subtle Bodies* also suggests that the time of male friendship and the time of mourning might be somehow linked. But by the end of the book the time of male friendship seems to have given way to another temporality, that of conception. As the narrative opens, Ned and Nina have been trying for their first child, and, as it closes, Nina finds out that she is pregnant.

In an interview, Rush suggests that although 'it's an old idea [...] I discovered when I began the book that the subject of male friendship is not a common one in literary fiction'.[4] Noting that 'the utopian function of friendship' pervades the 'old New Ages of Whitman and Edward Carpenter', and their celebrations of the democratic potential of comradely love, Rush claims that the theme of male friendship is largely absent from modern literature, and especially from the novel.[5] Speculating as to why this might be, Rush suggests that a 'reflexive tendency to analyze male friendships' as 'homosexual in nature would undoubtedly [have been] an inhibiting factor' throughout much of the twentieth century, while there 'has also been a shadow interpretation of many male friendships in literature as enactments of the search by a disillusioned son for a replacement father'. In other words, male friendship has often been read suspiciously, in literature as in life, as a cover story of sublimation or displacement of one kind or another, rather than as a relationship in its own right.

Rush is not alone in suggesting that the pathologising of homosexuality in the late nineteenth century made male friendship a site of cultural anxiety, and consequently a less popular and prominent literary theme. In fact, it has become something of a commonplace in histories of sexuality 'before homosexuality' to contrast the 'valences and nuances of love between men in pre-homosexual cultures' with the rigidity of the 'homosexual–heterosexual binary' of the twentieth century, and to suggest that male friendship became 'less visible and less of a topic to be discussed in literature' as a result.[6] In the twenty-first century, however, Rush wonders whether this is still the case. 'Times have changed radically', he asserts, 'and there is now more freedom to address the subject itself'. No longer such a source of defensive suspicion and misunderstanding, Rush argues, male friendship can again be explored in fiction.

This book argues that Rush is partly right. I demonstrate that male friendship does indeed re-emerge as a significant theme in late twentieth- and twenty-first-century American fiction, and I offer extended analyses of works by a broad and eclectic range of novelists, including Philip Roth, Paul Auster, Michael Chabon, Jonathan Lethem, Dinaw Mengestu, and Teju Cole. But I argue that the reasons behind this re-emergence are not only to do with changing societal attitudes towards male intimacy, as Rush implies. In fact, I argue that the tendency to understand the history of male friendship as only a facet of the history of sexuality obscures friendship's discrete philosophical and political genealogy. Moreover, it overlooks the central organising role friendship has played in how we imagine and practise citizenship, community, and democratic life more generally. Sharon Marcus makes a similar argument regarding friendship's place in the history of sexuality in *Between Women* (2007), her study of female friendship in Victorian fiction. Marcus notes that feminist critics from the 1970s through to the early 1990s placed women's friendships 'on a continuum with lesbian relationships'. And, while she acknowledges that the concept of a 'continuum' was 'once a powerful means of drawing attention to overlooked bonds between women', Marcus contends that it has also 'ironically obscured everything that female friendship and lesbianism did not share'.[7] Something similar might be said about recent critical studies of the literary and cultural history of male same-sex intimacy, wherein a corresponding concept of a 'continuum' between homosexuality and homosociality – derived from Eve Kosofsky Sedgwick's study *Between Men* (1985), to which Marcus's title alludes – has uncovered the historical congruencies between practices and representations of male friendship and homosexuality, but often at the risk of eliding the differences between them.[8]

Reading beyond the paradigm of sexuality, this book situates the re-emergence of male friendship in recent American fiction within three, interlinking critical contexts. As Rush notes, male friendship is 'an old idea', so I argue that, firstly, it is crucial to understand something of its importance in classical philosophy. Secondly, I suggest that portrayals of friendship between men in contemporary American fiction need to be contextualised within the long literary and cultural history of male friendship's distinctive, integral yet contested place in the US civic imaginary. And thirdly, I argue that the resurgence of interest in male friendship as a literary theme belongs to a broader cultural moment generally overlooked by literary critics, a moment in which not only novelists but also political theorists, sociologists, and philosophers turned to friendship to reimagine citizenship and political community. In *Subtle Bodies*, Ned and his college gang hope to 'somehow generaliz[e]' their friendship into a broader politics. In the next section of this Introduction, I show that, over the past four decades, there has been a far-reaching revival of critical interest in this very possibility.

Friendship, community, and liberalism's 'crisis of citizenship'

Joris – the cynical lawyer whom Ned has the most trouble convincing to sign his anti-war petition – is reading Morris Berman's bestseller *The Twilight of American Culture* (2000) (38). Mourning the collapse of civil society, Berman's diatribe draws a parallel between America at end-of-century and the final days of the Roman empire. Joris is similarly nihilistic. He tells Ned there is no point in political protest, or in fact in any form of civic participation: 'you can spend your whole life on it', he says, 'and you can die, and the next day the market is doing the same thing' (42). *Twilight of American Culture* takes its cues from Allan Bloom's *The Closing of the American Mind* (1987), the ur-text of the modern American jeremiad. But whereas Bloom's neo-conservative ire focuses on the university, Berman's critique is more eclectic, tackling not just education but corporate multinationalism and 'the replacement of intelligent citizens with mindless consumers'.[9] As Michiko Kakutani writes of the book's follow-up – the even bleaker *Dark Ages America* (2006) – *Twilight of American Culture* is 'the kind of book that gives the Left a bad name', a description that captures something of what Ned feels about Joris's fatalism.[10]

But there is another reason why Rush has Joris reading Berman's book. Joris realises that much of his pessimism stems from his increasing isolation after falling out of contact with the college gang. He acknowledges that 'he couldn't tell anyone' about difficulties in 'his private life, because he didn't have any friends' (38). Berman argues that Joris's situation is not unusual. In *Twilight*, he suggests that, 'real friendships require risk and vulnerability, and more and more Americans feel that they lack the psychological strength for that'. Instead, 'bottled rage and resentment are the norm as millions live in isolation, without any form of community'.[11] There 'is no genuine friendliness here, no community', Berman argues in *Dark Ages America*, because 'Americans care only about their individual lives'.[12]

Connecting a lack of friendship to a loss of community, and to a wider critique of liberal individualism, Berman (and Rush) echoes a concern that was widespread in late twentieth- and early twenty-first-century cultural criticism, political philosophy, and sociology. As Anthony Giddens, writing in the mid-1990s, notes, 'on each side of the political spectrum today we see a fear of social disintegration and a call for a revival of community'.[13] In *Liquid Modernity*, published in the same year as *Twilight*, Zygmunt Bauman similarly observes that Western liberal democracies are beginning to experience the 'corrosion and slow disintegration of citizenship'.[14] For Bauman, the problem is that 'somewhere along the line, friendship and solidarity, once upon a time major community-building materials, became too flimsy, too rickety or too watery for the purpose'.[15] This critique of liberalism's crisis of citizenship permeated mainstream American culture. Taking the decline of the local bowling league as symptomatic of a wider decline of civil society, Robert Putnam's bestseller *Bowling Alone* (2000) argues that modern Americans suffer from diminishing 'social capital' and, like Berman, concludes that the result is a loss of community.[16] Putnam's study draws on the findings of the sociologist Robert Bellah and his team in *Habits of the Heart* (1985), which decries the weakening 'sense of connection, shared fate, mutual responsibility, community' in a society where the 'individual can only rarely and with difficulty understand himself and his activities as interrelated in morally meaningful ways with those of other, different Americans'.[17]

The reasons given for this crisis of citizenship varied according to political perspective. Those on the Right pointed to the decline of 'family values', local voluntary association, faith, and morality – all of which are often traced to the cultural revolution of the 1960s, and the concomitant rise of feminism and identity politics – as causing a breakdown in the fabric of American society.[18] Those on the Left, meanwhile, identified as prime causes the 'privatization of the economy, the erosion of the welfare state, increased xenophobia in the face of rapid globalization and the passing of industrial labor' along with 'a relentless reemphasis on individualism and materialism' beginning in response to the political radicalism of the 1960s and 1970s.[19] A number of commentators summarise the transformation of citizenship and the political public sphere in America in the second half of the twentieth century using the same figure of chiasmus: the 1960s feminist-leftist maxim 'the personal is the political' has in subsequent decades been contorted into the conservative principle of 'the political is the personal'.[20]

However it has been explained, liberal democracy's crisis of citizenship became, as Giddens suggests, a serious concern across the political spectrum, with many arguing that the problem lay chiefly with the theory of liberalism itself. As Sybil Schwarzenbach summarises:

> in spite of the differences that might today distinguish many continental thinkers, socialists, Marxists, feminists, civic republicans, contemporary communitarians, and even conservative, religious fundamentalists from one another, one thing at least appears to unite them: the common belief that traditional liberalism has an inadequate conception of community.[21]

Addressing this inadequacy, commentators and theorists of all political stripes frequently reach for the same solution: a revitalised form of 'civic friendship'. In *Habits of the Heart*, for example, Bellah outlines a classical tradition in which 'friendship and its virtues are not merely private: they are public, even political, for a civic order, a city, is above all a network of friends'. Without such a network, 'a city will degenerate into a struggle of contending interest groups unmediated by any public solidarity'. In this tradition, friends must 'share a common commitment to the good' – a moral obligation that *Habits of the Heart* suggests is difficult to comprehend in a 'culture of utilitarian individualism'.[22]

More broadly, it is difficult to imagine friendship as a relationship with a political dimension, because 'the modern idea of friendship lies in its very freedom from public roles and obligations'.[23] On the whole, 'we think of friendship as a refuge from politics', rather than a site of its elaboration.[24] But *Habits of the Heart* offers a glimpse of the Aristotelian conception of civic friendship underpinning a whole swathe of 'communitarian' commentaries on liberal individualism from the past four decades that seek to revise the modern, privatised understanding of friendship. Communitarianism became something of a catch-all term in the 1980s and 1990s for a range of critiques that reasserted the importance of an active, engaged civic culture and challenged liberalism's atomistic conception of the individual, or what Michael Sandel, one of communitarianism's main proponents, calls 'the unencumbered self'.[25] A point of commonality among communitarians is an engagement with Aristotle's account of citizenship and political community in describing either an alternative or adjustment to liberalism's theory of the division between the private and public spheres. In the *Nicomachean Ethics*, Aristotle describes three categories of friendship: the useful, the pleasant, and the good. While friendships of the first two categories are common, friendships of the third kind are rare, taking time to build and trouble to maintain.[26] A friend of this category 'wishes for and does what is good or seems good for his friend for the friend's own sake'.[27] Elaborated through practices of generosity and reciprocity, such relationships engender a dynamic of mutual respect, care, and obligation, allowing for an understanding of the friend, in Aristotle's famous formulation, as 'another self'.[28] The lesser forms of friendship also involve aspects of this dynamic but in combination with other motivations; a good life will be composed of all three kinds of friendship. But Aristotle goes further, suggesting that friendship is necessary not only to the well-being of the individual but to the functioning and governance of the state. 'Friendship would seem to hold states together', he writes, 'and legislators would seem to be more concerned about it than about justice'. 'When men are friends', he argues, 'they have no need for justice'.[29] In both the *Politics* and the *Ethics*, friendship is pronounced to be the 'greatest good of the state', because of its 'binding effect on communities', and so 'community, justice, and friendship' are shown to be 'coextensive'.[30]

Reading Aristotle, it becomes clear that democracy 'finds its origin in a system of thought in which the idea of friendship is the major principle in terms of which political theory and practice are described, explained and analyzed'.[31] Over the past four decades, communitarian political theory has sought to test and build upon the connections Aristotle draws between friendship, citizenship, and community.[32] Alasdair MacIntyre, for example, offers a 'reconstructed version of Aristotle's conception of ethics', in which friendship is conceived of as 'being the sharing of all in the common project of creating and sustaining the life of the city, a sharing incorporated in the immediacy of an individual's particular friendship'.[33] For Michael Sandel, restoring friendship as a civic virtue would similarly make us aware of the 'constituent attachments' that shape who we are, and allow us to understand that 'knowing oneself [...] is a less strictly private thing' than liberal individualism assumes.[34] More recent studies also call for elaborating 'a new mode of citizenship in friendship understood not as an emotion but a practice', in Danielle Allen's phrase, and 'a set of hard-won, complicated habits that are used to bridge trouble, difficulty, and differences of personality, experience, and aspiration'.[35] Arguing that 'the problematic of a civic friendship between citizens is *the* forgotten problem of *modern* democratic theory', Sybil Schwarzenbach suggests that, 'for the construction of a plausible modern conception of a civic friendship between citizens, the vast repertoire of particular moral convictions hitherto relegated to the "private," the "personal," and the prepolitical "merely social" realm can no longer be excluded from the original data pool from which a political, reflective equilibrium begins'.³⁶

All of these theorisations of civic friendship call for a shift away from liberalism's familiar conception of 'negative liberty', in which the social contract protects the individual from the intrusions of other citizens and the state in order to maximise personal liberty, towards a conception of 'positive liberty', in which members of a political community acknowledge and negotiate the ways in which they are implicated in one another's freedom.³⁷ This particularist account of liberty counters the abstractions of liberal universalism and points instead to the '"thick" or embedded nature of ethicopolitical agency'.³⁸ Above all, these accounts of civic friendship each call for the reconstitution of the liberal dichotomy of public and private life. Each proposes that the virtues of personal friendship – justice, equality, empathy, reciprocity – should shape, inspire, and form the 'background condition' to interactions in and the institutions of the political public sphere.³⁹

The danger that these accounts of civic friendship risk is that they end up producing a normative conception of political community and citizenship. As Miranda Joseph notes in her critique of *Bowling Alone*, 'the social value of local community formation, for Putnam, is not in the challenges that such communities might offer to dominant regimes but rather in that they are sites of incorporation into hegemonic regimes'.⁴⁰ Bonnie Honig levels a similar charge at Sandel's communitarianism, suggesting that 'the ultimate aim of friendship in Sandel's community politics is to affirm and reinforce identification with community' in a process of 'perpetual reintegration'.⁴¹ Civic friendship therefore risks producing community and consensus at the expense of pluralism and democratic debate. This quandary animates Jacques Derrida's *The Politics of Friendship* (1997), the most prominent of a number of works of continental philosophy that have revisited the political philosophy of friendship.⁴² Surveying the Aristotelian classical tradition, Derrida is particularly troubled by the commonplace conceptual elision of the figure of the male friend, the brother, and the double. This elision institutes a political economy of sameness over difference, and is therefore, as Joseph and Honig also suggest, 'androcentric' and anti-pluralist.⁴³ Drawing on Carl Schmitt's account of the 'friend/enemy divide' as a structuring principle of political thought, Derrida demonstrates how the slippage between friendship and fraternity in particular produces a form of political community that is exclusionary, militaristic and repressive.[44] Yet he also suggests that the 'organising role' friendship plays in 'the definition of justice, democracy even' cannot be ignored.[45] Rather than abandon friendship as a political concept, Derrida asks his reader to instead reimagine a form of friendship 'beyond the principle of fraternity': 'Let us dream of a friendship that goes beyond this proximity of the congeneric double', he writes, towards 'a democracy to come'.[46]

A clue as to the shape of this 'democracy to come', and of the role of friendship in its elaboration, comes from the enigmatic apostrophe (traditionally though inaccurately attributed to Aristotle) that frames his study: 'O my friends, there is no friend'. This apostrophe 'negates friendship with the very same gesture by which it seems to invoke it'.[47] For Derrida, it therefore captures something of friendship's simultaneous necessity and impossibility as a structural concept in political philosophy, and gestures to his sense that friendship belongs to a 'temporality of that which cannot be fixed or even figured in the present'.[48] Analysing the canonical texts of friendship – Cicero's *De Amicita*, Montaigne's "On Friendship" – Derrida notes how many of these works are also works of mourning. This insight informs his conception of the experience of friendship as one shadowed by death; as he writes elsewhere, 'To have a friend, to look at him […] is to know in a more intense way […] that one of the two of you will inevitably see the other die'.[49] The time and experience of friendship is therefore at once utopian and mournful – forward-looking yet elegiac, a time of 'survival', but also of hope.[50]

In Derrida's deconstruction of the classical philosophy of friendship, the friend emerges as a less familiar figure, and the kinds of political community imaginable from such an altered conception of friendship are 'inoperative' and 'unavowable' rather than communitarian.[51] In an attempt to make it the grounds for a pluralistic politics of inclusion, what Derrida seeks to emphasise most is friendship's unknowability; as such, friendship represents one of the crucial terms of the 'political turn' in Derrida's later work, alongside 'cosmopolitanism' and 'hospitality' – both of which have received more attention from within literary studies.⁵² Leela Gandhi suggests that Derrida 'recognizes in the unscripted relation of "friendship" an improvisational politics appropriate to communicative, sociable utopianism, investing it with a vision of radical democracy'.⁵³ Accordingly, Gandhi's own study of fin-de-siècle radicalism follows Derrida in privileging 'the trope of friendship as the most comprehensive philosophical signifier for all those invisible affective gestures that refuse alignment along the secure axes of filiation to seek expression outside, if not against, possessive communities of belonging'.⁵⁴ In conceiving of friendship as the grounds for a politics of anticolonial resistance rather than of Aristotelian statehood and governance, Gandhi approvingly cites E. M. Forster's quintessentially liberal defence of personal freedom: 'if I had to choose between betraying my country and betraying my friend I hope I should have the guts to betray my country'.⁵⁵ Forster's sentiment finds something of an update in Michel Foucault's influential argument, in 'Friendship as a Way of Life' (1981), that friendship names a variety of 'intense relations' that 'short-circuit' the 'institutional codes' of 'law, rule, or habit', and the traditional nuclear family. Our 'sanitized culture' cannot allow a space for 'tenderness, friendship', Foucault writes, 'without fearing the formation of new alliances and the tying together of unforeseen lines of force'.⁵⁶ In this Foucaultian iteration, friendship is potentially a 'radical practice', one that 'might be capable of upending hierarchies, building community, and producing social change'.⁵⁷

Schematically, then, it is possible to distinguish two major strands to the resurgence of critical interest in the political philosophy of friendship emerging since the 1980s: the communitarian reading; and the Derridean–Foucaultian reading. Communitarianism revisits Aristotle's civic republicanism and attempts to update the classical conception of civic friendship for a modern polity. In so doing, communitarianism draws on a conservative discourse of personal responsibility, morality, and virtue. Yet many communitarian readings – especially those that engage with ideas of 'radical democracy' – also chime with a left-wing discourse of political agency, solidarity, and localism that are a legacy of experiments in collectivism and communal living from the 1960s and 1970s.⁵⁸ The Derridean–Foucaultian reading, meanwhile, attempts to defamiliarise the classical tradition upon which communitarianism rests. Derrida's critique makes less certain the kinds of community we find in and through friendship, and suggests that interactions between friends cannot be mapped and quantified in quite the way that Putnam's theory of 'social capital' would imply. Derrida thus develops a Foucaultian notion of friendship as an unpredictable relation of political opposition, one in which the institutional logics of the state and the family are queried and disrupted – friendship as a form of 'micro-political resistance', or a kind of 'molecular socialism', to recall Ned's term in *Subtle Bodies*.[59]

For all their purported oppositions, there are also significant overlaps between the two strands, such that the communitarian and Derridean–Foucaultian readings can be historicised as twinned critiques prompted by the same crisis of citizenship in late twentieth-century liberal democracy. Most obviously, both strands privilege friendship as the quintessential trope of 'democratic subjectivity', to borrow Derrida's phrase, and both employ friendship as the key figure for thinking through broader questions of citizenship, alliance, affiliation, and community. Despite their contrasting interpretations of Aristotle, both strands are drawn to friendship because it 'troubles the liberal conception of democracy with its distinct realms of political and cultural/private life'.[60] As Jon Soske and Joanna Walsh outline, friendships develop across 'multiple sites at once', forging links between the private sphere and 'the structures and networks that enable large-scale, formalised politics', traversing 'levels of analysis that social scientists and historians often treat separately: the local and the national, the economic and the political, the affective and the material, structure and agency'. In fact, they argue, 'friendship requires rethinking the question of *scale*' altogether.[61] A crucial facet of friendship's importance to political theorists and philosophers in this period is that it is a kind of interstitial social relation. Unsettling the familiar structures of the liberal imaginary, moving across and between the personal and the political, the local and the national, friendship reorders our sense of the foundations of and conditions for citizenship and political community.

In the chapters that follow, I argue that a broad range of contemporary writers are also drawn to friendship as a figure through which to query the scales of affiliation that shape American life, and to imagine how personal intimacies might inform public affiliations. In the rest of this Introduction, I outline two further frames of reference needed to fully understand the contemporary connection between friendship, politics, and the novel. Firstly, I turn more specifically to male friendship, and offer a *longue durée* account of its distinct role within American political, cultural and literary history. Focusing on contemporary literary studies, I then explore how an emphasis on the politics of male friendship in works by Roth, Auster, Chabon, Lethem, Mengestu, and Cole intervenes in current debates about the shape of the twenty-first-century literary field.

Male friendship in the American novel and civic imaginary

I have so far traced the re-emergence of civic friendship in late twentieth- and twenty-first-century political philosophy, and highlighted some points of contact between its place in mainstream American communitarianism and continental philosophy. This same period also saw a dramatic resurgence of critical interest in the social, political, and literary history of male friendship in America. As Janet Moore Lindman notes, a 'particularly active' area of research has been the history of male friendship and 'its relationship to sexuality, especially the homosocial and homosexual aspects of same-sex friendships'.[62] As I suggested earlier in reference to Sharon Marcus's *Between Women*, one origin point for this interest in male friendship is the work of feminist historians from the 1970s and 1980s who argued that a world of 'female love' and 'romantic friendship' flourished in nineteenth-century America.[63] Recent literary-cultural histories of male friendship by Axel Nissen and Caleb Crain, for example, have incorporated a version of the feminist 'romantic friendship' thesis into their work to argue that a world of 'male love' also developed in the period, and male friendship remains 'a consistently idealized model of same-sex relations' in queer studies.[64]

While the interrelation of the histories of friendship and sexuality is thus still a prominent topic, scholarly interest has also expanded in recent decades to include the political history of friendship in the

US, and specifically 'the overlapping ideals and practices of democracy and friendship' in the American civic imaginary.[65] Recent studies have considered the important role of 'friendship as a metaphor for political coexistence in revolutionary America', analysing how 'friendship remained a concept through which early Americans struggled to understand competing models of sociality and alliance' throughout the antebellum period and far beyond.[66] While historians of sexuality like Nissen and Crain have sought to emphasise the congruencies between practices of female and male friendship in the late eighteenth and early nineteenth centuries, when we turn to the *political* history of friendship in America in the same period, we see a starkly gendered division of roles. As Cassandra Good makes clear in *Founding Friendships* (2015), 'friendly bonds between men, in the tradition of ancient Greek and Roman history and philosophy, were deemed fundamental to political life'. While 'educated white women had a vital role to play in this new republic', Good writes, 'they were usually excluded from descriptions of civic friendship'.[67] Inspired by an 'Aristotelian concept of friendship as collective tissue', early Americans understood male friendships 'as crucial to the nation-building project and its creation of worthy republican citizens [...] encouraging empathy between citizens in a society that no longer cohered through shared loyalty to a monarch'.[68] While the separation from Britain was framed as a refusal of 'paternal authority', male friendship offered an alternative metaphor of civic association in the nascent independent nation.[69] Just as the rhetoric of the French Revolution interlinked *liberté* and *égalité* with *fraternité*, so too was the American Revolution galvanised by the egalitarian promise of friendship – even though of course this promise extended only to white men.

Given the complex and prominent role male friendship played in early American political discourse, it is not surprising to see the theme widely reflected in the nation's fiction. In the late eighteenth and early nineteenth centuries, 'the special task of American literature, like that of American politics, was the representation of bonds between men that kept men free – the provocation of sympathy, without any tethering to it'.[70] Ivy Schweitzer suggests that 'colonial and early national writers continually drew upon classical, Christian, and Enlightenment notions of friendship to fashion their accounts of American culture and politics and to script new modes of affiliation in the new world of colonial settlements, republicanism, and liberal democracy'.[71] Understanding male friendship as a 'politically-inflected cultural practice' that 'continually negotiates and mediates between liberty and equality, making the tension between the two possible to sustain', Schweitzer contends that it is in fictional portrayals of interracial male bonding that the cultural and political work of male friendship is most clearly visible.[72] She notes that, throughout nineteenth-century American literature, the 'mythology of male interracial friendship' is connected to a 'theoretical freedom from natural or biological obligation, social coercion, and institutional regulation', and that literary portrayals of interracial intimacy served as 'fictional embodiments of the Revolutionary ideal – however far from reality – enshrined in the Declaration of Independence: "all men are created equal"'.[73]

Schweitzer concentrates on a set of texts that she notes were 'elevated by later critics to "classic" status and inextricably linked with an American ideal of freedom and equality and the emerging nation itself'.[74] Here, she has in mind Leslie Fiedler's myth-and-symbol epic, *Love and Death in the American Novel* (1960), as well as his earlier article '"Come Back to the Raft Ag'in, Huck Honey!"' (1948), described by Ross Posnock as the 'most influential single essay ever written about American literature'.[75] The 'Fiedler thesis' held that, in contrast to the marriage plot structuring the European literary tradition, interracial 'immaculate male love' was at the heart of the American literary canon. Fiedler conceived of the 'counter-marriages' between James Fenimore Cooper's Natty Bumppo and Chingachgook in the *Leatherstocking* novels (1827–1841), Melville's Ishmael and Queequeg in *Moby-Dick* (1851), and Twain's Huck and Jim in *The Adventures of Huckleberry Finn* (1884) as an 'archetype' of 'classic' American literature, 'haunting almost all our major writers of fiction'.[76] A 'protest against the gentle tyranny of home and woman', these interracial friendships represent for Fiedler 'fragile utopian counter-spaces' that serve as a 'liminal site for male self-fulfilment in recoil from adult responsibility associated with female-dominated culture'.[77] Fiedler followed D. H. Lawrence in suggesting that these relationships were indicative of the 'immaturity' of American culture, but Lawrence also saw in the friendship of Natty Bumppo and Chingachgook a 'new relation' for the 'new world', and a 'clue' to a 'new society' away from 'the old authority of Europe'.[78] Fiedler similarly discerns in the relationship between Huck and Jim the democratic promise 'of a society in which, momentarily, the irreparable breach between black and white seems healed by love'.[79] Fiedler's argument has been 'bashed by critics both black and white' for its crude Freudianism, which often strays into racism and homophobia in its mapping of the American psyche. But despite his outmoded methodology, Lawrence Buell acknowledges that many critics have come to recognise that Fiedler nevertheless 'really seems to have been onto something significant about the (male) national imaginary'.[80]

Consistent with other cultural and literary histories of male friendship, Schweitzer argues that, by the late nineteenth century, 'friendship as the privileged site of sympathetic attachment became increasingly feminized, privatized, and removed from the public sphere of republican and democratic politics'.[81] She summarises the broader reasons for this transformation:

> [Male friendship's] power as a model for civic community waned in the face of liberal individualism, privatized domesticity, and the normativity of heterosexual marriage. By the twentieth century, Western culture developed an obsession with individual selfhood and sexual desire that marginalized friendship as a cogent social practice or civic ideal [...] [M]odern secular philosophy, especially liberal thought, emphasized individual selfhood and autonomy, relegating friendship and ethics to the private realm [...] and leaving the public sphere to the dictates of self-interest and market economics.[82]

This historicisation of male friendship has also been influential in the rise of so-called 'masculinity studies', which came to prominence in the 1980s and 1990s, and explores how the repertoire of same-sex intimacies available to heterosexual men had narrowed in the twentieth century. Most influentially, Michael Kimmel argues that the combination of the pathologisation of homosexuality and the 'economisation' of the male-dominated public sphere contributed to making 'homophobia, men's fear of other men,' the 'animating condition of the dominant definition of masculinity in America'.[83]

I have now shown how widespread the critical recovery of male friendship as a cultural practice, intellectual discourse, and object of study was in the last decades of the twentieth century, stretching across communitarian political theory, continental philosophy, histories of nineteenth-century American literature, emotion, and culture, and informing the rise of masculinity studies. What emerges most significantly from this recovery is an understanding of the dense interrelation of male friendship and politics in American history, and a clearer picture of the rich tradition of portrayals of male friendship – particularly interracial male friendship – in American literature. *The Politics of Male Friendship in Contemporary American Fiction* demonstrates how recent US fiction participates in this recovery, and explores how the contemporary novel has returned to male friendship as an evocative figure through which to reimagine forms of citizenship and political community.

In focusing exclusively on friendship between men, this book risks simply reproducing the exclusionary logic of civic friendship that I have shown marks its history in political thought. My decision to limit this study to male friendship is determined by three factors. Firstly and most importantly, the recent recovery of the history of friendship that I have been surveying reveals that male friendship has a distinct literary and philosophical lineage, and that the crucial tie between friendship and politics that is the subject of this book has historically been imagined as exclusively male – a factor that has shaped not only the practice of same-sex friendship for both men and women but also its place in the broader culture, whether in political philosophy or in the novel. Secondly, a specific set of historical conditions distinguish the history of male friendship in the twentieth and twenty-first centuries that require treating it as a discrete subject of inquiry, separate from female friendship and male–female friendship, chief among which is the pathologisation of homosexuality. While this book attempts to read beyond the paradigm of sexuality and to uncover the philosophical and political roots of contemporary portrayals of male friendship, it also recognises that this history has disciplined male intimacy in ways that have ultimately defined modern practices and representations of male friendship in ways quite different from female friendship. Thirdly, and more prosaically, this book also addresses a long-standing gender imbalance in the critical research of same-sex friendship, wherein female friendship has until very recently received much more scholarly attention; while there have been recent studies of political 'sisterhood' and interracial female friendship in contemporary fiction, there has been no such study of male friendship.[84]

Male friendship can be exclusionary in other ways, too. Critics of Fiedler's thesis have highlighted the violence that the fantasy of interracial male bonding obscures, and that the dream of black–white intimacy promulgated in the nineteenth-century novel was far removed from the historical reality. Critics of communitarianism have similarly noted that civic friendship's ambiguous mediation of the private and public spheres risks misrepresenting structural inequalities as problems to be solved at the level of personal relations, thus entrenching political discrimination. I argue that contemporary fiction recognises and engages with the limitations of male friendship as a political concept – and Chapters 3 and 4 pay particular attention to the issue of race. Nevertheless, I also argue that the authors I survey take seriously the utopian possibilities of friendship, even though the utopias they imagine are often male-only spaces. One of the through-lines connecting the nineteenth-century tradition of male bonding and the contemporary American novel is that male friendship continues to be a site of masculine fantasy, often imagined as an alternative to marriage and the other familiar scripts of heterosexual family life.

Yet crucial differences exist between the older tradition of male friendship in the American novel and its contemporary iterations. Whereas the interracial bonds of nineteenth-century fiction often appear to be a 'refuge' from history, male friendships in contemporary fiction are embedded *in* history.[85] Rather than taking place outside of society, the male friendships I survey are grounded in and mediate a range of other social and political structures, and exist within complex networks of other kinds of relations, including romantic partnerships, family bonds, mentorships, loose connections, neighbourhood camaraderies, local community, and citizenship. I argue that contemporary authors are drawn to male friendship as a figure through which to examine these interlinking forms and scales of affiliation shaping American society, and to critique their historical development within US liberal political culture. In the final section of this introduction, I explore how my concern with the novel's ability to speak to these wider processes of social formation chimes with a broader project in literary studies, aimed at assessing the changing political and historical imagination of contemporary fiction.

Critical paradigms

A number of critics in recent years have sought to map a 'post-postmodern aesthetics' emerging in American fiction of the past three or four decades, in 'the wake of postmodernism's waning influence'.[86] It has become commonplace to suggest that a prominent strand of contemporary fiction has spurned 'postmodern self-referentiality' and 'poststructural skepticism', and to argue that this rejection carries a critique of 'postmodernism's detachment from the social world'.[87] This movement away from postmodernism has been traced in the 'shifting status of irony' – often invoked, shorthand, as postmodernism's dominant affect – and in the emergence of a 'new sincerity' as a prominent contemporary cultural mode, capturing a 'renewed wish to return ethical intent to literature', and invested in 'generating empathy, communal bonds, ethical and political questions'.[88] Indeed, this broader link between the contemporary novel and a renewed interest in ethics and politics is crucial to most critical descriptions of post-postmodernism. Robert McLaughlin, for example, analyses recent fiction attempting to 'reenergise literature's social mission'.[89] Lee Konstantinou, meanwhile, tracks the development of 'postironic political commitment' in contemporary fiction, and Caren Irr surveys the recent 'resurgence of the political novel'.[90]

My focus on male friendship as a relationship of freely chosen association ideally modelling equality, and prefiguring a broader politics concerned with questions of community and citizenship, certainly speaks to the focus on ethical and political commitment that other critics have identified as characteristic of contemporary fiction. But most discussions of 'new sincerity' generally focus on a group of 'post-baby-boomer' authors who grew up in the 1970s, went to college and began writing in the heyday of high postmodernism and post-structuralism, with many subsequently honing their craft on postgraduate writing courses, and who came out the other side somewhat disaffected with both formal experimentalism and literary theory.[91] Rather than tell a simple story of a transition from postmodernism to post-postmodernism – as a study on, say, Don DeLillo, David Foster Wallace, Jennifer Egan, and Ben Lerner might – I complicate any argument for a generational shift in literary or intellectual outlook by bringing together writers of various ages to track the uneven development of post-1990s US fiction, and to highlight significant points of contact between writers whose careers began and developed in very different eras.

As well as post-postmodernism, another more established critical paradigm that this book queries is that of 'Jewish American fiction'. The novelists considered in the first three chapters are all Jewish, although the label 'Jewish American author' has been used to describe some of them more than others. Philip Roth always had a 'paradoxical' relationship with the identification, to put it mildly.[92] Part of a 'golden-age' of writers – along with Bernard Malamud and Saul Bellow – who were promoted, praised, and pigeonholed as Jewish American in the 1950s and 1960s, Roth always played with, up to, and against the categorisation, often insisting that he was simply an 'American' novelist, period. For Paul Auster, however, the issue seems hardly to have ever come up. Despite being from a similar background to Roth – born and raised in Newark, New Jersey, in a lower middle-class, religiously unobservant Jewish home – Auster's Jewishness is rarely mentioned in critical discussions of his work, in part it seems because his novels, unlike Roth's, appear to 'seldom address ethnicity or Jewish identity substantively'.[93] The same could be said of Jonathan Lethem. Growing up in a bohemian family in Brooklyn, Lethem felt that he 'made a very unconvincing Jew to other Jews – unobservant, un-Bar Mitzvah'd, attending Quaker Sunday school', while in his fiction 'Jewishness hovers enigmatically'.[94] By contrast, his close friend Michael Chabon is acknowledged as the leading light of a 'revival' of Jewish American fiction flourishing since the late 1990s.[95] This reputation was sealed with the publication of the Pulitzer-winning

The Amazing Adventures of Kavalier & Clay (2000), a novel which, according to D. G. Myers, represents Chabon's 'bid to enter the tradition' of Jewish American literature, because it deals prominently with recognisable Jewish themes, such as the immigrant experience in mid-twentieth-century America and the legacies of the Holocaust.[96]

The contrasting reception histories of these writers reveal that the critical application of the label 'Jewish American author' has less to do with whether the author is Jewish (though that's a necessary condition) than with the perceived Jewishness of the content or thematic preoccupations of their work. The problem with such a definition is the question of what counts as Jewish content.[97] Is it limited, say, to what I have described above as 'recognisable Jewish themes', such as the immigrant experience and the Holocaust? If so, then the chapters that follow present us with an irony, because these themes are explored in the most detail not by any of the Jewish authors discussed but by Dinaw Mengestu and especially Teju Cole, whose novel *Open City* (2011) – about a German-Nigerian psychiatrist in New York – is preoccupied with the memorialisation of the Holocaust. I do not leave behind the issue of Jewish identity; it is an important context throughout, and particularly in Chapter 3's examination of male friendship between Jewish and African American characters in Lethem's and Chabon's fiction. But in reading 'Jewish American' novels alongside fictions of African migration, I reveal unusual affinities between groups of writers rarely, if ever, discussed together, but whose work shares an interest in male friendship as a figure through which to explore broader themes of belonging, citizenship, and community.

I begin by looking at two novels from Roth's 'American Trilogy' (1997–2000), a series of historical fictions that have been read as part of a broader 'national turn' in Roth's later work in which he surveys the course of twentieth-century American liberalism. I analyse how the novels' attempts to address national politics are also framed as attempts to address a single male friend. Chapter 2 draws on the anthropology of the gift to examine forms of reciprocity between male friends in Paul Auster's fiction, arguing that Auster critiques liberal individualism by imagining networks of solidarity and alliance born of generosity. Chapter 3 turns to Jonathan

Lethem's *The Fortress of Solitude* (2003) and Michael Chabon's *Telegraph Avenue* (2012), two sprawling neighbourhood novels in which the central interracial male friendships are freighted with the legacies of 1960s and 1970s political radicalism. Chapter 4 broadens the book's focus by connecting friendship to cognate discourses of cosmopolitanism and globalisation through a close reading of Dinaw Mengestu's *The Beautiful Things that Heaven Bears* (2007) and Cole's *Open City*, arguing that the male friendships at the heart of these novels become sites for exploring issues of identity and belonging confronting their immigrant narrators. In the Conclusion, I briefly turn to Benjamin Markovits's *You Don't Have to Live Like This* (2015), a novel about gentrification in post-credit-crunch Detroit in which an interracial male friendship refracts my central themes of citizenship and community. Whether imagining civic ties within a neighbourhood, a nation, or a global public, for this diverse group of writers male friendships are relationships of democratic possibility through which the forms and scales of political life are mediated and contested. For Roth, thinking about these democratic possibilities leads back to the sentimental, 'fraternal' Popular Front politics of the 1940s and 1950s, by way of a conversation between two old friends, sitting out under a big sky in rural New England.

Notes

1 Norman Rush, *Subtle Bodies* (New York: Knopf, 2013). Subsequent references are given in the text as *SB* and in parentheses.
2 Jenny Hendrix, 'Empty Chairs at Empty Tables: Norman Rush's *Subtle Bodies*', *Los Angeles Review of Books*, 9 September 2013.
3 Nicholas Dames, 'Seventies Throwback Fiction: A Decade in Review', *n+1*, 21 (Winter 2014).
4 Tim Horvath, '*Subtle Bodies*: An Interview with Norman Rush', *Tin House*, 25 November 2013.
5 On comradeship in Whitman and Carpenter, see Kirsten Harris, *Walt Whitman and British Socialism: 'The Love of Comrades'* (London: Routledge, 2016), 30–64.
6 Axel Nissen, *Manly Love: Romantic Friendship in American Fiction* (Chicago: University of Chicago Press, 2009), 6, 14; Peter Nardi,

'Friendship', in Michael Kimmel and Amy Aronson (eds), *Men and Masculinities: A Social, Cultural, and Historical Encyclopaedia* (Santa Barbara: ABC-Clio Press, 2004), pp. 321–324 (321).
7 Sharon Marcus, *Between Women: Friendship, Desire, and Marriage in Victorian England* (Princeton: Princeton University Press, 2007), 29.
8 See Nissen, *Manly Love*; Caleb Crain, *American Sympathy: Men, Friendship, and Literature in the New Nation* (New Haven: Yale University Press, 2001); Jonathan Ned Katz, *Love Stories: Sex Between Men Before Homosexuality* (Chicago: University of Chicago Press, 2003); Eve Kosofsky Sedgwick, *Between Men: English Literature and Male Homosocial Desire* (New York: Columbia University Press, 1985).
9 Morris Berman, *The Twilight of American Culture* (New York: Norton, 2000), 35.
10 Michiko Kakutani, 'Grim View of a Nation at the End of Days', *New York Times*, 16 June 2006.
11 Berman, *Twilight of American Culture*, 55.
12 Morris Berman, *Dark Ages America: The Final Phase of Empire* (New York: Norton, 2006), 102.
13 Anthony Giddens, *Beyond Left and Right: The Future of Radical Politics* [1994] (Cambridge: Polity, 2007), 124.
14 Zygmunt Bauman, *Liquid Modernity* (Cambridge: Polity, 2000), 36.
15 Zygmunt Bauman, *In Search of Politics* (Stanford: Stanford University Press, 1999), 14.
16 Robert Putnam, *Bowling Alone: The Collapse and Revival of American Community* (New York: Simon & Schuster, 2000).
17 Robert Bellah et al., *Habits of the Heart: Individualism and Commitment in American Life* [1985] (Berkeley: University of California Press, 2008), xxxviii, 50.
18 Gerard Delanty notes that cultural criticism like *Bowling Alone* 'tends to look backwards to the time when liberal Protestant values held American society together'. Delanty, *Community* (London: Routledge, 2003), 65. See also Miranda Joseph, *Against the Romance of Community* (Minneapolis: University of Minnesota Press, 2002), 6–15.
19 Christopher Castiglia, *Interior States: Institutional Consciousness and the Inner Life of Democracy in the Antebellum United States* (Durham, NC: Duke University Press, 2008), 1; Magali Cornier Michael, *New Visions of Community in Contemporary American Fiction: Tan, Kingsolver, Castillo, Morrison* (Iowa City: University of Iowa Press, 2006), 14.
20 For examples of this figure of chiasmus, see Lauren Berlant, *The Queen of America Goes to Washington City: Essays on Sex and Citizenship*

(Durham, NC: Duke University Press, 1997), 177–178; Marianne DeKoven, *Utopia Limited: The Sixties and the Emergence of the Postmodern* (Durham, NC: Duke University Press, 2004), 190–191; Michael Kaplan, *Friendship Fictions: The Rhetoric of Citizenship in the Liberal Imaginary* (Tuscaloosa: University of Alabama Press, 2010), 5; Matthew Crenson and Benjamin Ginsberg, *Downsizing Democracy: How America Sidelined Its Citizens and Privatized Its Public* (Baltimore: Johns Hopkins University Press, 2002), 7.
21 Sibyl Schwarzenbach, *On Civic Friendship: Including Women in the State* (New York: Columbia University Press, 2009), 3.
22 Bellah et al., *Habits of the Heart*, 115–117.
23 Ray Pahl, *On Friendship* (London: Polity, 2000), 37.
24 Gregory Jusdanis, *A Tremendous Thing: Friendship from The Iliad to the Internet* (Ithaca: Cornell University Press, 2014), 21.
25 Michael Sandel, *Liberalism and the Limits of Justice* (Cambridge: Cambridge University Press, 1982), 182.
26 Aristotle, *Nicomachean Ethics*, Book VIII, 1156b, trans. Roger Crisp (Cambridge: Cambridge University Press, 2000), 145–147.
27 Lorraine Smith Pangle, *Aristotle and the Philosophy of Friendship* (Cambridge: Cambridge University Press, 2002), 142.
28 Aristotle, *Nicomachean Ethics*, Book IX, 1166a31–32, Crisp, 169.
29 Aristotle, *Nicomachean Ethics*, Book VIII, 1155a22–28, Crisp, 144.
30 Suzanne Stern-Gillet, *Aristotle's Philosophy of Friendship* (Albany: State University of New York Press, 1995), 45; David Riesback, *Aristotle on Political Community* (Cambridge: Cambridge University Press, 2016), 81.
31 Horst Hutter, *Politics as Friendship: The Origins of Classical Notions of Politics in the Theory and Practice of Friendship* (Waterloo: Wilfrid Laurier University Press, 1978), 2.
32 The rediscovery of Aristotle's philosophy of friendship has extended far beyond communitarian political theory. For a full bibliographic account, see Heather Devere, 'Amity Update: The Academic Debate on Friendship', *AMITY: The Journal of Friendship Studies*, 1:1 (2013), pp. 5–33.
33 Stephen Mulhall and Adam Swift, *Liberals and Communitarians* [1992] (Oxford: Blackwell, 1996), 81. See Alasdair MacIntyre, *After Virtue: A Study in Moral Theory* (London: Duckworth, 1981).
34 Sandel, *Liberalism and the Limits of Justice*, 182.
35 Danielle Allen, *Talking to Strangers: Anxieties of Citizenship since Brown v. Board of Education* (Chicago: University of Chicago Press, 2004), 157, xxi.

36 Schwarzenbach, *On Civic Friendship*, xiii, 8. Emphasis in original.
37 See Evert Van Der Zweerde, 'Friendship and the Political', *Critical Review of International Social and Political Philosophy*, 10:2 (2007), pp. 147–165 (153–155).
38 Leela Gandhi, *Affective Communities: Anticolonial Thought, Fin-de-Siècle Radicalism, and the Politics of Friendship* (Durham, NC: Duke University Press, 2006), 24. See also Mulhall and Swift, *Liberals and Communitarians*, 128–130.
39 Schwarzenbach, *On Civic Friendship*, 59.
40 Joseph, *Against the Romance of Community*, 12.
41 Bonnie Honig, *Political Theory and the Displacement of Politics* (Ithaca: Cornell University Press, 1993), 179.
42 See also Gilles Deleuze and Félix Guattari, *What Is Philosophy?*, trans. Hugh Tomlinson and Graham Burchell (New York: Columbia University Press, 1994), 1–35; Maurice Blanchot, *Friendship* [1971], trans. Elizabeth Rottenberg (Stanford: Stanford University Press, 1997).
43 See Samir Haddad, *Derrida and the Inheritance of Democracy* (Bloomington: Indiana University Press, 2013), 100–119.
44 Jacques Derrida, *The Politics of Friendship*, trans. George Collins [French, 1994; English, 1997] (London: Verso, 2005), 113–137.
45 Jacques Derrida and Geoffrey Bennington, 'Politics and Friendship: A Discussion with Jacques Derrida', 1 December 1997, http://hydra.humanities.uci.edu/derrida/pol+fr.html (inc http because no www).
46 Derrida, *The Politics of Friendship*, 12, vii.
47 Giorgio Agamben, *What Is an Apparatus?*, trans. David Kishik and Stefan Pedatella (Stanford: Stanford University Press, 2009), 26.
48 Pheng Cheah and Suzanne Guerlac, 'Introduction', in Cheah and Guerlac (eds), *Derrida and the Time of the Political* (Durham, NC: Duke University Press, 2009), pp. 1–37 (11).
49 Jacques Derrida, *The Work of Mourning*, ed. Pascale-Anne Brault and Michael Naas (Chicago: University of Chicago Press, 2001), 107.
50 Derrida, *The Politics of Friendship*, 12.
51 See Jean-Luc Nancy, *The Inoperative Community*, trans. Peter Connor, Lisa Garbus, Michael Holland, and Simona Sawhney (Minneapolis: University of Minnesota Press, 1991); Maurice Blanchot, *The Unavowable Community*, trans. Pierre Joris (Barrytown: Station Hill Press, 1988).
52 See, for example, Katherine Hallemeier, *J. M. Coetzee and the Limits of Cosmopolitanism* (Basingstoke: Palgrave Macmillan, 2013).
53 Gandhi, *Affective Communities*, 19.
54 Gandhi, *Affective Communities*, 10.

55 E. M. Forster, *Two Cheers for Democracy* (London: Edward Arnold, 1951), 66, quoted in Gandhi, *Affective Communities*, 10.
56 Michel Foucault, 'Friendship as a Way of Life', in *Ethics: Subjectivity and Truth*, ed. Paul Rabinow, trans. Robert Hurley et al. (New York: New York Press, 1997), pp. 135–140 (137–138).
57 Laura Forster, 'Radical Friendship', *History Workshop Online*, 10 June 2020.
58 See Paul Lichterman, *The Search for Political Community: American Activists Reinventing Commitment* (Cambridge: Cambridge University Press, 1996), 213–230; Chantal Mouffe, 'Democratic Citizenship and the Political Community', in Chantal Mouffe (ed.), *Dimensions of Radical Democracy: Pluralism, Citizenship, and Community* (London: Verso, 1992), pp. 225–239.
59 Todd May, *Friendship in an Age of Economics: Resisting the Forces of Neoliberalism* (Lanham: Rowman & Littlefield, 2012), 59.
60 Jon Soske and Joanna Walsh, 'Thinking About Race and Friendship in South Africa', in Soske and Walsh (eds), *Ties that Bind: Race and the Politics of Friendship in South Africa* (Johannesburg: Wits University Press, 2016), pp. 3–30 (13).
61 Soske and Walsh, 'Thinking About Race and Friendship in South Africa', 12. Emphasis in original.
62 Janet Moore Lindman, 'Histories of Friendship in Early America: An Introduction', *Journal of Social History*, 50:4 (2017), pp. 603–608 (604).
63 See Caroll Smith-Rosenberg, 'The Female World of Love and Ritual: Relations between Women in Nineteenth-Century America', *Signs*, 1:1 (Autumn 1975), pp. 1–29; Lillian Faderman, *Surpassing the Love of Men: Romantic Friendship and Love Between Women, from the Renaissance to the Present* (London: Women's Press, 1981).
64 Heather Love, *Feeling Backward: Loss and the Politics of Queer History* (Cambridge, MA: Harvard University Press, 2007), 76. See Crain, *American Sympathy*, and Nissen, *Manly Love*.
65 Dana Nelson, 'Cooper's Leatherstocking Conversations: Identity, Friendship, and Democracy in the New Nation', in Leland Person (ed.), *A Historical Guide to James Fenimore Cooper* (Oxford: Oxford University Press, 2007), pp. 123–155 (133).
66 Jusdanis, *A Tremendous Thing*, 19; Castiglia, *Interior States*, 24.
67 Cassandra Good, *Founding Friendships: Friendships Between Men and Women in the Early American Republic* (Oxford: Oxford University Press, 2015), 3.
68 Jusdanis, *A Tremendous Thing*, 49; Richard Godbeer, *The Overflowing*

of Friendship: Love Between Men and the Creation of the American Republic (Baltimore: Johns Hopkins University Press, 2009), 12.
69 Holly Jackson, American Blood: The Ends of the Family in American Literature, 1850–1900 (Oxford: Oxford University Press, 2014), 4.
70 Crain, American Sympathy, 2.
71 Ivy Schweitzer, Perfecting Friendship: Politics and Affiliation in Early American Literature (Chapel Hill: University of North Carolina Press, 2006), 22.
72 Schweitzer, Perfecting Friendship, 9, 6.
73 Schweitzer, Perfecting Friendship, 9, 134.
74 Schweitzer, Perfecting Friendship, 8.
75 Ross Posnock, 'Innocents at Home', Bookforum (Summer 2003).
76 Leslie Fiedler, Love and Death in the American Novel [1960] (Champaign: Dalkey Archive Press, 2003), 349.
77 Fiedler, Love and Death in the American Novel, 194; Lawrence Buell, The Environmental Imagination: Thoreau, Nature Writing, and the Formation of American Culture (Cambridge, MA: Harvard University Press, 1995), 35.
78 D. H. Lawrence, Studies in Classic American Literature [1923], ed. Ezra Greenspan, Lindeth Vasey, and John Worthen (Cambridge: Cambridge University Press, 2003), 58.
79 Fiedler, Love and Death in the American Novel, 353.
80 Lawrence Buell, The Dream of the Great American Novel (Cambridge, MA: Harvard University Press, 2014), 510, n. 12. See also Robyn Wiegman, American Anatomies: Theorizing Race and Gender (Durham, NC: Duke University Press, 1995).
81 Schweitzer, Perfecting Friendship, 10. See also Jusdanis, A Tremendous Thing, 52–53; Godbeer, The Overflowing of Friendship, 196.
82 Schweitzer, Perfecting Friendship, 10–11.
83 Michael Kimmel, 'Masculinity as Homophobia: Fear, Shame, and Silence in the Construction of Gender Identity', in Mary Gergen and Sara Davis (eds), Toward a New Psychology of Gender (New York: Routledge, 1997), pp. 223–245 (237).
84 See Sharon Monteith, Advancing Sisterhood?: Interracial Friendships in Contemporary Southern Fiction (Athens: University of Georgia Press, 2000).
85 Schweitzer, Perfecting Friendship, 136.
86 Adam Kelly, 'Beginning with Postmodernism', Twentieth-Century Literature, 75:3–4 (Fall/Winter 2011), pp. 391–422 (392); Andrew Hoberek, 'Introduction: After Postmodernism', Twentieth-Century Literature, 53:3 (Fall 2007), pp. 233–247 (233).

87 Robert McLaughlin, 'Post-Postmodern Discontent: Contemporary Fiction and the Social World', *symplokē*, 12:1/2 (2004), pp. 53–68 (55, 58); Ian Williams, '(New) Sincerity in David Foster Wallace's "Octet"', *Critique: Studies in Contemporary Fiction*, 56:3 (2015), pp. 299–314 (301).

88 Amy Hungerford, 'On the Period Formerly Known as Contemporary', *American Literary History*, 20:1–2 (Spring/Summer 2008), pp. 410–419 (415); Adam Kelly, 'Moments of Decision in Contemporary American Fiction: Roth, Auster, Eugenides', *Critique: Studies in Contemporary Fiction*, 51:4 (2010), pp. 313–332 (328); Mary K. Holland, *Succeeding Postmodernism: Language and Humanism in Contemporary American Literature* (London: Bloomsbury, 2013), 17.

89 McLaughlin, 'Post-Postmodern Discontent', 55.

90 Lee Konstantinou, *Cool Characters: Irony and American Fiction* (Cambridge, MA: Harvard University Press, 2016), 275; Caren Irr, *Toward the Geopolitical Novel* (New York: Columbia University Press, 2013), 3.

91 See Nicholas Dames, 'The Theory Generation', *n+1*, 14 (Summer 2012).

92 David Brauner, *Philip Roth* (Manchester: Manchester University Press, 2007), 12.

93 Alys Moody, 'Eden of Exiles: The Ethnicities of Paul Auster's Aesthetics', *American Literary History*, 28:1 (Spring 2016), pp. 69–93 (69).

94 Jonathan Lethem, 'My Egyptian Cousin', *London Review of Books*, 24:24 (12 December 2002), p. 22; Blake Eskin, 'Brooklyn Dodger', *Tablet*, 22 October 2003.

95 Derek Parker Royal, 'Introduction', in Royal (ed.), *Unfinalized Moments: Essays in the Development of Contemporary Jewish American Narrative* (West Lafayette: Purdue University Press, 2011), pp. 1–11 (2).

96 D. G. Myers, 'Michael Chabon's Imaginary Jews', *The Sewanee Review*, 116:4 (Fall 2008), pp. 572–588 (578).

97 See Hana Wirth-Nesher, 'Defining the Indefinable: What Is Jewish Literature?', in Wirth-Nesher (ed.), *What Is Jewish Literature?* (Philadelphia: The Jewish Publication Society, 1994), pp. 3–12.

1

'The love alternative': Philip Roth's *I Married a Communist* (1998) and *The Human Stain* (2000)

'the joining of the public and the private'

'I knew the phone would be off the hook the day Kakutani's review of IMAC [*I Married a Communist*] appeared', Jack Miles wrote in a letter faxed to his friend Philip Roth on 6 October 1998.[1] In that morning's *New York Times*, the paper's chief book reviewer had judged Roth's latest novel to be lacking the 'capacious social vision' of his previous book, the Pulitzer Prize-winning *American Pastoral* (1997).[2] Michiko Kakutani wrote that *I Married a Communist* was a 'smaller, less ambitious work' that remained 'hogtied to a narrow, personal agenda'. While it 'purports to do for the cold war period what [*American Pastoral*] did for the era of Vietnam', the novel was in fact Roth's 'revenge on his former wife, Claire Bloom', for her tell-all memoir of their marriage, *Leaving a Doll's House* (1996). But what Kakutani was 'incapable of appreciating', according to Miles, was the novel's 'portrayal of male friendship'. 'Friendship between men' is 'a common subject, but, as I believe I have said to you once already, friendship between the older and the oldest [...] is not a common subject at all in fiction'. Back in June that same year, Miles wrote to Roth to say that he thought *I Married a Communist*'s 'picture of friendship between an ageing man and an old man' one of its great strengths.[3] The intimacy between the novel's two narrators – Nathan Zuckerman, Roth's perennial 'alter brain', now in his early sixties, and his former high-school English teacher, ninety-year-old Murray Ringold – reminded Miles of the father–son relationship at the centre of Roth's memoir, *Patrimony* (1991).[4] 'But there are differences, obviously', he acknowledged.

'The old student and the old teacher are not just looking back together. Each is looking back through the other's eyes.'[5]

Kakutani's negative appraisal of *I Married a Communist* accords with the critical consensus that has emerged around the novel, while also reflecting a curious disjuncture within the broader reception history of the American Trilogy. As Philipp Löffler observes, while the series 'became a contemporary classic within the first years after its completion [...] when critics speak about the trilogy', they in fact 'mostly mean *American Pastoral* and *The Human Stain*, not knowing exactly what to do with *I Married a Communist*'.[6] It is by now a 'critical commonplace' that Roth began a 'career resurgence' with the trilogy's publication.[7] 'Much celebrated for Roth's turn toward social issues', the series was praised for moving 'beyond the narrow psychosexual concerns' of his earlier work and instead turning 'outward (and backward) to consider America's transformation during the postwar era'.[8] Although 'Roth's fiction has always been characterised by the tension between the individual capacity for self-determination and the deterministic forces of history', in the trilogy he seemed for the first time to 'write the individual into the fabric of history'.[9] Addressing the central 'historical moments in postwar American life', the three novels cumulatively offer a panoramic and 'intensely disenchanted view of the course of postwar liberalism', marking a significant 'historical' and 'national' turn in Roth's fiction.[10] Roth himself suggested that the books reveal 'something that had never been freed in my work before [...] the joining of the public and the private'.[11]

As Löffler intimates, however, the rapid canonisation of the American Trilogy has really rested on the reception of *American Pastoral* and *The Human Stain*; the 'middle' novel of the trilogy has been far from 'central' to most critical accounts.[12] In this chapter, I argue that this oversight is due to the fact that most discussions of the novel follow Kakutani in overlooking the male friendship that structures *I Married a Communist*. Miles suggests that, by missing the friendship between Nathan and Murray, Kakutani misses something important about the novel's historical imagination, because the novel's analysis of the political culture of the late 1940s and early 1950s is very deliberately shown to emerge from a conversation between friends, whose sense of the past and sense of themselves changes when seen 'through the other's eyes'. Rather than a work of straightforward historical realism, then, *I Married a Communist* is concerned with modes of historical sense-making – a preoccupation it shares with many historical fictions written after the so-called end of history.[13] But its focus on friendship marks it as a novel of the 1990s in other ways, too. In what follows, I read the novel alongside some of the late twentieth-century communitarian critiques of liberal individualism discussed in my Introduction. I also connect the novel to contemporaneous revisionist histories of the Popular Front, to suggest that Roth's depiction of male friendship is part of his broader survey of 'the course of postwar liberalism', and integral to his exploration of 'the joining of the public and the private'. I argue, in other words, that Nathan and Murray's friendship has a politics, a politics that complicates existing critical accounts of the novel's portrayal of the sentimental civic culture of the Popular Front.[14]

Miles's letter also notes that depictions of late-in-life male friendship are rare in fiction. When we think of literary portrayals of male friendship, we likely still think of Leslie Fiedler's heroic 'buddies', and his analysis of classic American fiction as a literature of 'boys' books'.[15] But in the American Trilogy – a series clearly in dialogue with nineteenth-century American literature – friendship between men belongs to the experience of old age, rather than that of youthful innocence.[16] The concluding volume of the trilogy, *The Human Stain*, is also the story of a friendship between two men at different stages of old age. In the final part of this chapter, I will argue that its central relationship, between Nathan and Classics professor Coleman Silk, is similarly important to understanding the novel's historical imagination. Nathan's narrative task in that novel appears to be that of an observer, piecing together the facts of Coleman's personal history. But it quickly becomes apparent that his role extends far beyond this; often we see Nathan imagining scenes, inventing conversations, and misconstruing events.[17] His narrative position seems similar in *American Pastoral*, where he more readily admits that his portrayal of his old high-school football idol, Seymour 'Swede' Levov, is largely fictional. By 'gazing into [the Swede's] life', Nathan writes near the book's opening, 'I dreamed a realistic chronicle'.[18] Nathan's portraits of the Swede and Coleman might seem to be further variations in his ongoing project of vicarious 'counterliving' – his trademark narrative art of conjuring alternative histories and fictive biographies of those around him through a high-wire combination of invention and impersonation.[19] Versions of counterliving play out throughout the 'Zuckerman Books'.[20] In *The Ghost Writer* (1979), twenty-three-year-old Nathan, staying at the home of his literary idol E. I. Lonoff, imagines that the writer's assistant, Amy Bellette, is in fact Anne Frank (and imagines himself married to her). In *The Counterlife* (1986), the recursive, reiterative narratives of the lives (and apparent deaths) of Nathan and his brother Henry overlap such that their stories become 'twinnishly' entwined.[21] 'We are all the invention of each other', Nathan suggests in that novel, 'everybody a conjuration conjuring everyone else'.[22]

While it is true that Nathan's 'manipulative and even mischievous side has carried over' into the trilogy from the previous books, *The Human Stain* is not simply another experiment in counterliving.[23] This becomes clearer when the novel is read alongside *I Married a Communist*, the book that immediately precedes it in the trilogy, rather than *American Pastoral*, as is more often the case. I argue that it is Nathan's friendship with Coleman that gives the novel its particular (and peculiar) form, and it is their relationship that comes to define the novel's engagement with history. I suggest that the novel might be reread not only as a 'national epic' but as an elegy for, and a bearing witness to, a singular, personal friendship.[24] Thinking about the demands made by friendship in each of these novels – and especially by the death of the friend – reframes critical accounts of the trilogy's exploration of American identity and history. If these novels address the nation, I argue that they do so by first addressing the friend.

Examining the role of male friendship in these novels challenges much of the existing commentary on masculinity and gender in Roth's work. While many critics might agree with Roth's own assessment that 'the lives of men has been my subject', few have judged same-sex friendship to be important to his portrayal of male identity.[25] Roth is often 'caricatured as a great propagandist of patriarchy', and most critiques of gender relations in his work have focused on his depictions of women, and the charge that his fiction is misogynistic.²⁶ Recently, however, some critics have suggested that his work 'can appear as much a prescient critique of misogynist attitudes as a purveyor of them', because his novels knowingly satirise 'the acute, even hysterical, sensitivity of the masculine self to its own insecurity and vulnerability'.²⁷ Certainly, many of Roth's male characters seem to be ensnared rather than emboldened by what Peter Tarnopol, the protagonist of *My Life as a Man* (1974), calls 'the myth of male inviolability'.²⁸ 'Under the terms of the myth', Debra Shostak writes, 'a man's sense of power relative to other men is key' to attaining a stable sense of male identity.²⁹ In this defensive conception of masculinity, 'affection represents a threat to the male self', leaving little room for same-sex friendship.³⁰

Often in Roth's earlier work, encounters between men seem fraught with suspicion and not a little homosexual panic. This is revealed in Roth's recurrent interest in doubles, or 'secret sharers' – the Conradian term used in *Zuckerman Unbound* (1981) to describe the uncanny Alvin Pepler, a motormouth ex-marine and aspiring writer who claims that Nathan has stolen details from his personal life for his novels.³¹ Set in 1969 against the backdrop of recent political assassinations, their connection comes to seem increasingly insidious when Nathan suspects Alvin of being behind a plot to kidnap his mother. Their encounters are laced with a certain sexual threat, too, that emerges through the mock-Shakespearean motif of a handkerchief. When they first meet at a diner, Nathan offers Alvin his handkerchief, which he takes to wipe his mouth.³² The trope recurs during Nathan's date with the actress Caesara O'Shea, when he leafs through her copy of Kierkegaard's *On the Life of an Actress* and reads aloud, 'she knows that her name is on everyone's lips, even when they wipe their mouths with their handkerchiefs!' Later, Nathan receives a package from Alvin containing his handkerchief, now 'damp' and 'matted' with a 'stale acrid odour he had no difficulty identifying'.³³

A perverse, comic love triangle of sorts emerges, then, between Nathan, Caesara, and Alvin – akin to that later staged between 'Philip Roth', his doppelgänger Moishe Pipik, and Pipik's lover Jinx, in *Operation Shylock* (1993).³⁴ Roth's use of doubles and triangles in each of these novels confirmed for some readers the commonplace criticism that his work is solipsistic.³⁵ But these intense, uneasy male relationships might also be read as forming part of a broader strain of 'homosocial discourse' running through Roth's oeuvre. Drawing on Eve Kosofsky Sedgwick's suggestion of the 'potential unbrokenness of a continuum between homosocial and homosexual' desire, David Brauner argues that 'Roth's representation of male sexuality is more complex, ambiguous, and ambivalent than has been generally recognised'.[36] Brauner identifies an example of what Sedgwick, following René Girard, calls the 'triangulation' of desire, in Roth's first novel, *Letting Go* (1962), between the narrator Gabe Wallach, his friend Paul Herz, and Paul's wife, Libby.[37] Gabe is writing his doctoral thesis on Henry James, and the trio's interweaving relationships play out under the sign of 'the Master': a key symbol throughout is Gabe's copy of *The Portrait of a Lady*, which passes between all three characters.[38] In *The Ghost Writer* – a novel partly modelled on James's 'artist tales' – Roth offers a variation on this theme.[39] We find Nathan reading Lonoff's copy of James's short story 'The Middle Years' (1893), which involves a triangular relationship between the ageing novelist Dencombe, his admirer Dr Hugh, and the doctor's patient, the Countess.[40] Their situation parallels the emerging relationship between Nathan, Lonoff – whom, with an 'amorous impulse', Nathan has a sudden urge to kiss after their first evening together – and Amy Bellette.[41] Although the overt Jamesian influence falls away in Roth's later work, this connection between masculine intimacy and literary influence remains strong, not least in *I Married a Communist*'s succession of male mentors and teachers.

Brauner's emphasis on the fluidity of male sexuality in Roth's fiction adds nuance to existing accounts of gender in his work. In particular, viewing a relationship like Nathan and Lonoff's as homosocial counters the tendency to read any intimacy between a younger and older man in Roth's fiction as filial, a tendency that, as Norman Rush also noted, has often obscured literary representations of male friendship from critical analysis. It must be said that Nathan often does this himself. In *The Ghost Writer*, having fallen out with his own father – 'the first of my fathers' – he seeks 'patriarchal validation elsewhere', and hopes to prove himself worthy of being Lonoff's 'spiritual son'.[42] But as the Zuckerman books progress, the father–son relationship becomes comically overdetermined, something of a worn-out Jewish joke. 'Are you *always* fighting with your father?' asks one of Nathan's girlfriends in *The Anatomy Lesson* (1983), flipping through the books on his shelves and noticing that 'every single line about a father is underlined'.[43] In this metacritical moment, Roth underlines that his readers should not do the same with his books, and that there is a world of masculine intimacy in his work beyond the Oedipal drama.

But thinking of the late-in-life male friendships Nathan shares with Murray and Coleman as only facets of a broader 'queering' of Roth, as Brauner does, risks underestimating the importance of these relationships to Roth's broader interest in 'joining the public and the private'. Ross Posnock suggests that the later Zuckerman books are 'less defensively homophobic' than the earlier novels, and are instead preoccupied with the elaboration of 'modes of being that cultivate some degree of intimacy' beyond the din of what Nathan calls 'the sexual caterwaul'.[44] In the trilogy, Nathan has been left impotent and incontinent from prostate cancer surgery, and, although he is keen to emphasise that his decision to retreat to a secluded cabin in the Berkshires preceded his diagnosis, the 'cancer blows' have intensified his isolation (*HS* 43). As sexual desire begins to flicker and fade (though it is by no means extinguished) in these later Zuckerman novels, the possibility emerges of other kinds of same-sex intimacy, and, with them, other kinds of storytelling. In old age, male friendship appears, if only briefly, to offer an alternative to isolation, and to thwarted desire. *Eros* wanes in these novels, but Nathan's capacity for *philia* waxes.

'What is it, this genealogy that isn't genetic?'

Set in the late 1940s and early 1950s, and pivoting around Henry Wallace's disastrous campaign as a third party candidate in the 1948 presidential election, *I Married a Communist* tracks the extravagant rise and fall of Ira Ringold, aka 'Iron Rinn', famed radio actor, vociferous Wallace supporter, and Communist firebrand. Ira is a high-profile casualty of McCarthyism, although his downfall is precipitated more directly by his vengeful wife, the

Hollywood star Eve Frame, whose ghostwritten schlock memoir, *I Married a Communist*, 'reveals' her husband to be a Communist agent – as well as a serial philanderer, the true reason for her hostility.[45] 'The most unreflective of all Roth's unreflective characters', Ira is a strident rabble-rouser, but far from the intellectually agile political tactician Frame frames him as.[46] If the former ditch-digger had not been politicised during his time in the army – under the influence of his ideological mentor, the Irish Communist Johnny O'Day – Ira might well have fallen in with Longy Zwillman and the other local Jewish gangsters back in the working-class neighbourhood of Newark where he grew up.[47] Instead, he becomes invested 'heart and soul' in the Communist project, a loyalist who uncritically 'obey[s] every one-hundred-eighty-degree shift in policy' (*IMC* 181).

Ira meets fifteen-year-old Nathan in the autumn of 1948, before Wallace's crushing defeat, and before McCarthyism put an end to the broad, fragile coalition of postwar 'Popular Front liberalism' of which Wallace had become the 'unlikely standard bearer'.[48] The novel is a *bildungsroman*, charting young Nathan's 'initiation' into the 'big show' of being a man, with Ira as his heroically flawed guide (32). *The Ghost Writer* was also a *bildungsroman* of masculine initiation, though not into the public sphere of politics but rather into the sequestered retreat of high art. Through Nathan's relationship with Ira – and those he develops with Murray, O'Day, and his English tutor at the University of Chicago, Leo Glucksman – *I Married a Communist* retrospectively reveals Lonoff to be only one in a series of male mentors Nathan has sought out. Roth has suggested that the subject of *I Married a Communist* is 'education, tutelage, mentorship', while Nathan also reflects on his predilection for teachers.[49] Thinking about 'the men who schooled me, the men I came from', he asks himself, 'what is it, this genealogy that isn't genetic?' He goes on to suggest that adolescence affords the opportunity to 'choose new allegiances and affiliations', but concludes that each of these 'chosen parents' must ultimately be 'cast off' for 'the orphanhood that is total, which is manhood. When you're out there in this thing all alone' (217). But analysing Nathan's old-age friendship with Murray challenges this conception of adulthood-as-isolation. Their relationship indicates how the novel looks beyond filial bonds to consider what other kinds of 'allegiances and affiliations' might structure a life and a political community. Through their friendship, the novel ultimately calls into question Nathan's notion of masculine independence, and his decision to live apart from the world.

As well as noting the novel's similarities to *The Ghost Writer*, critics have also pointed to the resemblance between Ira and the Swede in *American Pastoral*. Structurally, both characters appear to play comparable roles within their narratives and, thematically, each seems to represent both an individualistic will to self-transformation, and the 'impossibility of transcending historical circumstances'.[50] 'Whereas a de-ethnicized immersion into white-bread America had been the Swede's pastoral', Derek Parker Royal writes, 'Ira's becomes a socially just and politically progressive America'.[51] But while it was easy to see why the 'honourable, decent, deluded' Swede was afforded the role of tragic hero, critics struggled to appreciate the pathos in the story of a 'hothead' like Ira.[52] In a letter to Roth, Saul Bellow dismissed Ira as a 'cast-iron clutz', suggesting that he was 'probably the least attractive of all your characters'.[53] The novel's politics, meanwhile, have often been taken to be as simplistic as Ira's own. In contrast to the complex portrayal of the Swede's 'weak' liberalism in *American Pastoral*, James Wood argues that *I Married a Communist* reveals Roth to be a writer lacking 'a sensitive or original political imagination'; the book is less a political novel, Wood asserts, than a hectoring 'essay about politics'.[54] More frequently, the novel's evocation of the postwar Popular Front milieu has been taken to be mere backdrop. Although the book 'purports' to be about the fate of progressive politics at the start of the Cold War, Linda Grant writes, its real focus is Eve's betrayal of Ira, which, like Kakutani, Grant reads as a thinly veiled attack on Claire Bloom.[55] While the trilogy's first instalment seemed an astutely self-conscious metafictional reflection upon the epistemological uncertainties of historical knowledge after the end of history, *I Married a Communist* was judged to be a vindictive *roman à clef* disguised as shallow historical realism.[56]

Readings such as these – which, on the one hand, minimise the depth and seriousness of the novel's engagement with politics and history, and, on the other, minimise its formal ingenuity and reflexiveness – largely rest upon a misperception of how the narrative's 'frame' relates to the themes of its 'main' plot. Unlike *American Pastoral*, *I Married a Communist* is narrated not only by Nathan but also by Murray, Ira's less combustible older brother. A former English teacher but a perpetual student, ninety-year-old Murray is taking a course for seniors on Shakespeare at the local college when he bumps into Nathan, the pair having not seen one another since their time together in the classrooms of Weequahic High. Over the course of six long summer evenings in 1997, the two sit together on the porch of Nathan's isolated cabin high up in the Berkshires and pool together what they know of Ira's story, with Murray's contributions narrated as direct speech, and sequestered in their quotation marks. The novel, then, is in the form of a conversation, or dialogue, such that the 'task of recounting' is shown to be 'communal', rather than Nathan's alone.[57] This 'dialogic' form of narration is not simply 'expositional', nor straightforwardly realist.[58] Rather, crafted retrospectively by Nathan after Murray's death (revealed only at the end of the novel), the narrative structure manifests a form of historical sense-making. In this unusual method of storytelling, Nathan and Murray's friendship of the 1990s becomes integral to the novel's exploration of the political culture of the late 1940s and early 1950s.

'the fate of the community'

Ira's story is not only told by Murray but bookended by an account of his older brother's personal misfortune. The lurid tale of Ira's very public downfall is preceded and followed by Murray's own, very different experience of political persecution and betrayal – a watchword throughout the novel. Four years after Ira was 'blacklisted from radio for being a Communist, Murray had been dismissed from his teaching job', and forced to make his living selling vacuum cleaners door to door (4).[59] But Murray is not simply collateral damage of his brother's catastrophe. In fact, his left-wing political activism far predates Ira's, and runs much deeper. Murray 'threw [him]self into organizing' his union as soon as he became a teacher at Weequahic, remaining stoical about his private misfortune because of the union's enduring strength: 'now, if the *union* had failed, that would have affected me' (5, 14). In contrast to his brother's 'inflated' revolutionary internationalism, Murray says that his 'political beliefs were pretty localised', more 'sociological' than ideological, and more concerned with 'the fate of the community' than the fate of the world (12). Nowadays, Murray says, the union is 'a big disappointment', because this localist egalitarianism had narrowed to a focus solely on pay – the union in the 1990s is 'a money-grubbing organization' (14).

Murray's historical perspective also has a localist orientation, apparent in his 'sociological' reminiscences about life in Newark's old Italian First Ward, where he and Ira grew up, members of the neighbourhood's only Jewish family. While Ira often talks in grand abstractions – about the 'common man', 'the Negro', and 'the capitalists' – Murray deals in details and particulars. For example, he recalls 'the canary funeral' held for the Italian cobbler Russumanno's pet bird, and how the funeral procession went 'past Del Guerico's grocery store [...] past Melillo's fruit and vegetable stand, past Giordano's bakery' (61–62).[60] As Jack Miles suggests in his letter to Roth, Murray resembles *Patrimony*'s Herman Roth, 'the great rememberer of the family's past', for whom the old stories of local life in Newark are 'a sacred text'.[61] But Murray is much more closely based on one of Roth's own high-school teachers, Bob Lowenstein. In his eulogy for Lowenstein – published in the *New York Times* as 'In Memory of a Friend, Teacher, and Mentor', a title suggestive of the different facets of their relationship – Roth recounts not only the early influence of his homeroom teacher but also the story of how, like Nathan and Murray, they reconnected as friends in the 1990s. 'In the spirit of Bob Lowenstein', Roth writes of their friendship, 'I will put the matter in plain language, directly as I can: I believe we fell in love with each other'.[62] A 'radical and intellectual' like Murray, Lowenstein was awarded a PhD in Romance Languages from Johns Hopkins in 1933 and, after failing to secure a college teaching job, returned to his home state of New Jersey to teach high school.[63] Quickly involving himself in the nascent unionisation effort, Lowenstein became an executive board member of his local branch, helping to make Weequahic a stronghold for the radical Newark Teacher's Union.[64] Lowenstein's unionism was 'shaped by his political egalitarianism', Steve Golin explains in his history of Newark teachers' unions, and so maintained a 'larger political perspective'.[65] His 'Jewish-flavored version of unionism' gave way to an 'Italian-flavored version' as the demographics of Newark changed in the 1960s, focusing more on what Lowenstein called 'bread and butter issues' such as pay – the circumscribed kind of unionism Murray describes as a 'big disappointment'.[66]

By beginning with a detailed account of Murray's unionism closely based upon Lowenstein's personal history, Roth indicates how the novel will offer a portrayal of the period's political culture that moves beyond familiar narratives of McCarthyism. 'Not simply another novel about the red scare', *I Married a Communist* depicts a much broader Popular Front civic culture, grounded in local activism like Murray's, and flourishing well beyond the confines of the Communist Party.[67] In foregrounding Murray's history, Roth also foregrounds his relationship with Nathan. Their friendship becomes part of the novel's broader exploration of civic affiliation and political community, so it is telling that, in talking to Nathan, Murray is reminded not of the classroom they once shared but of the union meetings he used to attend (261). Staging another kind of political dialogue, their friendship manifests a form of democratic engagement that comes to define the novel's late twentieth-century perspective on the Popular Front culture of the late 1940s. Below, I explore the suggestive congruency between Roth's approach in the novel to mid-century coalition politics and a strain of left-wing revisionist historicism that rose to prominence in the post-Cold War era.

The spirit of the common man

The Popular Front was a loose alliance of the antifascist Left, anchored in the industrial collectivism of the Congress of Industrial Organizations (the CIO), that flourished in America in various guises from the mid-1930s until the start of the Cold War.[68] Histories of the Popular Front written from the 1950s through to the 1980s emphasised the centrality of the American Communist Party (the CPUSA) to this coalition.[69] In these histories, the

Popular Front was 'made up of Communists and fellow-travelling liberals; the center was red, the periphery, shades of pink'.[70] This 'traditionalist' interpretation followed 'the lead of Cold War era scholars like Theodore Draper', who maintained that the Popular Front was a Soviet directive adopted by the CPUSA, rather than a genuinely grassroots labour movement.[71] In this account, it was Earl Browder, General Secretary of the CPUSA from 1934 to 1945, who was largely responsible for instigating the Party's shift in political strategy (the Popular Front has long been associated with what both conservatives and the anti-Stalinist Left dismissively called 'Browderism').[72] According to Draper, in fact, there was no 'Popular Front *sui generis*', only 'the Popular Front of the Communist Party'.[73] These 'top-down' histories of the Popular Front emphasised the role of Party leaders, drew heavily on Comintern and Cominform cables, and, in short, searched for 'the Moscow gold that kept it all running'.[74]

In the 1990s, a new understanding of the period's political culture emerged. 'After 1989', Graham Cassano notes, 'one of the ironic effects of the end of the cold war was the new space produced for rethinking Marxism, and part of this general trend was a reevaluation of the history of the CPUSA and the Popular Front'.[75] Instead of a political tactic of the Communist Party, the Popular Front was reassessed as a diverse social democratic alliance 'uniting industrial unionists, Communists, independent socialists, community activists, and emigre anti-fascists around laborist social democracy', in which the 'categories of left and liberal, socialist and democrat became blurred'.[76] Revisionists inverted the traditionalist perspective to argue that 'Popular Front history is not a subset of the history of the Communist party [...] rather, the history of the Communist party is a subset of the history of the Popular Front social movement'.[77] Conceiving of the Popular Front as a 'bottom-up' movement of interlocking projects of social democracy precipitated a focus on the variety of regional and local forms of civic action and alliance that flourished in the period. A number of revisionist histories therefore focused on single cities, or individual industries or unions, to tell the story of the movement.[78]

Equally characteristic of the revisionist approach was an emphasis on the wide-ranging influence of the Popular Front in mainstream

American culture – what Michael Denning calls the 'cultural front' of the movement. In Hollywood, on Broadway, on the airwaves, and in literature, writers and performers allied or sympathetic to the Popular Front were instrumental in crafting the movement's political style, a populist pluralism that drew on the patriotic appeal of Roosevelt's New Deal.[79] 'Popular Front culture offered a sentimental, egalitarian, and schematic world view', Maurice Isserman summarises, epitomised for him by Paul Robeson's rendition of Earl Robinson's 'Ballad for Americans', first aired on Norman Corwin's CBS radio programme 'The Pursuit of Happiness' in 1939.[80] Robeson's jaunty paean to ethnic pluralism has come to typify the 'all-embracing Popular Front civic culture' of the period, and to stand for the 'Popular Front structure of feeling' that permeated American mass culture.[81] Postwar literary critics such as Lionel Trilling and Irving Howe – representatives of the liberal and radical anti-Stalinist Left respectively – 'scorned most of the output of the Popular Front as bathetic and simplistic', Michael Kazin observes, but 'whatever its flaws, this unashamedly demotic art did much to re-infuse the national culture with an anti-authoritarian, pluralist spirit that soon became ubiquitous'.[82]

I Married a Communist offers a revisionary account of the Old Left that closely correlates to this strain of 1990s historicism. Roth pays sustained attention to the aesthetic forms of the Popular Front, and takes seriously the idea of a popular civic culture. In foregrounding Murray's unionism and his 'sociological' political perspective, the novel also signals its interest in the kinds of local civic association that were the focus of contemporaneous revisionist histories. If this congruency seems unlikely, it is worth recalling just how widespread the 'revisionary position' had become in mainstream American intellectual culture by the mid-1990s. Roth needn't have been reading Michael Denning to be aware of the issues at stake; he could have just picked up a copy of the *New York Review of Books*, where the increasingly rancorous debate between traditionalist and revisionist historians was playing out in the letters pages. For example, in June 1994, a number of the 'new historians' wrote in response to Draper's dismissive review of two recent revisionist histories, accusing him of a 'fixation' on the Soviet influence in the Popular Front.[83] Among the respondents was Isserman, who noted that it was not only historians who had come of age politically during the heyday of the New Left who were reconsidering the legacy of the Popular Front, but also prominent leftists of the previous generation, including Irving Howe.

Roth's turbulent relationship with Howe is well documented and its effects on his fiction have been far-reaching.[84] Some critics have read the American Trilogy as offering a final refutation to the famous charge Howe made in 1972 that Roth's work evidenced the author's 'thin personal culture'.[85] Conversely, Edward Alexander suggests that *American Pastoral* amounts to 'the existential realization of Howe's criticism of the moral and political style of the New Left'.[86] But there are also connections between *I Married a Communist* and Howe's changing conception of the 'political style' of the Old Left. As Isserman intimates, like most on the anti-Stalinist Left, Howe had been suspicious of the Popular Front and dismissive of its 'middle-brow' intellectual culture. A critical history of the CPUSA Howe co-wrote in 1958 held to a traditionalist critique of the Popular Front as a 'political masquerade' orchestrated by the Soviets, even as it acknowledged that the movement's 'appeal to the emotions of antifascist fraternity [...] was extremely successful'.[87] But in a 'Note on "Browderism"' published in 1985, Howe reconsidered his position, suggesting that the contemporary Left might benefit from pursuing 'a policy somewhat like that of the Popular Front (call it "coalition politics")'.[88] 'In contrast to Draper', Isserman notes, 'Howe gave the new historians a serious reading', and consequently came to reflect upon how his initial appraisal of the Popular Front was itself a product of Cold War ideology.[89]

'the feeling for community'

I Married a Communist follows Howe and the revisionist historians in a recuperative turn towards the Popular Front. Through his relationship with Ira, Nathan becomes immersed in the movement's 'cultural front', listening to the 'high demotic poetry' of Norman Corwin's radio plays, reading the popular historical fictions of the Communist writer Howard Fast, and even meeting Paul Robeson at a Wallace rally (39).[90] Fifty years later, Nathan is able to lightly satirise his youthful political piety and the populist fervour of the times: 'Rank and file – three little words that thrilled me' (42, emphasis in original). But the novel takes seriously the movement's various attempts to render a genuinely democratic style – indeed, Roth's interest in the Popular Front is as much aesthetic as it is political. Of Corwin's famous play commissioned to celebrate VE Day, Nathan writes:

> I wouldn't care to judge today if something I loved as much as I loved *On a Note of Triumph* was or was not art; it provided me with my first sense of the conjuring *power* of art and helped strengthen my first ideas as to what I wanted and expected a literary artist's language to do: enshrine the struggles of the embattled. (And taught me, contrary to what my teachers insisted, that I could begin a sentence with 'And'.) (38, emphasis in original)

Nathan's conception of literary language and the power of art develops well beyond these 'first ideas' in the intervening half-century, not least under the influence of subsequent mentors like Glucksman and Lonoff. But that playful final sentence, beginning with a Corwin-esque 'And', suggests that the influence of the Popular Front's demotic style remains important to the narrative. I suggest that the unusual structure of Roth's novel represents an attempt to forge a democratic aesthetic that borrows from Corwin and the Popular Front, but that is also reflective of the political culture of the 1990s.

As such, the novel's 1997 frame is crucial to understanding the intervention Roth is making in the broader revisionary recuperation of the Popular Front I have sketched. Arguing that Roth is a key figure in what he calls, following Mark McGurl, 'the high cultural pluralist program' of modern American fiction, Philipp Löffler suggests that the 1997 'retrospective' established in the novel's frame is important, because it 'allows Roth [...] to make a powerful revisionist claim about the centrality of the individual self', in distinction to the 'obdurate universalism' of Ira's Communist ideology.[91] Contrary to 'Ira's totalizing view of history', Nathan and Murray pretend to be interested not in 'historical truth', Löffler argues, but rather in the uses to which history can be put in 'processes of individual self-fashioning'.[92] But while Löffler is right to emphasise the novel's revisionary cultural pluralism, the dichotomy he sets up between liberal individualism and Communist universalism misses the way in which the dynamic of Murray and Nathan's conversation offers a political alternative to both of these positions.

History is made intersubjectively, the novel suggests; the process of 'individual self-fashioning' Löffler highlights is in fact a joint venture. Murray is able to contextualise Nathan's understanding of his youthful relationship with Ira by sharing his own partial account of his brother's history; each provides details of which the other is unaware, and, in so doing, each demonstrates their provisional hold on the past: 'Your life story is in and of itself something that you know very little about', Nathan reflects (15). This echoes a scepticism concerning our capacity for knowing ourselves and others that resonates through the trilogy. 'Getting people right is not what living is all about anyway', Nathan writes in *American Pastoral*, 'It is getting them wrong that is living [...] That's how we know we're alive: we're wrong' (*AP* 35). In that novel, it is the Swede's brother, Jerry, who corrects Nathan's mistaken assumptions about his childhood hero. Initially, Murray seems to play a similar role. But whereas Jerry's revelations become the grist for Nathan's 'realist chronicle', in *I Married a Communist* we stay steadfastly rooted to Nathan and Murray's ongoing conversation. It is a conversation full of revelations, corrections, digressions, and, above all, feeling. As Murray reveals the death of his daughter Lorraine, Nathan tenderly considers his old teacher's skull, the way it 'looked so fragile and small now. Yet within it were cradled ninety years of the past' (77). The moment carries an echo of Murray's performance, back in the classroom at Weequahic High in the late 1940s, of the 'scene at the end of act 4 of *Macbeth*', in which Ross informs MacDuff that Macbeth has slaughtered his family. Nathan clearly remembers 'the simple line that would assert itself, in Murray Ringold's voice, a hundred times, a thousand times, during the remainder of my life: "But I must also feel it as a man"' (314–315). Their late-in-life friendship extends and enriches this emotional education. The pair's conversation elaborates a ruminative, compassionate, and respectful form of engagement that carries an echo of the sentimental, fraternal feeling of the Popular Front, but that also accounts for the losses, personal and political, accrued in the intervening half-century.

Roth's association of conversation and male friendship is longstanding. In a note to *The Counterlife*, he writes that the 'greatness' of 'male friendships' is that they 'don't compel consummation' like sexual relationships, but are instead 'endless talk'.[93] In a 1974 interview, meanwhile, he reflects that 'the best of adolescence was the intense male friendships [...] because of the opportunity they provided for uncensored talk', suggesting a link between 'the amalgam of mimicry, reporting, kibitzing, disputation, satire, and legendizing' that characterised his adolescent friendships and 'the work I do now'.[94] The tenor of Murray and Nathan's conversation is of course very different, forming the basis of a very different kind of friendship, and therefore producing a very different kind of story. Rather than the richly inventive comedy of adolescence, there is 'something of the Socratic dialogue' about the old men's exchange.[95] As in Plato's dialogues, conversation becomes a form of friendship, and the relationship between friends becomes a mode of broader philosophical and political enquiry.

It is just this kind of conversation that Ira is unable to take part in. 'Extremely disinclined to lose' a 'political argument' (177), Ira 'rarely speaks to anyone in particular', Elaine Safer observes, but instead 'pontificate[s] in long monologues, mostly in the inflated language of agitprop'.[96] Even as a boy, Nathan tires of Ira's ranting – 'I'd heard it all before, these exact words many times' – and after a week together he can't 'wait to get out of earshot' (190). By contrast, Nathan becomes increasingly attuned to Murray's voice, and even to his silences, the 'eloquence of an old man evenly expiring' (75). Their conversation recognises the making of history as pluralistic, while also demonstrating our reliance on others in making sense of our selves, which is to say that their friendship is concerned with questions of citizenship and community.

Forming part of the novel's broader exploration of the American civic imaginary, the men's friendship points to an affinity between *I Married a Communist* and the communitarian political philosophy I analysed in my Introduction. Critiquing liberalism's atomistic conception of the individual – what Michael Sandel called 'the unencumbered self' – communitarians reasserted the importance of citizenship, stressing 'the ways in which our selves are socially embedded and constructed within a community'.[97] In more conservative accounts, this 'community' resembled a Tocquevillian conception of civil society, founded on the ties of family, the church, and a broader network of voluntary association. These often nostalgic appeals to traditional 'family values' frequently came couched in a broader elegy for the decline of morality in contemporary culture. Other critiques looked not to family and faith but to the freely chosen bonds of friendship to imagine a revitalised political community. In these accounts, civic friendship protects and promotes important liberal democratic values, such as individual rights, justice, and pluralism, yet also challenges the liberal dichotomy of the private and public spheres by suggesting that our political affiliations should be shaped by, rather than separate from, our personal relations.[98]

American Pastoral's evocation of the 'decline' of Newark – especially after the race riots of the 1960s – echoes the elegiac tone of some communitarian accounts of the fragmentation of civil society.[99] The Swede's father, Lou, is a 'lifetime Democrat' and a New Deal liberal, but his sense of the growing disorder in American culture chimes with popular neoconservative critiques from the 1980s and 1990s:

> We grew up in an era when it was a different place, when the feeling for community, home, family, parents, work ... well, it was different [...] The lack of feeling for places like what is going on in Newark – how does this happen? You don't have to revere your family, you don't have to revere your country, you don't have to revere where you live, but you *have* to know you have them, you have to know that you are *part* of them. (*AP* 364–365, emphasis in original)

Critiquing this 'lack of feeling' remains important to the political intervention Roth makes in *I Married a Communist*, where being able to 'feel it as a man' is central to the lesson Nathan learns from Murray. But while Lou mourns the collapse of Newark and is dismayed by the cultural politics of the New Left, *I Married a Communist* reframes the history of postwar American liberalism to imagine a point of contact between the sentimental civic culture of the Popular Front and the communitarianism of the 1990s. Like both conservative and progressive communitarian critiques, the novel substantiates a localist perspective attuned to the particularities of place. But rather than an elegiac account of the loss of community, in its depiction of Nathan and Murray's friendship *I Married a Communist* offers a portrayal of a civic relation in which a 'feeling for community' might be reimagined. Tracing a link between the late 1940s and the late 1990s, the novel suggests that the contemporary Left's project of revitalising citizenship and community might learn something from the sentimental politics of the Popular Front.

'My only friend is the revolution'

With this connection between the civic culture of the 1940s and 1990s in mind, Roth's careful evocation of Popular Front aesthetics comes to seem self-reflexive. Ira is associated with the cultural front from his first appearance in the novel, when we see him in one of his earliest theatrical roles, playing the part of Abraham Lincoln in a performance of the Lincoln–Douglas debates at the Weequahic High auditorium, with Nathan in the audience. The 1930s were marked by a 'passionate addiction to Lincoln', Alfred Kazin observed, in which the Republican president emerged as the fulfilment of the period's search for a 'useable American past', a 'champion of the needy' at a time of economic depression, and 'a symbol of the broadened responsibility of the state – in short, a hero of the left'.[100] President Roosevelt 'frequently wrapped himself in the mantle of the Civil War president', quoting Lincoln in his Fireside chats, and even hiring as one of his speechwriters Robert Sherwood, whose 1938 Broadway hit *Abe Lincoln in Illinois* was a 'pivotal factor in the crystallisation' of Lincoln's populist image.[101] In contrast to this 'liberal Lincoln', the CPUSA's Earl Browder claimed in a speech delivered on Lincoln's birthday in 1936 that, 'If the tradition of Lincoln is to survive […] this will be due not to the Republicans nor to the Democrats, but to the modern representatives of historical progress, the Communists'.[102]

Ira's Lincoln, then, would have been one among many left-leaning portrayals of the president in the period. But as well as gesturing to the Popular Front's predilection for historical appropriation, Ira's Lincoln also reflects back upon the novel's own revisionary search for a 'useable past'. Nathan and Murray are also engaged in a kind of political dialogue, and, through Ira's participation in the Lincoln–Douglas debate, the novel 'stages' another conversation about civil rights, representation, and citizenship, one taking place at a national scale.[103] This emphasis on dialogue re-emerges when Nathan first meets Ira in person, when he cycles by Murray's house on his way home from the library. Ira is helping Murray take down his screen doors, and Nathan is at first struck by the physical impression made by 'the two shirtless brothers', with Ira wearing nothing more than 'a prizefighter' (18). But it is also the brothers' intellectual muscle that impresses Nathan. The Ringolds practise the kind of 'critical thinking' Murray espouses in his classroom, demonstrating to young Nathan a form of combative literary engagement: 'Not opening a book to worship it or be elevated by it [...] No, *boxing* with a book' (27, emphasis in original). Kasia Boddy argues that 'boxing with a book' portrays education as a robust one-to-one exchange akin to a 'continuous Socratic debate'.[104] Patrick Hayes, meanwhile, suggests that it 'models a form of engagement in which – to borrow a Blakean phrase that Roth is fond of quoting – "opposition is true friendship"'.[105] Most notably, Bob Lowenstein himself suggests a similar conception of pedagogy in his poem 'Boxing Lessons', which he sent to Roth in 1997, having read an early draft of *I Married a Communist*:

> My father taught me the hard way
> his 'do' was punitive, his 'don't'
> more so. I balked, flat-footed as
> a mule. When I got out from under
> his control, I sought out trainers
> in ring lore known for their ability
> to teach.
>
> From crafty Socrates
> I learned sound footwork, how to lead,
> to feint, and – his special art –
> to counterpunch. I later made
> the rounds of other masters of
> the trade and honed my basic skills.[106]

Shot through with a machismo reminiscent of Murray's way of speaking, Lowenstein's poem imagines education as a series of man-to-man tussles, first with the father, then with major figures from philosophy (next in the ring in the following stanza is 'Michel (that's Mike) Montaigne'). Citing Socrates as one of these interlocutors, Lowenstein alludes to the philosophical dialogue, a form the novel also explores through Nathan and Murray's conversations. Plato's dialogues – and especially the early dialogue on friendship, the *Lysis* – conceive of 'friendship as a mode of cultural transmission that subverts the biological' and, like Lowenstein's poem, the novel delineates a network of male relationships beyond the family that together form a 'genealogy that isn't genetic', including not only the mentorships and tutelages of Nathan's youth but also his old-age friendship with Murray.[107] It is an education that never stops: 'The man who first taught me to box with a book', Nathan writes of Murray, 'is back now to demonstrate how you box with old age' (78).

The classicism of this formative scene of masculine initiation looks forward to the sustained engagement with ancient Greek tragedy in *The Human Stain* – in which Coleman Silk is not only a combative Classics professor who teaches that 'all of European literature springs from a fight', but, in a previous life, a promising boxer and wily 'counterpuncher' (*HS* 4, 100). But the book with which Nathan, Ira and Murray are boxing is not some great work of classical philosophy or literature but an example of popular historical fiction, Howard Fast's *Citizen Tom Paine* (1943). Murray approaches Fast's novel through the kind of close reading we might associate with mid-twentieth-century New Criticism. In one scene he is analysing the 'cryptogrammatic g's, the subtlety of their disintensification' in a line from *Twelfth Night*, and he encourages a similar concentration from Nathan upon a line of Paine's about George III, quoted by Fast: 'I should suffer the misery of devils, were I to make a whore of my soul by swearing allegiance to one whose character is that of a [...] brutish man' (302, 27). If you 'looked at one word', and 'asked yourself some questions about that word', Murray suggests, you can eventually see 'through the word' to reveal the 'source' of the writer's 'power' (28). 'Whore' is the word they close read together to get to the source of Paine's power – which, in Ira's reckoning, is his 'audacity'. But 'allegiance' might be the operative word here, given the novel's broader exploration of the 'allegiances and affiliations' of political life; certainly, the question of where one's political allegiances lie is crucial to Fast's interest in Paine.

In the 1940s and early 1950s, Howard Fast was among the country's 'most celebrated novelists' and, until his resignation in 1957, 'the single most important literary figure in the American Communist Party'.[108] Like Ira, Fast was Jewish and working-class, and he was blacklisted for his political beliefs. In 1947 (just a year before Nathan checks out his copy from his local branch of the Newark Public Library on Chancellor Avenue), *Citizen Tom Paine* was banned from public libraries across New York State.[109] Only a few years earlier, the novel had been a bestseller 'taught to a generation of America's school children'.[110] Charting Paine's political career in America and France, *Citizen Tom Paine* was the most successful example of what Fast called his 'one-man reformation of the historical novel'.[111] As Ira observes, Fast was 'with Wallace from the start' (26) and, as Priscilla Murolo explains, his politics inspired his fictional 're-visions of US history, introducing readers to a national legacy of revolt'.[112]

'*Citizen Tom Paine*', Nathan writes, 'was not so much a novel plotted in the usual manner, as a sustained linking of highly charged rhetorical flourishes tracing the contradictions of an unsavoury man' (25). As Aimee Pozorski suggests, 'what makes this passage so striking is its self-referentiality [...] this description of Fast's novel might well be a description of [Roth's]'.[113] This self-referentiality extends to Nathan's reading of Paine's 'unsociability':

> That was Paine as Fast portrayed him, savagely single-minded and unsociable, an epic, folkloric belligerent [...] frequenting brothels, hunted by assassins, and friendless. He did it all alone: 'My only friend is the revolution.' By the time I had finished the book, there seemed to me no other way than Paine's for a man to live and die [...] *He did it all alone.* (25, emphasis in original)

Nathan can now poke fun at his youthful valorisation of Paine's 'heroic suffering', but, in late middle age, he has returned to an idealisation of isolation summed up in the repeated phrase, 'He did it all alone'. In *The Ghost Writer*, twenty-three-year-old Nathan admires Lonoff's 'winnowing of the insatiable self' and resolves to follow his example: 'Purity. Serenity. Simplicity. Seclusion [...] I looked around me and thought, This is how I will live'.[114] In *I Married a Communist*, Nathan delineates a more elaborate genealogy for his reclusion. The idea of the isolated retreat in the woods 'has a history', he writes, 'It was Rousseau's. It was Thoreau's. The palliative of the primitive hut' (72). But there is a more immediate model for his solitude. Nathan wonders whether Murray will recognise his cabin as 'an upgraded replica' of Ira's shack, to which the actor periodically retreated, and which itself had been based upon Johnny O'Day's utilitarian Leninist 'cell' (228). Ira's shack adheres to a vision of the pastoral that Nathan had sought to demythologise in *American Pastoral*. The shack is an 'antidote' to city life, a sanctuary to which Ira retreats to 'sweat out the bad vapors' (*IMC* 51). Nathan similarly suggests that he can 'decontaminate and absolve' himself in his cabin (72). But the trilogy insists that contamination – what Roth calls the 'human stain' – is inevitable, and we should be wary of 'the fantasy of purity' (*HS* 242). 'Unless you're an ascetic paragon like Johnny O'Day or Jesus Christ', Murray says, 'purity is petrifaction [...] purity is a lie' (*IMC* 318). Nathan insists that 'my seclusion is not the story here', yet, over the course of the novel, his friendship with Murray calls into question his decision to live alone (71). Reintroducing Nathan to 'the pleasures of companionship', Murray challenges the picture of the unencumbered self Nathan has cultivated, suggesting that it is a form of escapism akin to Ira's Communism. 'Beware the utopia of isolation', he warns near the novel's close, 'Beware the utopia of the shack in the woods' (315).

With Murray's warning in mind, it is worth reconsidering Nathan's reading of *Citizen Tom Paine*. In the passage quoted above, Nathan draws attention to Fast's emphasis on Paine's isolation, but there is also an emphasis on the idea of friendship. Following Murray's practice of close reading, we can say that the passage develops a 'tension' between two potentially competing registers of friendship: friendship as a personal relation (Paine is 'friendless'); and friendship as a metaphor of political association ('my only friend is the revolution').[115] In a moment, I will consider how Paine's own work explores these registers, but it is first important to read Fast's novel a little more closely than Nathan does to show how his summary is somewhat limited. Fast's Paine is certainly the 'folkloric belligerent' described by Nathan, a defiant iconoclast sometimes depicted as 'completely alone; alone and unafraid'.[116] But at other times, Paine – introduced in France to his fellow revolutionaries as 'the friend of man' – is shown to seek the company and affection of others. He was 'no recluse', Fast writes, 'that was not for Paine; for Paine was the feeling of his fellow man, their nearness, their voices and their smiles and good intimacies'.[117] As the elderly Paine returns to America from France, he reflects that 'when he is old, a man wants a friend or two about him'; 'a man', he says, 'wants to die in a friendly place'.[118] Fast's picture of Paine's old age, then, is quite different from the one Nathan creates from himself, derived from 'those old Chinese paintings of the old man under the mountain' who 'goes into the woods' and is 'drawn down into austerity' (*IMC* 72).

In Paine's own work the idea of friendship is often invoked to attempt to conceive of a new basis for association, both between citizens and between nation states. As I discussed in my Introduction, friendship became important in early American efforts to imagine a 'new kind of democratic relationship' following the dissolution of what Paine calls 'the evil of monarchy and hereditary succession'.[119] *Common Sense* (1776) is the work that Ira recommends to Nathan – unsurprisingly, given that Paine's pamphlet was written in a 'strikingly demotic populist voice' that was much admired by Popular Front writers.[120] But Paine's title was 'multivalent', Richard Godbeer explains, referring 'not only to the basic and readily comprehensible principles on which its arguments were constructed, but also to Americans' common capacity for sensation'.[121] Paine's use of the phrase therefore linked his work to the 'common sense school of philosophy', and its theory of natural affection and sympathy.[122] Arguing that 'man, were he not corrupted by government, is naturally the friend of man', Paine's work 'creates a space in which friendship might discover politically radical meanings through the discourse of intuitive feelings'.[123] Declaring that 'what Athens was in miniature, America will be in magnitude', the idea of a *polis* defined by *philia* often plays a part Paine's thinking about civic ties and national alliances.[124] In his first *Crisis* pamphlet (1776), it is with 'the warm ardor of a friend' that he addresses those who have remained loyal to the cause of independence; elsewhere, when imagining American relations with the rest of the world after it ceases to be a British territory, he encourages his fellow citizens to carry their 'friendship to a larger scale'.[125]

Nathan's introduction to Paine's work via Fast's novel is part of his initiation into what he calls 'the big show, into my beginning to understand what it takes to be a man on the larger scale' (*IMC* 32). The novel clearly suggests a parallel between Paine's defiance of British paternalism and Nathan's developing independence from his father: 'once little Tom Paine has been let into the company of men', Nathan writes, 'the father is finished' (32). But Paine's emphasis on friendship seems to get lost along the way, and it takes the reappearance of Murray to remind Nathan that independence and isolation are not the same thing. Reading Paine more closely, we can see why he is a useful figure for historical appropriation for both Fast's and Roth's political novels, beyond his obvious resonance as a symbol of defiant independence. His articulation of the natural sympathy of man and the stress his political philosophy lays upon the importance of intuitive feelings to civic association chimes with the sentimental political culture of the Popular Front; but it also speaks to a communitarian emphasis on personal relations and civic friendship. Just as Fast had, Roth seeks to trace a political lineage from the country's founding to the present and, in its close reading of *Citizen Tom Paine*, *I Married a Communist* reflexively comments upon this ongoing search for a useable American past. In drawing a connection between Fast's historical fiction and his own, Roth thus foregrounds the role of the novel-form itself in the elaboration and transmission of a political culture, and in the making of national history.

'Take a bow, little guy'

Young Nathan does not initially aspire to write historical fictions like Fast, but patriotic radio dramas in the style of Norman Corwin's *On a Note of Triumph*:

The form of Corwin's play was loose, plotless [...] written in the high colloquial, alliterative style that may have derived [...] from the effort of American playwrights of the twenties and thirties to forge a recognizable native idiom [...] a poeticised vernacular that, in Norman Corwin's case, combined the rhythms of ordinary speech with a faint literary stiltedness. (38)

Later in the novel, we sample Nathan's own highly derivative dialogue play, *The Stooge of Torquemada*. Nathan is not the first Roth character to have imitated the 'poet laureate of radio'; Alexander Portnoy also recalls attempting to write a 'prose-poetry' play 'inspired by my master, Norman Corwin', with the mock-Popular Front title *Let Freedom Ring!*.[126] Like Nathan, Portnoy is a 'sucker for manly intimacy' (*IMC* 233) and, under the influence of his Ira-like brother-in-law Morty, he too begins to 'evangelize for Henry Wallace'.[127] But the tone of Roth's evocation of the sentimental political culture of the Popular Front is quite different in the later novel. Roth is not simply parodying Corwin any more, but is instead suggesting a deeper affinity between the 'poeticized vernacular' of *On a Note of Triumph* and *I Married a Communist*.[128] Nathan and Murray's 'dialogue' is a kind of updated version of Nathan's first Corwinesque 'dialogue plays'; their conversation might also be said to 'combine the rhythms of ordinary speech with a faint literary stiltedness', and like Corwin's radio dramas, their conversation is attuned to questions of national identity and community.[129]

Corwin was the most influential of a group of progressive writers and producers who made network radio 'the site of the left's greatest success in the culture industry'.[130] Though never a Communist like Fast, Corwin also supported Wallace as 'the last and best bulwark against fascism in America', following the death of Roosevelt in 1945.[131] *On a Note of Triumph* was his grand paean to the ordinary GI – the 'little guy' – who had 'beaten the brownshirt bully boys' against the odds.[132] Broadcast to over sixty million Americans, the drama blended a sentimental ethnic patriotism with a celebratory, utopian internationalism to evoke 'a mystical vision of citizenship'.[133] Nathan quotes the play's closing 'prayer' – though notably omits its famous final line, a plea 'That man unto his fellow man shall be a friend forever' – before reflecting on the appeal of Corwin's work, and of the radio generally:

The power of that broadcast! There, amazingly, was *soul* coming out of a radio. The Spirit of the Common Man had inspired an immense mélange of populist adoration [...] Corwin modernized Tom Paine for me by democratizing the risk, making it a question not of one just wild man but a collective of all the little just men pulling together [...] A thrilling idea. And how Corwin laboured to force it, at least imaginatively, to come true. (41, emphasis in original)

Nathan summarises here how Corwin's work captured the 'pluralist promise' of 'radio's unique nationalising address'.[134] In the 1930s and 1940s, Americans 'looked to radio not only to reflect but to resolve some of the tensions they felt about the nature of [the country's] institutions, the location of social power, [...] and the future of its democracy'.[135] Radio's 'invisible national reach' and 'universal and simultaneous address' became the 'perfect symbol of national unity', while the medium's 'preoccupation with voices, reception practices and the interests of "the people"' seemed to 'gesture toward a model of participatory democracy – a national town meeting in the air'.[136] At the same time, the 'mobility of radio voices across the borders between the intimate world of domesticity, solitude, and one-to-one conversation, and the public world of politics, sociability and mass communication' seemed to 'conjure a new social space both public and private, national and local', located in 'the middle distance opening up between publicity and intimacy'.[137]

Of course the novel is another medium capable of a distinctive combination of national address and individual interpellation, and I read the narrative frame of *I Married a Communist* as an attempt to forge a novelistic version of radio's singular evocation of a middle distance between intimacy and publicity.[138] Nathan suggests that the 'book of my life is a book of voices' (222), but, as Robert Chodat observes, 'which of these voices are public, which voices are private, [and] which voices evolve from one into the other' remains an open question.[139] Nathan reflects that the appeal of Corwin's radio dramas, and of the sentimental political culture of the period, was the sense that 'history had been scaled down and personalized' (39). Framing a national history through an intimate conversation between two friends, the novel looks back to the democratic aesthetics of the Popular Front, and to the radio in particular, to reflexively consider what role literature might play in imagining the scales of civic affiliation and action that form a political community.

As a freshman at Chicago, Nathan encounters some forthright opinions on this subject, when he lets his English tutor, Leo Glucksman, take a look at his radio play. 'Who taught you art is in the service of *"the people"*?', Glucksman demands after reading Nathan's 'propagandist crap', 'Art is in the service of *art*' (218, emphasis in original). Dismayed by the idea of 'the culture of the peasants and the workers', Glucksman insists that Nathan strive for 'aesthetic mastery over everything that drives you to write in the first place – your outrage, your politics, your grief, your love!' (219). Swapping Corwin for Kierkegaard, Glucksman teaches Nathan that 'the public' is a 'monstrous abstraction' to be reviled. Glucksman may appear a much-needed Trillingite counterweight to Nathan's infatuation with Ira's working man's argot. But if Nathan's fluency in Corwin-esque corniness is inauthentic, so too is Glucksman's cultivation of a liberal imagination. Though still a PhD student, Glucksman dresses in 'a three-piece black suit and a crimson bow tie' (217), recalling the observation of Ted Solotaroff – a classmate of Roth's when they were both enrolled in the doctoral programme at UChicago – that all graduate students in the 1950s 'came on as though [they] were thirty'.[140] Solotaroff reflects on how Trilling acted as a 'guide' to young Jewish intellectuals into the 'Anglo-American literary tradition', a role Glucksman also plays for Nathan.[141] Through this process of cultural assimilation, Trilling and other Jewish literary critics were able to 'pass' in the WASP academy.[142] But Glucksman is passing in another way as well. When Nathan visits his tutor in his room late one evening, Glucksman makes a sexual advance:

> 'Oh, Nathan,' Leo said tenderly. 'My dear friend.' It was the first time he had called me anything other than 'Mr. Zuckerman.' He sat me down at his desk and, standing over me just inches away, watched while [...] I undid the buttons of a mackinaw already wet and heavy with snow. Maybe he thought that I was preparing to undo everything. (238–239)

The association of high culture and homosexuality is a little tired, to be sure, and Glucksman can appear at times as much a caricature as Ira sometimes does. But this is partly Roth's point: the tutors, Nathan realises, are equally 'uncompromising' in their ideals (224). And this passage is also worth pausing over because of the curious weight given the term 'friend'. Glucksman and Nathan aren't friends, after all, nor does Glucksman have friendship in mind when he uses the word. For a Kierkegaardian like Glucksman, friendship is only ever a ruse, or an extended form of self-love (hence, perhaps, Roth's association of the term with homosexuality here).[143] This conception of human nature underpins Glucksman's view of art, of 'the public', and of politics more broadly. That is to say, thinking about how Glucksman (mis)uses the term 'friend' reveals much about his wider worldview. This is true elsewhere in the novel. When, for example, Murray suggests that the anti-union schools superintendent was 'no friend of mine', we should understand the charge as a meaningful one; and, when he recalls that no city was 'friendlier' in the 1940s than Newark, he is saying something significant about his civic values (5, 283).[144]

Glucksman's dismissal of the sentimentality of the Popular Front recalls the opinion of Goldstine, an old army buddy of Ira's who was once sympathetic to Communism but is now a factory boss. Goldstine tells Nathan not to believe the 'fairy tale about people's *brotherhood*' peddled by the Communists, because 'we know what our brother is, don't we? He's a shit. And we know what our friend it, don't we? He's a semi-shit' (95, emphasis in original). In isolation, the distinction Goldstine draws between brothers and friends may seem odd. But as part of Roth's foregrounding of the term 'friend' throughout the book – whether in the examples noted above, or in Nathan's summary of *Citizen Tom Paine* – Goldstine's commentary can be read as part of the novel's broader interest in the question of what kind of loyalties should structure a political community. Murray is celebrated as 'the very best of loyal brothers', but the novel also warns how 'a twisted sense of loyalty' leads him to betray his principles to protect his brother when, as a young man, Ira commits murder (323, 303). Yet nor does the novel dismiss the Popular Front's idealisation of what Michael Denning calls 'masculine brotherhood', whether in Fast's historical novels or in Corwin's radio dramas.[145] Rather, through Murray and Nathan's conversations, Roth attempts to recall and recover something of this demotic cultural style, while also gesturing to another kind of political loyalty. In Murray and Nathan's friendship, the novel offers an alternative both to 'the fairy tale of people's brotherhood', and to Goldstine's political nihilism.[146]

'My last task'

In my reading it is therefore Murray rather than Ira who is the more significant character in understanding the novel's political imagination. But like the trilogy's other heroic men, Nathan's old teacher is not without his flaws. Late in the novel we learn that Murray's wife Doris was murdered during a mugging in Newark, where the Ringolds had remained even after the 'white flight' from the city following the race riots in the late 1960s. 'I wouldn't leave', Murray explains, 'just because it was now a poor black city full of problems', and he acknowledges that consequently 'Doris paid the price for my civic virtue' (316, 317). Doris's murder is one of the novel's darker tragic ironies, one from which Jack Miles pleaded with Roth to spare Murray. In a handwritten postscript to a letter, Miles writes:

> Imagine how different an effect would be created if Doris did not die – mugged maybe – but instead provided her husband a wonderful, long autumn in Arizona [where Murray moves after Doris's death] and if, *after* that marvelous, starry conclusion – Nathan received word of [Murray's] death in a letter from Doris who would, of course, remember him and who might provide a remarkable fact or two of her own.[147]

Roth did not use Miles's idea – at least, not for Murray's story. There is, however, a similarity between Miles's plan for Doris's role and the part played by Coleman Silk's sister Ernestine at the end of *The Human Stain*, to which I turn in a moment. Yet although Roth does not spare him a tragic ending, Murray remains an enduring example to Nathan. Miles even suggests to Roth that:

> Murray is, within this book and perhaps within your oeuvre, the love alternative. You have a moment for the acknowledgment of this or wonderment at it when Nathan says [...] 'I wished I had invited him

to stay with me. But I didn't have the heart ...' Nathan shouldn't change. He should stay that way. He shouldn't invite Murray to stay. But Murray should be allowed to be, to the end, someone who always would invite Nathan to stay with him, who would have the heart. There are such people, and there is such a way.[148]

Miles astutely picks out the term 'heart', which echoes back to Murray's most pressing question to Nathan: 'Why do you live up there alone like that? Why don't you have the heart for the world?' (315). We never quite get an answer, although Nathan's battle with cancer, and the travails of his younger years documented in earlier Zuckerman books, offer some indications as to why he lives alone. Contrary to Miles, however, I think Nathan does change over the course of the trilogy. Aaron Chandler argues that Nathan undergoes a 'sentimental education' during the trilogy, marked by an 'intensification of intimacy between [Nathan] and his principal subject in each book'.[149] This culminates with what Nathan describes as his 'serious friendship' with Coleman Silk (*HS* 43). 'Having a "heart for the world"', Chandler suggests, 'is precisely what Zuckerman gains as the novels progress'.[150] Nathan may not have the heart to let Murray stay over, but he has the heart to write a novel in which the emotional registers of civic life are scrutinised, and in which the relationship between friendship and politics is explored in the very structure of the narrative he tells. He may not invite Murray to stay over, but Nathan offers him something else: the novel itself is a kind of 'gift' of their friendship, an idea I explore in more detail in the next chapter, in relation to Paul Auster's work.

Roth gave a eulogy for Lowenstein, and *I Married a Communist* is Nathan's tribute to Murray. This comparison clarifies something often overlooked: that Murray has died before Nathan begins writing the novel. The conversational immediacy of the narrative structure suggests that the novel is inspired by Murray's reappearance, and on one level this is obviously right: 'that's how the past showed up this time', Nathan says when they bump into each other in town, 'in the shape of a very old man' (3). But on another, it is Murray's absence rather than his presence that prompts Nathan's narrative. Near the end of the novel, Murray insists on recounting the tragic circumstances of Ira's final years in detail, because 'I'd like to tell it right. To the end [...] My last task. To file Ira's story with Nathan Zuckerman'. Nathan replies that 'I don't know what I can do with it', to which Murray says, 'That's not my responsibility. My responsibility is to tell it to you' (265). The question of responsibility itself, it seems, is at stake here. Taking on the responsibility of telling Ira's convoluted story of political fervour and betrayal, Nathan also tries to do justice to Murray's life – to his teaching, his politics, and to the friendship they share.

'the million circumstances of the other fellow's life'

A concern with responsibility re-emerges in *The Human Stain*, another novel written by Nathan after the death of a male friend. Coleman Silk resembles both the Swede and Ira in his tragic quest for 'self-definition', and in his attempt to slip free from his historical moment and ethnic origins.[151] Only at Coleman's funeral does Nathan learn that his friend was born to African American parents and passed his adult life as Jewish. Made by Coleman's sister Ernestine, this revelation recalls Murray's disclosure of his brother's secret, that Ira committed murder as a young man. But the narrative implications of the revelations are markedly different. While Ira's crime 'makes sense' to Nathan and comes as no 'surprise' (*IMC* 297), the revelation of Coleman's identity transforms his friend into an 'uncohesive person' (*HS* 333). 'I couldn't imagine anything that could have made Coleman more of a mystery to me than this unmasking. Now that I knew everything, it was as though I knew nothing' (333). Nathan's narrative task becomes not so much to 'make sense' of Coleman's life as to present his 'mystery' in all its confounding complexity.

While critics have stressed the similarities between Coleman and the protagonists of the other novels in the trilogy, little has been made of his resemblance to Murray. Like Murray, Coleman is a dedicated teacher, a Classics professor at Athena College (where Murray took his course on Shakespeare), and like *I Married a Communist*, *The Human Stain* opens in the classroom. Just as Murray is 'brash', 'natural', and 'clear-cut' (*IMC* 1) in his teaching style, so Coleman is 'direct, frank, and unacademically forceful'

(*HS* 4). He too encourages a combative form of literary engagement, modelled on his experience as an amateur boxer, and mirrored in his physique. While Murray is 'rangy' and 'athletic' (*IMC* 1), Coleman, aged seventy, retains some of 'the bounce of the high school athlete' (*HS* 15). Coleman is not politically active like Murray, but is in his own way a 'revolutionary' force at Athena (25).[152] He too is forced from his job by a politically motivated witch hunt. Having asked if two perpetually absentee – and, unbeknownst to Coleman, African American – students really exist, or are 'spooks', he is dismissed on a trumped-up and ironic charge of racism. He is a victim of the 'censorious' moral hypocrisy of the summer of 1998 (the summer of the Monica Lewinsky affair) which the novel portrays as another iteration of 1950s McCarthyism. 'It is too late in the century to call him a Communist', Nathan writes, 'though that is the way it used to be done' (290). Murray also links the two eras when he describes the 1994 funeral of Richard Nixon, whom he reviles for his involvement with the House Un-American Activities Committee. Murray reserves particular vitriol for two of Nixon's eulogists, Henry Kissinger and Bill Clinton, both of whom are mentioned in *The Human Stain* (*IMC* 227). Having tried to write about his dismissal in his abandoned memoir, *Spooks*, Coleman has found he 'can't maneuver the creative remove' to write about himself. 'Kissinger can unload fourteen hundred pages of this stuff every other year', he says, 'but it's defeated me' (*HS* 19). Coleman instead asks Nathan to chronicle his story, *The Human Stain* representing Nathan's attempt to write 'the book [Coleman] had asked me to write in the first place, but written not necessarily as he wanted it' (213).

Nathan does not share a history with Coleman as he did with Murray, though it transpires that they grew up a few miles from each other in Newark, and attended the same after-school boxing club a few years apart (*HS* 204). Although the two men are closer in age, something of the teacher–student dynamic of the previous novel remains, and the narrative set-up of their friendship is strikingly similar: two older men sitting on a porch high up in Berkshires, talking about the 1940s and 1990s. While Nathan holds his marathon conversations with Murray out on his cabin porch, in *The Human Stain* he ventures over to Coleman's isolated house on the other 'side of the mountain' (3). Their friendship develops casually over a couple of months, Coleman inviting Nathan over 'to listen to music, or [...] to play [...] a little gin rummy [...] and sip some cognac' out on his 'cool screened-in side porch' (3–4, 18). While it is the Soviet Army Chorus's rendition of the Russian folksong 'Dubinushka' that leads Murray to disclose the tragic death of his daughter Lorraine to Nathan (*IMC* 74), it is Sinatra's sugary rendition of 'Bewitched, Bothered, and Bewildered' that moves Coleman to take Nathan into his confidence (*HS* 24). He declares that he is having an affair with Faunia Farley, a thirty-four-year-old janitor at Athena, a revelation sure to further scandalise the local academic community. His Viagra-fuelled final fling leads Coleman to do away with his *Spooks* project and even become a little sentimental, reading Nathan a love letter from an old girlfriend, Steena Paarlson, whom he met in 1948, the year in which much of *I Married a Communist* is set. Later, this pre-civil-rights historical context becomes the background to Nathan's attempt to portray Coleman's decision to pass as Jewish, and indicative of the novel's – and the trilogy's – broader twinning of the late 1940s and late 1990s.

In thrall to his nostalgia, and buoyed by his affair, Coleman asks Nathan to dance with him:

> 'I hope nobody from the volunteer fire department drives by', I said.
>
> 'Yeah,' he said. 'We don't want anybody tapping me on the shoulder and asking, "May I cut in?"'
>
> On we danced. There was nothing overtly carnal in it, but because Coleman was wearing only his denim shorts and my hand rested easily on his warm back as if it were the back of a dog or a horse, it wasn't entirely a mocking act. There was a semi-serious sincerity in his guiding me about on the stone floor. (26)

Like boxing, dancing figures a form of dexterous intimacy that becomes 'a central metaphor in the novel, one directly linked to the narrative act'.[153] Nathan imagines Faunia dancing with Coleman to the same sentimental 'evening-long Saturday FM program' (203). Later, he pictures her dancing at the foot of Coleman's bed in a scene that itself echoes Coleman's description of a swaying striptease performed by Steena Paarlson back in 1948. Sashaying to

Artie Shaw and Roy Eldridge's rendition of Gershwin's 'The Man I Love', Steena dances 'to a black man's version of a Jewish man's version of a black-inspired musical idiom', Jonathan Freedman writes, her performance keying into the broader 'discursive matrix' of race, ethnicity, and identity at play in the novel.[154] Nathan and Coleman's foxtrot is also a 'black and Jewish dance' in which ethnicity is problematised.[155] Given the novel's range of allusions to nineteenth-century US literature and post-Second World War Jewish American intellectual culture, it is not too far-fetched to interpret Nathan and Coleman's friendship as Roth's version of the kind of interracial male bonding that Leslie Fiedler suggested was at the heart of classic American fiction. Certainly, as a reader of '*Commentary*, *Midstream*, and the *Partisan Review*' in the late 1940s, Coleman would surely have come across Fielder's famous article in which he first formulated his thesis, '"Come Back to the Raft Ag'in, Huck Honey!"', published in *Partisan Review* in 1948 (131).[156] But their friendship also forms part of the trilogy's broader exploration of postwar Jewish and African American relations, a 'Rothian theme' for 'almost half a century'.[157] *American Pastoral* focuses on the 'shifting racial landscape' of Newark following the 1960s race riots, while the most deeply held of Ira's political convictions is his anti-racism.[158] Nathan's relationship with Coleman, then, continues Roth's examination of 'the de-ethnicising' or 'whitening of Jewish identity' in postwar America.[159]

When they first dance, however, Nathan knows nothing of Coleman's secret. Rather, the pair appear to be two Jewish men of a similar age, raised a few miles apart in New Jersey, with similar political outlooks and conceptions of literary value. But their friendship is formed not so much by these shared cultural markers as by a shared understanding of what Nathan calls 'an essential part of being a man' – sex (27). Surprised at Coleman's candour regarding his affair with Faunia, Nathan reflects:

> I thought, He's found somebody he can talk with ... and then I thought, So have I. The moment a man starts to tell you about sex, he's telling you something about the two of you. Ninety percent of the time it doesn't happen, and probably it's as well it doesn't, though if you can't get a level of candor on sex and you choose to behave instead as if this isn't ever on your mind, the male friendship is

incomplete. Most men never find such a friend. It's not common. But when it does happen, when two men find themselves in agreement about this essential part of being a man, unafraid of being judged, shamed, envied, or outdone, confident of not having the confidence betrayed, their human connection can be very strong and an unexpected intimacy results. (27)

This 'serious friendship' upends Nathan's project of 'radical seclusion'. Murray had reminded him of the 'pleasures of companionship', but it is his friendship with Coleman that brings Nathan 'out from under the stalwartness of living alone' (45). As in the earlier novel, a male friendship allows Nathan to regain a 'heart for the world', in all its hostility and incomprehensibility: 'I did no more than find a friend', he writes, 'and all the world's malice came rushing in' (45).

But, as in *I Married a Communist*, Nathan realises the true extent of his feelings for his friend only in retrospect: Coleman is dead before the book begins. In an interview conducted some years after *The Human Stain*'s publication, Roth reflects on the unique process of 're-estimation' that accompanies the death of friends:

> The death of friends is a very, very difficult thing to come to grips with [...] Your friends are your friends for life, as it were. You're all in this thing together. You're equals [...] and you have a kind of feeling for friends unlike the feeling you have for family. You're quite astonished, I think, by the depth of the feeling when someone dies, what you felt for a friend. And also the re-estimation which happens when someone dies happens all the time with friends, I think. I don't mean that you suddenly think, gosh, he was a wonderful fellow, and I always thought he was a son of a bitch. Not that. Nothing as crude as that. But rather, you suddenly see them clearly, vividly. And it's very strong medicine.[160]

Nathan experiences a similar sense of recognition, although he does not so much see Coleman 'clearly' as clearly see how little he ever understood his friend. In my Introduction, I noted the elegiac tone that characterises the philosophical and literary tradition of friendship, in which many of the canonical texts on friendship are works of consolation. 'The experience of friendship' in this tradition, Simon Critchley writes, 'is intimately connected with the experience of loss, of mourning', such that 'the voice of the friend' always reaches us from 'beyond the grave'.[161] *The Human Stain* is a work of mourning that has its moment of origin in Nathan's visit to the grave of his 'utterly transformed friend' (338). He listens for Coleman's voice: 'Out there at his grave [...] I waited and I waited for him to speak until at last I heard him asking Faunia what was the worst job she'd ever had [...] And that is how all this began' (338).

Nathan is 'Roth's original ghost writer', David Coughlan argues, and a certain spectrality has figured in all the Zuckerman books, from *The Ghost Writer* to *Exit Ghost* (2007).[162] Nathan's account of his friendship with Coleman – who insists that he used the word 'spooks' in its 'primary meaning' as 'a specter or ghost', rather than as a racial epithet – is also shadowed by death (6). As Sinatra begins to sing and Coleman invites him to dance, Nathan thinks, 'What the hell [...] we'll both be dead soon enough', flitting back to the sight of Coleman, 'out of his mind with grief and rage', after the death of his wife Iris. 'Maybe why I gave him my hand and let him [...] push me dreamily around [...] was because I had been there that day when her corpse was still warm and seen what he'd looked like' (25–26). That deathly warmth permeates their dance, felt when Nathan rests his hand upon Coleman's 'warm back' (26). There is a spectral quality to the scene that prefigures what Nathan, citing Keats's last letter, will describe in *Exit Ghost* as a sense of living 'a posthumous existence'.[163] Nathan also quotes Keats to Coleman, when the professor waxes lyrical over the 'ignitable' Faunia. '"La Belle Dame sans Merci hath thee in thrall"', Nathan says, alluding to the line spoken by the 'death pale warriors' in the knight's 'latest dream' in Keats's poem (*HS* 27).[164] Coleman may well dance him 'right back into life', as Nathan says, but only by fostering a 'keen awareness of the narrative implications surrounding death'.[165]

At Coleman's funeral, Nathan listens to a eulogy given by Herb Keble, Athena's first African American professor and Coleman's first appointment as Dean. Having failed to defend Coleman when he was accused of racism, Keble uses his eulogy to apologise for his cowardice, and to glorify Coleman as 'an American individualist par excellence' in the tradition of New England's literary forefathers, 'Hawthorne, Melville, and Thoreau' (310). But Nathan does not buy Keble's remorse, nor his characterisation of Coleman. Strong-armed by Coleman's children in their bid to salvage their father's reputation, Nathan realises that Keble's eulogy is part of a concerted effort to, as he puts it in a nicely ironic phrase, 'kosher the record' (312). Just as I suggested that, with Roth's eulogy for Bob Lowenstein in mind, *I Married a Communist* might be read as Nathan's tribute to Murray, so too can *The Human Stain* be read as Nathan's counter-eulogy for the 'counter-confessional' counterpuncher Coleman, complicating the neat re-estimation Keble attempts in his funeral address (100). Rather than simplifying Coleman's story into a 'conventionalized narrative' Nathan attempts to do justice to Coleman's singular life by recognising the 'blizzard of details that constitute the confusion of a human biography' (147, 22). Rather than 'mythologize' Coleman as an 'American individualist', Ross Posnock observes, Nathan 'instead inquires into the costs' of Coleman's 'oppositional individualism', a reckoning that inevitably reflects back upon Nathan's own decision to live alone.[166]

Nathan gains a clear account of some of these costs from Coleman's sister Ernestine. Their conversation near the end of the novel is recorded at length, recalling the dialogic structure of *I Married a Communist*. Like Murray, Ernestine is a dedicated public-school teacher whose talk is permeated by local history and an old-fashioned patriotic liberalism: 'In my childhood, as in yours', she tells Nathan, 'it was recommended that each student who graduated from high school in New Jersey get [...] a diploma and a copy of the Constitution' (329). Decrying the 'urban renewal' of East Orange, Ernestine sounds like Murray reminiscing about the old First Ward, indicative of the novels' shared political perspective (330). Listening to Ernestine, Nathan comes to see Coleman not only in the broader context of his national historical moment, but in the context of his local and family history. Subsequently, his decision to pass is 'presented not so much as a betrayal of the entire black race as a betrayal of a particular set of people'.[167]

As in *I Married a Communist*, then, male friendship becomes a prism through which Roth explores the allegiances and loyalties that can structure a life and a political community. Through friendship, both novels examine the ways in which people are embedded in a particular set of historical circumstances, but also in a particular network of personal relationships. Nathan's friendships with Murray and Coleman offer an alternative to his conception of adulthood-as-isolation, although it is an alternative that can only be recognised too late. David Coughlan argues that the Zuckerman books always 'begin with death' and are 'directly concerned with the responsibility of the writer to the dead'.[168] But in *I Married a Communist* and *The Human Stain*, Nathan's responsibility is that of a writer *and* a friend. Alluding to Chekhov's definition of the task of the writer, Nathan captures these overlapping obligations in *The Human Stain*: 'the dance that sealed our friendship was also what made his disaster my subject [...] And made the proper presentation of his secret my problem to solve' (45).[169] Quoting this passage, Andy Connolly concludes that 'Zuckerman thus finds in Coleman's history a suitable canvass [*sic*] for once again exploring the relationship between personal acts of self-transformation and authorial models for reinventing life'.[170] But Coleman is not just a 'canvass' to Nathan. 'His difficulties mattered to me, and this despite my determination [...] to have not even a life of my own to care about, let alone somebody else's' (*HS* 43). In properly presenting Coleman's secret, Nathan must do justice to their 'serious friendship'. And if, as Connolly suggests, this represents an imaginative opportunity, it also represents a haunting responsibility, a dubious gift.

Notes

1 Jack Miles, Letter to Roth dated October 6, 1998, 'Jack Miles Correspondence', Box 24, Folder 13, Philip Roth Papers, Library of Congress, Washington, DC. According to the 'Chronology' included in the Library of America editions of Roth's work, Miles – a professor of religion and author of *God: A Biography* (1995) – first wrote to Roth in 1974, after reading Roth's essay, 'Imagining Jews'. This began a long correspondence and a 'lasting intellectual friendship'.

2 Michiko Kakutani, 'Manly Giants vs. Zealots and Scheming Women', *New York Times*, 6 October 1998. Kakutani had praised *American Pastoral*; see 'A Postwar Paradise Shattered from Within', *New York Times*, 15 April 1997.

3 Miles, Letter to Roth dated June 29, 1998, 'Jack Miles Correspondence'.
4 See Charles McGrath, 'Zuckerman's Alter Brain: An Interview with Philip Roth', *New York Times*, 7 May 2000.
5 Miles, Letter to Roth dated June 29, 1998.
6 Philipp Löffler, *Pluralist Desires: Contemporary Historical Fiction and the End of the Cold War* (Rochester: Camden House, 2015), 97.
7 David Gooblar, *The Major Phases of Philip Roth* (London: Continuum, 2011), 131.
8 Mark Shechner, 'Roth's American Trilogy', in Timothy Parrish (ed.), *The Cambridge Companion to Philip Roth* (Cambridge: Cambridge University Press, 2007), pp. 142–158 (142); Matthew Shipe, '*Exit Ghost* and the Politics of "Late Style"', *Philip Roth Studies*, 5:2 (Fall 2009), pp. 189–204 (191).
9 David Brauner, *Philip Roth* (Manchester: Manchester University Press, 2007), 148; Derek Parker Royal, 'Pastoral Dreams and National Identity in *American Pastoral* and *I Married a Communist*', in Royal (ed.), *Philip Roth: New Perspectives on an American Author* (Westport: Praeger, 2005), pp. 185–208 (185).
10 McGrath, 'Zuckerman's Alter-Brain', 8; Sean McCann, *A Pinnacle of Feeling: American Literature and Presidential Government* (Princeton: Princeton University Press, 2008), 187. On the 'historical turn' in Roth's work, see Laura Tanenbaum, 'Reading Roth's Sixties', *Studies in American Jewish Literature*, 23 (2004), pp. 41–54 (41–44); Gooblar, *Major Phases*, 131–134. On the 'national turn' in Roth's later fiction, see Bryan Cheyette, *Diasporas of the Mind: Jewish and Postcolonial Writing and the Nightmare of History* (New Haven: Yale University Press, 2013), 161–203 (161).
11 David Remnick, 'Philip Roth at 70' [Interview], dir. Deborah Lee, BBC4, 7 May 2003.
12 See David Brauner, 'Essay Review: The Canonization of Philip Roth', *Studies in the Novel*, 39:4 (Winter 2007), pp. 481–488 (481–482). The way in which the novel is often excised from critical treatments of the trilogy is demonstrated by a collection of essays by leading Roth scholars edited by Debra Shostak, *Philip Roth: American Pastoral, The Human Stain, The Plot Against America* (London: Continuum, 2011).
13 See Samuel Cohen, *After the End of History: American Fiction in the 1990s* (Iowa City: University of Iowa Press, 2009), 1–30; Löffler, *Pluralist Desires*, 1–19.
14 Two studies have addressed the novel's political and historical context. See Anthony Hutchison, *Writing the Republic: Liberalism*

and *Morality in American Political Fiction* (New York: Columbia University Press, 2007), 96–112; Andy Connolly, *Philip Roth and the American Liberal Tradition* (Lanham: Lexington Books, 2017), 61–112.

15 Leslie Fiedler, *Love and Death in the American Novel* [1960] (Illinois: Dalkey Archive Press, 2003), 352.

16 'Placing Zuckerman is the Berkshires, home to Hawthorne, Melville and Thoreau, Roth moves himself [...] into the tradition of the American Renaissance writers'. Catherine Morley, *The Quest for Epic in Contemporary American Fiction: John Updike, Philip Roth, and Don DeLillo* (London: Routledge, 2009), 86.

17 A 'close reading suggests that much of what transpires is just as much a matter of the narrator's imagination as it is of recorded fact'. Derek Parker Royal, 'Plotting the Frames of Subjectivity: Identity, Death, and Narrative in Philip Roth's *The Human Stain*', *Contemporary Literature*, 47:1 (Spring 2006), pp. 114–140 (118).

18 Philip Roth, *American Pastoral* [1997] (London: Vintage, 2000), 87. Subsequent references are given in the text as *AP* and in parentheses. On this shift of focalisation, see Gary Chase Johnson, 'The Presence of Allegory: The Case of Philip Roth's *American Pastoral*', *Narrative*, 12:3 (October 2004), pp. 233–248 (244).

19 I borrow the term 'counterliving' from Ross Posnock. See Posnock, *Philip Roth's Rude Truth: The Art of Immaturity* (Princeton: Princeton University Press, 2006), 15. Debra Shostak argues that the idea of the counterlife is integral to Roth's 'dialogic' imagination. See Shostak, *Philip Roth: Countertexts, Counterlives* (Columbia: University of Southern Carolina Press, 2004), 6–19.

20 The Zuckerman books are *The Ghost Writer* (1979), *Zuckerman Unbound* (1981), *The Anatomy Lesson* (1983), *The Prague Orgy* (1985) (collected as *Zuckerman Bound* in 1989), *The Counterlife* (1986), The American Trilogy, and *Exit Ghost* (2007). Zuckerman also appears as the creation of another of Roth's novelist-narrators, Peter Tarnopol, in *My Life as a Man* (1974).

21 Philip Roth, *The Counterlife* [1986] (London: Jonathan Cape, 1987), 46.

22 Roth, *The Counterlife*, 145.

23 Royal, 'Plotting the Frames', 118.

24 Morley, *The Quest for Epic*, 98.

25 Quoted in Shostak, *Philip Roth*, 21.

26 Elizabeth Moran, 'Death, Determination and "the End of Ends?": Nathan Zuckerman from *My Life as a Man* to *Exit Ghost*', *Philip*

Roth Studies, 11:2 (Fall 2015), pp. 5–30 (8). For an overview, see David Gooblar, 'Introduction: Roth and Women', *Philip Roth Studies*, 8:1 (Spring 2012), pp. 7–15.

27 Debra Shostak, 'Roth and Gender', in Timothy Parrish (ed.), *The Cambridge Companion to Philip Roth* (Cambridge: Cambridge University Press, 2007), pp. 111–126 (112); Velichka Ivanova, 'My Own Foe from the Other Gender: (Mis)representing Women in *The Dying Animal*', *Philip Roth Studies*, 8:1 (Spring 2012), pp. 31–44 (32).

28 Philip Roth, *My Life as a Man* (New York: Holt, Rinehart and Winston, 1974), 173.

29 Shostak, 'Roth and Gender', 111.

30 Ivanova, 'My Own Foe from the Other Gender', 39.

31 Eve Kosofsky Sedgwick makes the link between doppelgängers and homosexual panic in her discussion of Henry James and the 'paranoid Gothic'; see *Epistemology of the Closet* [1990] (Berkeley: University of California Press, 2008), 186. On doubles in Roth's work, see Josh Cohen, 'Roth's Doubles', in Timothy Parrish (ed.), *The Cambridge Companion to Philip Roth* (Cambridge: Cambridge University Press, 2007), pp. 82–93. 'Secret sharer' alludes to the Joseph Conrad short story of the same title, often read as being about homosexual desire.

32 Philip Roth, *Zuckerman Bound: A Trilogy and Epilogue* [1985] (London: Vintage, 1998), 152.

33 Roth, *Zuckerman Bound*, 198, 258.

34 See Ann Basu, *States of Trial: Manhood in Philip Roth's Post-War America* (London: Bloomsbury, 2015), 21.

35 See for example Robert Alter, 'The Spritzer: Review of *Operation Shylock*', *The New Republic*, 5 April 1993, p. 31. For a subtler reading of Roth's doubles, see Mark McGurl, *The Program Era: Postwar Fiction and the Rise of Creative Writing* (Cambridge, MA: Harvard University Press, 2009), 51–55.

36 Eve Kosofsky Sedgwick, *Between Men: English Literature and Male Homosocial Desire* (New York: Columbia University Press, 1985), 1; Brauner, 'Queering Philip Roth: Homosocial Discourse in "An Actor's Life for Me," *Letting Go*, *Sabbath's Theater,* and the "American Trilogy"', *Studies in the Novel*, 48:1 (Spring 2016), pp. 86–106 (88).

37 Sedgwick, *Between Men*, 26.

38 On *Portrait*'s broader significance in the novel, see Hayes, *Philip Roth*, 63–71. On the importance of James to Roth and Jewish American intellectuals in the 1950s, see Jonathan Freedman, *The Temple of Culture: Assimilation and Anti-Semitism in Literary Anglo-America* (Oxford: Oxford University Press, 2000), 117–154.

39 See Hana Wirth-Nesher, 'The Artist Tales of Philip Roth', *Prooftexts*, 3:3 (September 1983), pp. 263–272 (268–269).
40 On 'homosocial pleasure' in 'The Middle Years', see Leland Person, *Henry James and the Suspension of Masculinity* (Philadelphia: University of Pennsylvania Press, 2003), 139–149 (142).
41 Roth, *Zuckerman Bound*, 54. See Brauner, 'Queering Roth', 104, n. 7.
42 Roth, *Zuckerman Bound*, 57, 7.
43 Roth, *Zuckerman Bound*, 370.
44 Posnock, *Philip Roth's Rude Truth*, 48; Philip Roth, *The Human Stain* (London: Vintage, 2000), 37. Subsequent references are given in the text as *HS* and in parentheses.
45 Daniel Leab notes that the 'absolutely awful' *I Married a Communist* – retitled *The Woman on Pier 13* for general release in 1950 – was 'among the crudest of the anti-communist films' of the Cold War era. Alfred Hornung suggests a number of similarities between the film's plot and Ira's backstory. Leab, 'How Red Was My Valley: Hollywood, the Cold War Film, and *I Married a Communist*', *Journal of Contemporary History*, 19 (1984), pp. 59–88 (66); Hornung, 'The Personal is the Fictional: Philip Roth's Return to the 1950s in *I Married a Communist*', in Gerd Hurm and Ann Marie Fallon (eds), *Rebels without a Cause? Renegotiating the American 1950s* (Bern: Peter Lang, 2007), pp. 77–95.
46 Mark Shechner, *Up Society's Ass, Copper: Rereading Philip Roth* (Madison: University of Wisconsin Press, 2003), 176.
47 'Ira's Longy Zwillman was Johnny O'Day', Murray says. Philip Roth, *I Married a Communist* (London: Jonathan Cape, 1998), 67. Subsequent references are given in the text as *IMC* and in parentheses.
48 Thomas Devine, *Henry Wallace's 1948 Presidential Campaign and the Future of Postwar Liberalism* (Chapel Hill: University of North Carolina Press, 2013), 291; Michael Denning, *The Cultural Front: The Laboring of American Culture in the Twentieth Century* (London: Verso, 1996), 10.
49 Philip Roth, 'In Memory of a Friend, Teacher, and Mentor', *New York Times*, 20 April 2013.
50 Brauner, *Philip Roth*, 151.
51 Royal, 'Pastoral Dreams', 191.
52 Howard Jacobson, 'Is *American Pastoral* Philip Roth at His Best?', *The Guardian*, 11 November 2016. 'Hothead' is Roth's own affectionate description for Ira; he has suggested that *Communist* is 'a favourite among his books'. See Claudia Roth Pierpont, *Roth Unbound: A*

Writer and His Books (New York: Farrar, Straus & Giroux, 2013), 234.

53 Saul Bellow, Letter to Roth, January 1, 1998, in Benjamin Taylor (ed.), *Saul Bellow: Letters* (New York: Viking, 2010), 540.
54 Hutchison, *Writing the Republic*, 126; James Wood, 'The Sentimentalist: Review of *I Married a Communist*', *The New Republic*, 12 October 1998, pp. 38–42 (39, 42).
55 Linda Grant, 'The Wrath of Roth', *The Guardian*, 4 October 1998.
56 On *American Pastoral* as historical metafiction, see Cohen, *After the End of History*, 61–90; on *Communist*'s historical realism, see Shechner, *Up Society's Ass, Copper*, 174–185.
57 Royal, 'Pastoral Dreams', 200.
58 Shostak notes the novel's 'dialogic situation, in which the meaning of the story emerges from the interaction between speaker and listener'. *Philip Roth: Countertexts, Counterlives*, 250. By contrast, Roth Pierpont suggests that 'Murray's side of the story consists of expositional chunks'. *Roth Unbound*, 235.
59 This recalls Roth's accounts of the fate of literary dissidents under Soviet totalitarianism in Czechoslovakia. See Philip Roth, 'A Czech Education', in *Why Write?: Collected Nonfiction 1960–2013* (New York: Library of America, 2017), pp. 368–370 (369).
60 Much of Murray's local knowledge is drawn from Michael Immerso, *Newark's Little Italy: The Vanished First Ward* (New Brunswick: Rutgers University Press, 1997); for the canary funeral, see 107–109. Roth cites Immerso's book as a 'primary source' in the novel's frontmatter.
61 Shechner, *Up Society's Ass, Copper*, 127; Philip Roth, *Patrimony: A True Story* (London: Jonathan Cape, 1991), 190.
62 Roth, 'In Memory of a Friend, Teacher, and Mentor'.
63 Steve Golin, *The Newark Teachers Strikes: Hopes on the Line* (New Brunswick: Rutgers University Press, 2002), 10–11.
64 In *The Plot Against America* (London: Jonathan Cape, 2004), Aunt Evelyn is a 'substitute elementary school teacher [...] who'd been active several years earlier in founding the left-wing, largely Jewish Newark Teachers Union, whose few hundred members were competing with a more staid, apolitical teachers' association' (86).
65 Golin, *The Newark Teachers Strikes*, 11.
66 Golin, *The Newark Teachers Strikes*, 28–29.
67 Aimee Pozorski, *Roth and Trauma: The Problem of History in the Later Works (1995–2010)* (London: Continuum, 2011), 67.

68 See Robert Zieger, *The CIO, 1935–1955* (Chapel Hill: University of North Carolina Press, 1995), 141–212.
69 See John Earl Haynes and Harvey Klehr, 'The Historiography of American Communism: An Unsettled Field', *Labour History Review*, 68:1 (April 2003), pp. 61–78.
70 Denning, *The Cultural Front*, 5.
71 John Barrett, 'Rethinking the Popular Front', *Rethinking Marxism*, 21:4 (2009), pp. 513–550 (535). See Theodore Draper, *The Roots of American Communism* (New York: Viking, 1957).
72 Maurice Isserman, *Which Side Were You On?: The American Communist Party During the Second World War* [1982] (Urbana: University of Illinois Press, 1993), 4–8.
73 Theodore Draper, *American Communism and Soviet Russia* [1960] (New York: Vintage, 1986), 470–471.
74 Denning, *The Cultural Front*, xviii.
75 Graham Cassano, 'Returning to the Popular Front', *Rethinking Marxism*, 21:4 (2009), pp. 476–479 (477).
76 Denning, *The Cultural Front*, 4; Doug Rossinow, *Visions of Progress: The Left-liberal Tradition in America* (Philadelphia: University of Pennsylvania Press, 2008), 145.
77 Michael Denning, 'Afterword: Reconsidering the Significance of the Popular Front', *Rethinking Marxism*, 21:4 (2009), pp. 551–555 (554).
78 See, for example, Gary Gerstle, *Working-Class Americanism: The Politics of Labor in a Textile City, 1914–1960* (Princeton: Princeton University Press, 1989).
79 See Rossinow, *Visions of Progress*, 146; Denning, *The Cultural Front*, 125.
80 Isserman, *Which Side Were You On?*, 22. David Eldridge notes that 'Ballad for Americans' became 'the Popular Front's unofficial anthem'. *American Culture in the 1930s* (Edinburgh: Edinburgh University Press, 2008), 115.
81 Zieger, *The CIO*, 154; Denning, *The Cultural Front*, 26.
82 Michael Kazin, *American Dreamers: How the Left Changed a Nation* (New York: Knopf, 2011), 158.
83 Paul Lyons, Maurice Isserman, and Theodore Draper, 'The Old Left: An Exchange', *New York Review of Books*, 23 June 1994, pp. 62–63 (63), in response to Draper, 'The Life of the Party', *New York Review of Books*, 13 January 1994, pp. 45–51.
84 See R. Clifton Spargo, 'How Telling: Irving Howe, Roth's Early Career, and the Dialectic of Impersonation in *The Anatomy Lesson*', *Philip Roth Studies*, 5:2 (Fall 2009), pp. 251–279.

85 Irving Howe, 'Philip Roth Reconsidered', *Commentary*, December 1972, pp. 69–77 (73).
86 Edward Alexander, *Classical Liberalism and the Jewish Tradition* (New Brunswick: Transaction, 2003), 142.
87 Irving Howe and Lewis Coser, *The American Communist Party: A Critical History* [1958] (New York: Da Capo Press, 1974), 386, 325.
88 Irving Howe, *Socialism and America* (New York: Harcourt Brace Jovanovich, 1985), 103.
89 Isserman, 'The Old Left: An Exchange', 63.
90 'Don't lose your courage, young man,' Robeson tells Nathan (33).
91 Löffler, *Pluralist Desires*, 106, 102. See McGurl, *The Program Era*, 56–58.
92 Löffler, *Pluralist Desires*, 102, 107.
93 Philip Roth, '*The Counterlife*: Notes' [October 5, 1985]. Box 79, Folder 2, Philip Roth Papers.
94 Philip Roth, *Reading Myself and Others* [1975] (London: Vintage, 2000), 4.
95 Kasia Boddy, *Boxing: A Cultural History* (London: Reaktion Books, 2008), 379. Elaine Safer, however, argues that Nathan and Murray's 'lengthy endeavors to attain insight tend to parody the Socratic dialogue'. Safer, *Mocking the Age: The Later Novels of Philip Roth* (Albany: State University of New York Press, 2006), 111.
96 Safer, *Mocking the Age*, 109.
97 Michael Sandel, *Liberalism and the Limits of Justice*, 182; Sandra Marshall, 'The Community of Friends', in Emilios Christodoulidis (ed.), *Communitarianism and Citizenship* (Aldershot: Ashgate, 1998), pp. 208–219 (209).
98 See Thomas Spragens, *Civic Liberalism: Reflections on Our Democratic Ideals* (Lanham: Rowman & Littlefield, 1999), 175–212. On the overlap between friendship networks and the long American tradition of voluntarism 'combining individual self-reliance and group belonging', see Claude Fischer, *Made in America: A Social History of American Culture and Character* (Chicago: University of Chicago Press, 2010), 95–150, esp. 132–133 (96).
99 See Brian McDonald, '"The Real American Crazy Shit": On Adamism and Democratic Individuality in *American Pastoral*', *Studies in American Jewish Literature*, 23 (2004), pp. 27–40 (34–36).
100 Alfred Kazin, 'What Have the '30s Done to Our Literature?', *New York Herald Tribune Books*, 31 December 1939, pp. 1–2 (1); Alfred Haworth Jones, *Roosevelt's Image Brokers: Poets, Playwrights, and the Use of the Lincoln Symbol* (Port Washington: Kennikat Press,

1974), 49; Barry Schwartz, *Abraham Lincoln in the Post-Heroic Era: History and Memory in Late Twentieth-Century America* (Chicago: University of Chicago Press, 2008), 33.
101 Jones, *Roosevelt's Image Brokers*, 65, 5.
102 Jones, *Roosevelt's Image Brokers*, 42; Earl Browder, *Lincoln and the Communists* (New York: Workers Library, 1936), 7.
103 Nathan describes watching Ira discuss politics with African Americans on Newark street corners as witnessing 'the Lincoln-Douglas debates in a strange new form' (92).
104 Kasia Boddy, 'Philip Roth's Great Books: A Reading of *The Human Stain*', *Cambridge Quarterly*, 39:1 (March 2010), pp. 39–60 (59). Boddy notes that, in the *Protagoras*, Plato 'likens the moves and countermoves of Socratic debate to a boxing match'. Boddy, *Boxing*, 7. Jerry jokingly likens Nathan to Socrates in *American Pastoral* (64).
105 Hayes, *Philip Roth*, 19. Roth uses the phrase to describe his friendship with Bernard Malamud. See Roth, *Shop Talk* (London: Vintage, 2001), 125.
106 Bob Lowenstein, 'Boxing Lessons' [Sent to Roth 28/2/97], in 'Bob Lowenstein Correspondence, 1996–99', Box 20, Folder 6, Philip Roth Papers.
107 Tom MacFaul, *Male Friendship in Shakespeare and His Contemporaries* (Cambridge: Cambridge University Press, 2007), 7.
108 Phillip Deery, *Red Apple: Communism and McCarthyism in Cold War New York* (New York: Fordham University Press, 2014), 39.
109 See Deery, *Red Apple*, 40; Julia Mickenberg, *Learning from the Left: Children's Literature, the Cold War, and Radical Politics in the United States* (Oxford: Oxford University Press, 2005), 283, n. 3.
110 Andrew MacDonald, *Howard Fast: A Critical Companion* (Westport: Greenwood Press, 1996), 50.
111 Quoted in MacDonald, *Howard Fast*, 49.
112 Priscilla Murolo, 'History in the Fast Lane: Howard Fast and the Historical Novel', in Susan Porter Benson, Stephen Brier, and Roy Rosenzweig (eds), *Presenting the Past: Essays on History and the Public* (Philadelphia: Temple University Press, 1986), pp. 53–67 (54).
113 Pozorski, *Roth and Trauma*, 68.
114 Roth, *Zuckerman Bound*, 4.
115 'Tension' became a key term for the New Critics; see Allen Tate, 'Tension in Poetry', *Southern Review*, 4 (January 1938), pp. 101–116.
116 Howard Fast, *Citizen Tom Paine* [1943] (London: Bodley Head, 1945), 211.
117 Fast, *Citizen Tom Paine*, 216.

'The love alternative' 77

118 Fast, *Citizen Tom Paine*, 242.
119 Gurion Taussig, *Coleridge and the Idea of Friendship, 1789–1804* (Newark: University of Delaware Press, 2002), 146; Thomas Paine, *Political Writings*, ed. Bruce Kuklick (Cambridge: Cambridge University Press, 1989), 11.
120 Robert Lamb, *Thomas Paine and the Idea of Human Rights* (Cambridge: Cambridge University Press, 2013), 13; Kuklick, 'Introduction', in Paine, *Political Writings*, vii. On the Popular Front's historical appropriation of Paine, see Harvey Kaye, *Thomas Paine and the Promise of America: A History & Biography* (New York: Hill and Wang, 2005), 218–222. Fraser Ottanelli notes that the CPUSA celebrated 'Thomas Paine Day' on 18 September 1937. See *The Communist Party of the United States: From the Depression to World War II* (New Brunswick: Rutgers University Press, 1991), 123.
121 Richard Godbeer, *The Overflowing of Friendship: Love Between Men and the Creation of the American Republic* (Baltimore: Johns Hopkins University Press, 2009), 151.
122 See Jay Fliegelman, *Prodigals and Pilgrims: The American Revolution Against Patriarchal Authority 1750–1800* (Cambridge: Cambridge University Press, 1982), 103–108.
123 Thomas Paine, *The Rights of Man, Part II* [1792] (Cambridge: Cambridge University Press, 2012), 76–77; Taussig, *Coleridge and the Idea of Friendship*, 146.
124 Paine, *The Rights of Man, Part II*, 33.
125 Paine, *Political Writings*, 18.
126 Philip Roth, *Portnoy's Complaint* [1969] (London: Vintage, 2005), 169, 170.
127 *Portnoy's Complaint*, 168. See also Marshall Berman, 'Dancing with American: Philip Roth, Writer on the Left', *New Labor Forum*, 9 (Winter 2001), pp. 46–56.
128 Roth recalls listening to *On a Note of Triumph* as 'one of the most thrilling experiences of my childhood'. Pierpont notes that the script was 'the first book he ever bought'. *Roth Unbound*, 21.
129 Pierpont describes Murray's speech as 'stiff and oddly literary'. *Roth Unbound*, 234.
130 Denning, *The Cultural Front*, 91.
131 Michael Keith and Mary Ann Watson (eds), *Norman Corwin's One World Flight: The Lost Journal of Radio's Greatest Writer* (London: Bloomsbury, 2009), 193–194.
132 Norman Corwin, *On a Note of Triumph* (New York: Simon & Schuster, 1945), 10.

133 Neil Verma, *Theater of the Mind: Imagination, Aesthetics, and American Radio Drama* (Chicago: University of Chicago Press, 2012), 81.
134 David Goodman, *Radio's Civic Ambition: American Broadcasting and Democracy in the 1930s* (Oxford: Oxford University Press, 2011), 181; Michele Hilmes, *Radio Voices: American Broadcasting, 1922–1952* (Minneapolis: University of Minnesota Press, 1997), 230.
135 Elena Razlogova, *The Listener's Ear: Early Radio and the American Public* (Philadelphia: University of Pennsylvania Press, 2011), 2.
136 Jason Loviglio, *Radio's Intimate Public: Network Broadcasting and Mass-mediated Democracy* (Minneapolis: University of Minnesota Press, 2005), xix.
137 Loviglio, *Radio's Intimate Public*, xvi.
138 This link between the radio and the novel's narrative structure is emphasised when Nathan, having dropped Murray back into town for the final time, sees the 'citronella candle' burning on his porch where they have been talking, and is reminded of 'the radio dial' of the 'cathedral-shaped table radio' he had in his room as a boy (320).
139 Robert Chodat, 'Fictions Public and Private: On Philip Roth', *Contemporary Literature*, 46:4 (Winter 2005), pp. 688–719 (717).
140 Theodore Solotaroff, 'The Journey of Philip Roth', *Atlantic Monthly*, April 1969, pp. 64–72 (67), quoted in Gooblar, *Major Phases*, 38.
141 Theodore Solotaroff, 'The New York Publishing World', in Bernard Rosenberg and Ernest Goldstein (eds), *Creators and Disturbers: Reminiscences by Jewish Intellectual of New York* (New York: Columbia University Press, 1982), pp. 401–419 (409). Solotaroff notes that 'reading [Trilling] you felt that you hadn't betrayed your heart by abandoning your radicalism' (409).
142 See Freedman, *The Temple of Culture*, 164.
143 On Kierkegaard and friendship, see Graham Smith, *Friendship and the Political: Kierkegaard, Nietzsche, Schmitt* (Exeter: Imprint Academic, 2011), 79–128, esp. 95–100.
144 Chodat makes a similar point. See 'Fictions Public and Private', 708.
145 Denning, *The Cultural Front*, 117. In *Citizen Tom Paine*, Fast has Paine imagine 'a united states of Europe allied to a united states of America, a brotherhood of man' (184). *On a Note of Triumph*'s closing prayer includes the imperative to 'Post proofs that brotherhood is not so wild a dream as those who profit by postponing it pretend'.
146 On Goldstine's nihilism, see Sorin Radu Cucu, *The Underside of Politics: Global Fictions in the Fog of the Cold War* (New York: Fordham University Press, 2013), 109.

147 Jack Miles, Letter to Roth dated January 1, 1997, 'Jack Miles Correspondence', Box 24, Folder 13, Philip Roth Papers. Emphasis in original.
148 Miles, Letter to Roth dated January 1, 1997.
149 Aaron Chandler, 'Pursuing Unhappiness: City, Space, and Sentimentalism in Post-Cold War American Literature', PhD Thesis, University of North Carolina (2009), 68.
150 Chandler, 'Pursuing Unhappiness', 68.
151 Royal, 'Plotting the Frames', 137.
152 Earlier, Coleman is described as 'revolutionizing the curriculum' (5).
153 Royal, 'Plotting the Frames', 125.
154 Jonathan Freedman, *Klezmer America: Jewishness, Ethnicity, Modernity* (New York: Columbia University Press, 2008), 182.
155 Ranen Omer-Sherman, *Diaspora and Zionism in Jewish American Literature: Lazarus, Syrkin, Reznikoff, and Roth* (Hanover: Brandeis University Press, 2002), 257.
156 See Leslie Fiedler '"Come Back to the Raft Ag'in, Huck Honey!"', *Partisan Review*, 15 (June 1948), pp. 269–276.
157 Berman, 'Dancing with America', 48.
158 Jennifer Glaser, *Borrowed Voices: Writing and Racial Ventriloquism in the Jewish American Imagination* (New Brunswick: Rutgers University Press, 2016), 96. When asked by Nathan what 'Negroes [are] actually like', Ira says that the 'characteristic I was most aware of [was] their warm friendliness' (C, 93).
159 Emily Miller Budick, *Blacks and Jews in Literary Conversation* (Cambridge: Cambridge University Press, 1998), 1; Glaser, *Borrowed Voices*, 95, 96.
160 Terry Gross, '*Fresh Air* Remembers Novelist Philip Roth', 25 May 2018, www.npr.org/2018/05/25/614398904/fresh-air-remembers-novelist-philip-roth.
161 Simon Critchley, *Ethics, Politics, Subjectivity: Essays on Derrida, Levinas and Contemporary French Thought* (London: Verso, 1999), 257.
162 David Coughlan, *Ghost Writing in Contemporary American Fiction* (Basingstoke: Palgrave Macmillan, 2016), 98.
163 Philip Roth, *Exit Ghost* (London: Vintage, 2007), 221; John Keats, 'Letter to Charles Brown, November 30, 1820', in *Keats's Poetry and Prose*, ed. Jeffrey Cox (New York: Norton, 2009), 533.
164 John Keats, 'La Belle Dame sans Merci', in *Keats's Poetry and Prose*, 343. Nathan also quotes 'The Eve of St Agnes' in describing Coleman and Faunia (212).

165 Royal, 'Plotting the Frames', 127.
166 Posnock, *Philip Roth's Rude Truth*, 222.
167 Chodat, 'Fictions Public and Private', 709.
168 Coughlan, *Ghost Writing in Contemporary American Fiction*, 98.
169 Roth quotes Chekhov's distinction between 'the solution of the problem and a correct presentation of the problem' in *Reading Myself and Others*, 16.
170 Connolly, *Philip Roth and the American Liberal Tradition*, 176.

2

The gift of friendship: Paul Auster's fiction and film

'I keep wanting to give you things'

In the final section of the previous chapter, I began to explore the relationship between friendship and mourning and, more broadly, to consider the kinds of obligations and responsibilities that shape relations between friends and citizens. In the first half of this chapter, I turn to three novels by Paul Auster in which these issues are also at stake, and in which one male friend is tasked with accounting for the life of another. I approach these novels, and some of Auster's other works, by way of the gift. Like friendship, the concept of the gift became the focus of renewed critical attention across a range of disciplines towards the end of the twentieth century, and ever since has enjoyed a particular vogue among literary critics and novelists thanks to Lewis Hyde's bestselling book *The Gift* (1983).[1] Hyde argues that, unlike a commodity, a gift fosters a 'feeling-bond' between people and 'creates a community', rather than a set of market relations.[2] Articulating an ethic of generosity, Hyde suggests that the gift substantiates a form of sociability based on reciprocity and beyond the logic of economic self-interest. Yet, as Derrida cautions in *Given Time* (1992) and *The Gift of Death* (1996), distinguishing between a 'gift economy' and a market economy might be less straightforward than Hyde suggests. Even well-intentioned acts of generosity might imbricate both donor and donee in a dynamic of restricting indebtedness; like other economic relations, the gift might only be a form of proprietorial social control. In the second half of this chapter, I continue to think through the equivocal promise of the gift by considering the circulation of money in

Auster's work. For Auster, money focalises the issues of value, reciprocity, and debt that both define and trouble the gift. I show that his fiction holds to the possibility that money might elaborate forms of haphazard solidarity and community between people, in which the working up and off of debts indexes emotional ties as well as financial obligations. Money, however, is not the only currency of friendship in Auster's work. Throughout the chapter, I consider how the concept of the gift becomes a model for thinking about the relationship between authors, texts, and readers in his fiction, and about the circulation of literature within the wider culture.

I turn first to another form of exchange: correspondence. As in the previous chapter, I begin with letters passing between two male friends, but whereas before I drew on the private correspondence of Jack Miles and Philip Roth, in this chapter I draw on *Here and Now* (2013), the published correspondence of Auster and J. M. Coetzee, which covers the period from 2008 (shortly after the pair first met) to 2011. 'Reading a writer's letters can sometimes be embarrassing', Auster notes in a review of Kafka's *Letters to Friends, Family, and Editors* (1977). 'We feel we are intruding on a private realm, seeing things that were never meant for our eyes'.[3] This is not the case with *Here and Now*, however, where readers are left to guess quite where the private realm ends and the public realm begins, Auster and Coetzee leaving the question of whether these letters were written for publication unanswered. In one exchange, Coetzee notes that he writes 'books in which people write (and mail) paper letters', hinting that *Here and Now* might be a kind of collaborative postmodern fiction, in which Paul Auster and J. M. Coetzee write an epistolary novel of a correspondence between 'Paul Auster' and 'J. M. Coetzee'.[4] Discussing a new edition of Samuel Beckett's correspondence that Coetzee is reviewing, Auster complains that the volume's 'cumbersome editorial apparatus' carves a 'distinction between "work" and "life"' (48). It is a distinction neither writer observes in his own work, and, as a public performance of a private correspondence, *Here and Now* continues to blur the line between the two.

In other ways, however, their correspondence is quite quaintly old-fashioned, taking the form of a series of exchanges on a variety of literary, political, and philosophical topics. But as Martin Riker notes in his review, 'friendship is the book's overarching subject'.[5] Coetzee's opening letter begins:

> I have been thinking about friendships, how they arise, why they last – some of them – so long, longer than the passional attachments of which they are sometimes (wrongly) considered to be pale imitations. I was about to write a letter to you about all this, starting with the observation that, considering how important friendships are in social life [...] it is surprising how little has been written on the subject.
>
> But then I asked myself whether this was really true. So before I sat down to write I went off to the library to [...] check. And, lo and behold, I could not have been more wrong. The library catalog listed whole books on the subject [...] But when I took a step further [...] I recovered my self-respect somewhat [...] what these books had to say about friendship was of little interest [...] Friendship, it would seem, remains a bit of a riddle. (1)

In its false starts, befuddled negations, and convoluted syntax, Coetzee's letter also remains a bit of a riddle. He wonders whether he discovered little of interest during his library trip because, 'unlike love or politics, which are never what they seem to be, friendship is what it seems to be. Friendship is transparent' (3). But his own rumination on friendship is anything but transparent. In his reply, Auster challenges Coetzee's characterisation, suggesting that men's friendships in fact often occupy 'an ambiguous zone of notknowing'. 'At least three of my novels deal directly with male friendship, are in a sense stories *about* male friendship', Auster writes, observing that each novel – *The Locked Room* (1986), *Leviathan* (1992), and *Oracle Night* (2004) – dramatises 'this no-man's land of not-knowing that stands between friends' (4). These three novels are the focus of the first half of this chapter and, in each, male friendship is far from a 'transparent' relation. Despite his scepticism however, in the same letter Auster offers an idealised portrait of the 'absolute equality' of the 'best and most lasting friendships': 'you are both giving more than you receive, both receiving more than you give, and in the reciprocity of this exchange, friendship blooms' (6). Imagining friendship as a practice of generosity – as a kind of gift – Auster seems to also comment on the reciprocal exchange he is beginning with Coetzee. In a later letter he writes, 'For reasons I can't quite grasp, I keep wanting to *give you things*' (128, emphasis in original).

The association of friendship, epistolarity, and the gift has a long history. In classical Rome, Amanda Wilcox writes, correspondence was 'self-consciously wielded as both the medium for friendship and the means of its display', familiar letters representing 'gifts of friendship' between correspondents, offered as a way of fostering affection at a distance.[6] Humanism developed this connection between letter-writing and friendship into what Kathy Eden calls a 'hermeneutics of intimacy', in which the 'familiar letter constructs a fiction of the affective presence of the absent individual', a fiction made compelling by the rhetorical ingenuity of the correspondents, and by the symbolic exchange of the texts themselves as gifts.[7] In humanism's conception of epistolary friendship, absence brings forth an emotional and imaginative fluency not afforded by proximity, and writing well becomes a way of eliding the distance between friends. Letters 'simultaneously articulate union (by connecting us to another) *and* disunion (the letter is sent in lieu of presence)', and so correspondence 'confirms even as it would mitigate separation'.[8] Letters cultivate a kind of intimate distance.

In 'Friendship' (1841), Ralph Waldo Emerson develops a similar conception of intimacy *in absentia*, connecting friendship, letters, and gifts. Elizabeth Hewitt notes that a dialectic between 'absolute intimacy' and 'radical solitude' operates as a 'kind of deep structure in Emerson's work', and that correspondence offers him an 'analogue' for 'the alternation between these two extremes of sociability'.[9] William Decker also argues that correspondence and friendship are 'inextricably bound' in Emerson's thought.[10] In his essay, Emerson's primary depiction of friendship is of the solitary 'scholar who sits down to write' and who, despite his 'years of meditation', cannot come up with 'one good thought' until he 'write[s] a letter to a friend – and forthwith troops of gentle thoughts invest themselves [...] with chosen words'.[11] For Emerson, epistolary friendship figures a form of 'social reciprocity', to use Hewitt's phrase, transcending earthly embodiment while guarding the self-reliant individual's sovereignty. 'To my friend I write a letter and from him I receive a letter', Emerson continues, 'It is a spiritual gift worthy of him to give and of me to receive'.[12]

Friendship therefore appears to function in Emerson's essay as a structure of thought as well as a personal relation. In his first letter to Auster, Coetzee quotes Charles Lamb saying something similar a little more curtly: 'One can have friends without wanting to see them' (*HN* 2).[13] More broadly, Emerson's conception of epistolary friendship gestures to the possibilities of textually mediated intimacy, and to imagining the epistolary moment as a *mise-en-abyme* of the broader scene of reading and writing; that is, to imagining the epistle, as Derrida does, as 'not a genre, but all genres, literature itself'.[14] The reciprocal relation of address and reply inherent to letter-writing between correspondents might be at work in all texts between authors and readers; every text might be a letter from a friend, or a kind of 'spiritual gift'. Versions of this intersubjective model of literary encounter were elaborated in the 1980s and 1990s within what became known as 'ethical criticism'. In *The Company We Keep* (1988), Wayne Booth suggests that 'all books are gifts from would-be friends', though only a few will offer the kind of 'perfect' friendship esteemed by Aristotle.[15] Considering the 'consequences of saying that I have a positive obligation to an implied author', Booth's study draws on the twinned critical metaphors of friendship and the gift to articulate a neo-Aristotelian, humanist account of the novel's social value – of how novels render readers more 'finely aware and richly responsible', as Martha Nussbaum puts it, facilitating a 'new freshness of sympathy' to the 'social world around them'.[15]

Dorothy Hale observes that Booth and Nussbaum's ethical criticism owes much to the liberal pluralism of Lionel Trilling – which Nathan Zuckerman sampled at Chicago – for whom novel reading similarly fosters a humanist appreciation of social 'variety and modulation'.[17] Hale observes that 'Trilling's defence of the social value of literature is rooted in a pre-structuralist sense of the liberal individual', while Booth and Nussbaum's ethical criticism explicitly pits itself against post-structuralism, or what Nussbaum calls 'the fashionable recent dogma that literary texts refer only to other texts and not to the world'.[18] Recently, however, a 'new ethical criticism' has emerged that attempts to 'retain the post-structuralist's skepticism about knowledge [...] while bestowing upon epistemological uncertainty a positive ethical content'.[19] The new ethical criticism continues to draw upon an interpersonal metaphor of literary encounter, but whereas Booth and Nussbaum envisage texts as engaging readers in a form of friendship, the new ethical criticism imagines a confrontation with alterity that focalises a sense of uncertainty, problematising the process of readerly judgement.[20] Rather than figuring a 'positive obligation' to an implied author, in the new ethical criticism, literature elaborates a Levinasian sense of our 'infinite responsibility' to the Other.[21]

Yet Booth's notion of novels as gifts whose circulation substantiates ethical ties has remained evocative to literary critics and novelists. Booth punningly acknowledges that he has 'profited from' Lewis Hyde's book *The Gift*, and, as I suggested at the start of this chapter, Hyde's work has been important to the broader popularity of gift theory.[22] Like Booth, Hyde draws on Marcel Mauss's anthropological account of 'the gift economy' and his analysis of the 'threefold obligation to give, to receive and to reciprocate'.[23] Hyde argues that works of art 'exist simultaneously' within this kind of gift economy as well as a market economy, but maintains that, while 'the work of art can survive without the market [...] where there is no gift there is no art'.[24] As in the Trillingite liberal humanism of Booth and Nussbaum, for Hyde the work of art is central to the cultivation of a set of social values distinct from market principles.

Reissued in 1999 and 2007, *The Gift* continued to find 'an enthusiastic audience among contemporary authors hoping to overcome [...] the debilitating legacy of postmodernism' and fearing that 'commodification might now be an inescapable condition'.[25] David Foster Wallace, Zadie Smith, and Jonathan Lethem, among others, have read and written about Hyde's work.[26] Lee Konstantinou sees this enthusiasm for Hyde's 'ethic of generosity' as paradigmatic of a 'post-postmodern mode' in contemporary fiction that has sought to move beyond 'the cynical disposition of postmodern self-awareness'.[27] Adam Kelly's term for this mode of contemporary fiction is 'new sincerity' – another concept that owes a debt to Trilling – and he too traces Wallace's engagement with Hyde's work.[28] But Kelly also draws on Derrida's *Given Time* to argue that Wallace's understanding of the gift is more 'double-edged' than Hyde's.[29] Pushing 'Mauss's thesis to its logical extreme',

Derrida argues that 'the very fact that exchange is predicated on a structure of reciprocity and hence calculation renders [the gift] an impossibility'.[30] For Derrida, the gift 'ought not to appear as gift', either to 'the donee or to the donor' if it is to avoid recapitulating the logic of economic exchange: 'secrecy is the last word of the gift'.[31] Kelly argues that, for Wallace, 'reading is a transaction, an economy like any other', while 'at the same time', his fiction holds to the Derridean possibility that the work of art might circulate 'beyond the economic, into the realm of the gift of sincerity', but only if it 'remain[s] a secret beyond representation'.[32]

In his emphasis on secrecy, Derrida explores a long-held anxiety about the gift captured in its double etymology, meaning both 'present' and 'poison'.[33] If the gift substantiates an ethic of generosity and creates community, it might also implicate the receiver in a deleterious debt relation. 'The gift puts the other in debt', Derrida warns, 'with the result that giving amounts to [...] doing harm'.[34] 'We do not quite forgive the giver', Emerson writes in 'Gifts' (1844), because receiving a gift upsets our sense of being 'self-sustained'.[35] Attending more closely to the logic of the gift therefore problematises rather than clarifies what for Mauss and Hyde is its structuring principle of reciprocity. The gift might trace a 'feeling bond', but it might also elaborate a restrictive obligation.

I have set down the convoluted and overlapping critical histories of ethical reading, friendship, and the gift in some detail because these preoccupations are similarly intertwined in the texts I will discuss. In Auster's work, the responsibility the gift bestows upon its recipient is often ambiguous, and the relationship formed between donor and donee is frequently ambivalent – that is, when the gift is in fact recognised as such, because Auster also explores the gift's secrecy. Complex patterns of generosity and reciprocity crisscross his fictions, as money, letters, and works of literature are lent, borrowed, stolen, lost, and given away. At times, these circulations seem to substantiate the kinds of ethical bonds imagined by Booth, Nussbaum, and Hyde – friendships in which we recognise a mutuality and social interconnectedness, and in which an ethic of generosity is established akin to that described by Auster in his letter to Coetzee: 'you are both giving more than you receive, both receiving more than you give, and in the reciprocity of this exchange, friendship blooms'. But the near-tautology of this model of exchange hints at the more ambivalent role the gift plays in Auster's work. Often, giving and receiving seem to incur unaccountable or incalculable obligations, articulating something closer to the new ethical criticism's conception of alterity and 'infinite' responsibility than to the old ethical criticism's model of friendship.

A memorial in the shape of a book

As an example of the 'not-knowing' that he feels characterises friendship between men, Auster tells Coetzee an anecdote about his 'closest male friend', whom he resembles: 'both writers, both idiotically obsessed by sport'. When this friend finished writing a new book, he sent a copy to Auster, who was deeply moved to find that the novel was dedicated to him: 'my friend never said a word about it' (5). The friend was Don DeLillo and the novel was *Cosmopolis* (2003); DeLillo's gesture of friendship reciprocated Auster dedicating *Leviathan* to him a little over a decade earlier. The anecdote testifies to the closeness of their friendship, Auster writes, but also to the fact that 'I know this man and don't know him'. DeLillo's gesture of friendship threw into doubt even as it confirmed their relationship, exposing the limits of their intimacy. In his first letter to a potential new friend, Auster chooses to tell an anecdote about another, more elaborate textual exchange in which each friend addresses their novel to the other as a curious token of their relationship.[36] In doing so, Auster also draws us back to *Leviathan*, and to its preoccupation with writing to and of absent friends.

Leviathan is structured around the fifteen-year friendship of the author-turned-terrorist Benjamin Sachs and fellow-writer Peter Aaron, the novel's narrator.[37] Aaron begins writing the story of Sachs's life immediately after reading a news item in the *New York Times* about a man blowing himself up in a car on a road in Wisconsin, his body bursting into 'dozens of small pieces' (1). Instinctively, Aaron knows that the unidentified man is Sachs, and the FBI are on their way to the same conclusion. When two federal agents come calling, Aaron tries to 'give away' as little as possible of what he knows about Sachs, while in the novel he has just started writing, he promises to 'give the true story'. As *Leviathan* unfolds, however, Aaron's attempts to at once conceal and reveal the truth become conjoined, and what we are 'given' instead is a 'tangled and complicated' narrative in which 'everything is connected to everything else' (3, 51). There were 'no witnesses' to the explosion in Wisconsin, the *Times* reports, but Aaron will try to bear witness to Sachs's life, 'picking up the pieces and gluing them back together again' (40). At the same time, he stresses how little he really knows about his 'closest friend': 'I don't want to present this book as something it's not [...] even though Sachs confided a great deal to me [during] our friendship, I don't claim to have more than a partial understanding of who he was' (22). Like Nathan in the American Trilogy, Aaron acknowledges his limited capacity for knowing the lives of others, and, just as Nathan's mistaken assumptions about the Swede, Ira, and Coleman gather an epistemological significance over the course of the trilogy, so too does Sachs come to resemble 'an emblem of the unknowable itself' in the eyes of his friend (146).

Like *The Human Stain*, *Leviathan* consists of five chapters, Aaron charting Sachs's tragic transformation from promising young novelist into the 'Phantom of Liberty', a Unabomber-esque vigilante who gains notoriety for blowing up scale models of the Statue of Liberty in public parks across small-town America. Published shortly after DeLillo's *Mao II* (1991), *Leviathan* is similarly concerned with the relationship between literature and terrorism, and with the prospect of the novel's waning capacity to speak to the wider culture.[38] Though the theme is DeLillo-esque, Sachs's turn to terrorism results from a concatenation of coincidences more typical of Auster's fiction.[39] After losing his way on a woodland walk, Sachs is hitching a ride back to his Vermont summer house with local farmhand Dwight when they come across a car blocking their way on a back road. The driver shoots Dwight, and Sachs then kills the driver in self-defence, stealing his car to escape the scene. In the trunk, Sachs discovers bomb-making equipment, $165,000 in cash, and a passport in the name of Reed Dimaggio. It transpires that Dimaggio was also a writer, not of fiction but of a history of American radicalism, and a 'reappraisal' of the communist-anarchist Alexander Berkman proposing 'a moral justification for certain forms of political violence' (224). When he learns that Dimaggio subsequently turned from writing to ecological activism and was planning a series of violent protests, Sachs comes to sense a 'cosmic attraction' (224) between them, and Aaron speculates that in different circumstances they 'might even have been friends' (224). His initial impulse is not to carry out Dimaggio's political campaign but to write a book of his life. 'I planned it as an elegy', he tells Aaron, 'a memorial in the shape of a book [...] As long as I was devoting myself to Dimaggio, I would be keeping him alive. I would give him my life [...] and in exchange he would give my life back to me' (225).

But it is Aaron who ends up writing 'a memorial in the shape of a book'. *Leviathan* is his 'elegy' for his friend, and writing it imbricates him in the kind of 'exchange' Sachs describes, in which life and death are mysteriously entwined. In the previous chapter, I suggested that *I Married a Communist* represents Nathan's tribute to Murray, while *The Human Stain* is also a work of memorialisation. Just as there is something 'ghostly' about Nathan and Coleman's friendship, Aaron and Sachs's friendship seems to belong to the dimension of the spectral; in both novels, to write about the friend is to arrange a haunting. Having been in hiding during his Phantom campaign, Sachs reappears at his Vermont house, where Aaron happens to be staying while working on a novel, sitting 'in the same chair that Sachs used to sit in', and feeling Sachs's presence as that of a 'welcoming ghost' (218, 219). They settle down to talk in a scene reminiscent of the narrative set-up of *I Married a Communist* and *The Human Stain*, wherein Nathan listens to Murray and Coleman out under the Berkshire stars: 'We stayed up late again that night [...] two disembodied voices in the dark, invisible to each other [...] I remember the glowing ends of cigars [...] an enormous sky of stars overhead' (231).[40]

Sachs soon disappears again, leaving a letter atop the manuscript of Aaron's novel-in-progress. He apologises for 'sneak[ing] out', but writes that, 'when the time comes, you'll know how to tell [his story] to others' (236). Aaron reflects that Sachs wrote the letter because 'he had wanted our friendship to survive' (236). Letters, after all, invite reply, and, placed symbolically on Aaron's manuscript, Sachs positions *Leviathan* itself as a response, Aaron's side of the correspondence. *Leviathan* is in fact the title of Sachs's abandoned second novel, adopted by Aaron to 'mark what will never exist', while at the same time the novel stands metonymically for Sachs's physical absence (142). As Aliki Varvogli argues, Aaron attempts to 'fill in the gap left by his best friend's death by telling his story'.[41] Earlier, Aaron recalls that, when they were separated during their friendship, 'postcards and letters took the place of late-night talks', and a similar textual exchange frames the novel (52). Aaron tells the FBI agents that someone has been 'impersonating' him, 'answering letters in my name, walking into bookstores and autographing my books' (4). At the end of the novel, the agents reveal that the impostor was Sachs. 'Now why would a friend do something like that?' one of them asks. 'Because he missed me', Aaron replies, 'He went away on a long trip and forgot to buy postcards. It was his way of staying in touch' (244). Turning an author book-signing into a familiar correspondence, Sachs's impersonation suggests the peculiar kinds of intimacy a novel can create. 'A book is a mysterious object', Aaron reflects, observing how his own readers often identify with him through his work. 'All of a sudden, they imagine that you belong to them' (4).

A similarly ambiguous textual exchange between male friends is the focus of *The Locked Room*, the final volume of *The New York Trilogy* (1987).[42] An unnamed narrator tells the story of the disappearance of his friend Fanshawe, a promising young writer like Sachs, and the novel initially appears to also be a work of mourning. The narrator has not stayed in touch with Fanshawe since childhood – although in the intervening years he continues to feel his presence like 'a ghost […] inside me' – and so is surprised to discover that he is named as his friend's literary executor (202). Publishing Fanshawe's work provides the narrator with a steady income and a literary fame that has eluded him in his own career as a hack writer. Echoing Sachs's description of his exchange with Dimaggio, the narrator writes, 'The thought flickered through me that I could one day be resurrected in my own eyes, and I felt a sudden burst of friendship for Fanshawe across the years' (210). But Fanshawe is alive after all, and so the bequest of his work is transformed from a generous gift to a manipulative act. The narrator is 'haunted' by the knowledge of Fanshawe's survival, which threatens not only his literary career but his blossoming romantic relationship with Fanshawe's widow, Sophie (244). The couple had resolved 'not to feel indebted to Fanshawe', but instead to see the windfall from his work as 'an unlikely gift' (234). But in this intricate, claustrophobic narrative of writerly rivalry, the gift of friendship turns poisonous; the narrator remains in Fanshawe's debt, with no 'chance to pay [him] back' (236).

The narrator recounts a story from his childhood with Fanshawe that speaks to this uneasy dynamic of generosity and indebtedness at play between the friends. In the second grade, the pair are walking to a birthday party with a schoolmate, Dennis, a poor kid from a tough background who has no present to give. 'Without any explanation', the narrator recalls, Fanshawe 'turned to Dennis and handed him his present'. Rather than feel affronted, Dennis nods his head, 'as if acknowledging the wisdom of what Fanshawe had done' (212). Giving Dennis the present, the narrator suggests, 'was not an act of charity so much as an act of justice [...] the one thing had been turned into another. It was a piece of magic' (213). Fanshawe's mother sees it differently. 'The present had cost her money, and by giving it away Fanshawe had in some sense stolen that money from her' (214). Mrs Fanshawe confirms 'the logic of contract' rather than the logic of the gift, Alex Segal argues, whereas the narrator feels that Fanshawe's generosity constitutes 'the first truly moral act I had witnessed' (214).[43] Segal suggests that Fanshawe's actions adhere to Derrida's conception of the gift – in which the gift exists only if it is not recognised as such by either party – and posits that this scene speaks to the novel's broader 'thematization of responsibility'.[44] When he learns that he is Fanshawe's literary executor, the narrator asks, 'How could I be expected to take on such a responsibility, to stand in judgement of a man and say whether his life had been worth living?' (205). The 'magic' of the gift, the novel suggests, is a dark magic. Fanshawe demonstrates the gift's capacity to constitute a 'truly moral act', but the narrator's experience shows how it can also implicate the donee in a deadly relation of obligation.

While *The Locked Room* remains a tightly wound psychological tale of the anxiety of literary influence – replete with allusions not only to Hawthorne's apprentice novel *Fanshawe* (1828) but to Poe's stories of entrapped doubles – *Leviathan* is set against a much broader political backdrop. If the patterns of textual exchange between Aaron and Sachs recall those between the narrator and

Fanshawe, then *Leviathan*'s interest in forms of generosity, reciprocity, and indebtedness develops far beyond the earlier novel. Mark Osteen neatly captures the contrast between the books:

> The narrator of *The Locked Room* claims that 'No one can cross the boundary into another – for the simple reason that no one can gain access to himself'. *Leviathan* revises that perception by suggesting that only through others can one gain access to the locked room of the self.[45]

While *The Locked Room* might thus be said to speak to the exploration of solitude that is a keynote of Auster's early work, *Leviathan* is 'poised halfway between the personal and the political', Varvogli argues, and so speaks to the exploration of 'community' that Mark Brown suggests becomes a thematic preoccupation in Auster's later work, much as it does in Roth's.[46] Like the novels of the American Trilogy, *Leviathan* is a historical fiction that analyses the course of postwar liberalism through a central male friendship, and, like Roth's protagonists, Sachs is a representative historical figure.[47] Sachs 'embodies American Cold War history', Dustin Iler notes: 'he finds purpose in the New Left of the 1960s, becomes disillusioned with leftist politics in the post-Vietnam period, and after the Cold War's end is unable to imagine a future for himself or the nation'.[48] Born on the day of the bombing of Hiroshima, Sachs is proud of his 'father's socialist politics in the thirties, which [...] involved union organizing' (26–27). He meets his future wife, Fanny, at a peace rally in New York in 1966, and two years later is imprisoned for seventeen months for refusing the draft. His first novel, *The New Colossus*, is a historical fiction 'set in America between 1876 and 1890' – precisely a century before the period covered in *Leviathan* – and, while Aaron initially suggests that the work 'had nothing to do with the sixties, nothing to do with Vietnam', he later recognises that 'the anti-war moment' was the 'engine that pushed the book forward' (37, 40). Something similar might be said of *Leviathan*. In 'the Ronald Reagan era', Sachs comes to be 'seen as a throwback, out of step with the spirit of the times' (104). He 'holds fast to the ideals of the 1960s', Iler argues, even in 'the new American order of the 1980s', defined by 'selfishness' and 'chest-pounding Americanism' (104).[49]

Laurent Berlant describes the 'anti-federal but patriotic nationalism of Reagan Republicanism' which sought to 'shrink the state while intensifying identification with the utopian symbolic "nation"'.[50] She argues that Reaganism 'convinced a citizenry that the core context of politics should be the sphere of private life', resulting in what she calls 'the privatisation of U.S. citizenship'.[51] Reflecting in an interview on the political context of *Leviathan*, Auster suggests that 1980s conservatism represented 'the dismantling of everything we had fought for in the sixties'.[52] Berlant similarly frames Reaganite 'family values' as a reversal of the 1960s leftist-feminist maxim 'the personal is the political' into 'the political is the personal'.[53] *Leviathan* is also concerned with the shrinking scale of public life in 1980s America, together with the political mobilisation of citizenly symbolic identification with the nation state. These preoccupations are neatly captured in Sachs's choice of target for his vigilante campaign: scale models of the Statue of Liberty. Berlant elsewhere analyses 'Lady Liberty' as a 'popular site of collective fantasy that "solves" the problem of staging collective life' by facilitating 'the translation of subjects in time and history into an unmarked place [...] a whole body, indivisible although clearly divided, that represents the promise of the nation'.[54] Exploding the scale model statues, Sachs attempts to blow apart this fantasy of national identity, and to insist instead on a kind of revitalised civic culture that responds to the 'rugged individualism' of Reaganism. In a message sent to the press following the Phantom's latest attack, Sachs writes, 'Each person is alone and therefore we have nowhere to turn but to each other' (217).

As in *I Married a Communist*, this critique of contemporary liberalism is connected to a longer genealogy of political philosophy, albeit much more schematically than in Roth's novel. Aaron suggests that, if he had to summarise Sachs's political beliefs, he 'would begin by mentioning the Transcendentalists', and, just as Nathan traces the idea for his Berkshire hideaway back to Thoreau, Sachs takes inspiration from 'Civil Disobedience' (1849) (26). Like the American Trilogy, *Leviathan* is in dialogue with American Renaissance literature, and the novel's epigraph is drawn from Emerson's 'Politics' (1844): 'Every actual State is corrupt'.[55] Emerson's essay concludes by asking whether 'thousands of human beings might exercise towards each other the grandest and simplest sentiments, as well as a knot of friends, or a pair of lovers'. Elizabeth Hewitt interprets the essay as offering a 'conception of intimate sociability' that 'becomes a model by which to interrogate the possibilities of sociability more largely'.[56] Elsewhere in 'Politics', Emerson asks, given the inherent corruption of governments, 'could not a nation of friends even devise better ways?'.

The novel's title, meanwhile, is both an allusion to *Moby-Dick* and, according to Auster, 'a direct reference to Hobbes's notion of the state'.[57] In *Leviathan* (1651), Hobbes proposes a theory of the ambiguation of the individual subject in a collective fantasy of representation via the figure of an authoritarian sovereign. As Danielle Allen explains, 'Hobbes believes it is possible to stabilize the idea of "the people's will" only by severing it from any individual's subjectivity'.[58] Hobbesianism 'implies that as long as citizens trust their institutions they need not trust one another'.[59] Hobbesian political philosophy therefore forecloses 'the possibility of cultivating within citizens a culture of reciprocity', Allen argues, by basing its contractual definition of political bonds 'only on self-interest and fear, and not more broadly on practices like friendship'.[60] Indeed, a version of Aristotelian civic friendship is Allen's solution to Hobbes's derogation of citizenship. In the *Nicomachean Ethics*, she notes, 'practices of reciprocity coalesce in politics in the form of law and contract', but it is 'friendship's ability to achieve ethical, and not merely legal, exchange that outpaces justice'. Involving practices of 'self-sacrifice', 'generosity', and a 'willing[ness] to be in debt to one another', friendship elaborates a relation of 'ethical reciprocity' that 'limits' individual agency and yet 'generates consent and the experience of autonomy', a relation that becomes Aristotle's 'model for how political freedom [...] works'.[61] Only such a revitalised code of 'equitable exchange', Allen argues, can counter a Hobbesian corrosion of citizenship.

Leviathan explores the practices of exchange and reciprocity that might articulate a version of political community that is less like that based on a conception of negative liberty envisioned by Hobbes (or Reagan), and more like that outlined by Allen. Mark Brown is right to suggest that the novel portrays Sachs's 'abandonment of social contacts' as he transforms into the Phantom, and that his project of political activism fails because he 'is no longer able to recover the social connections that had formed the basis for his earlier self'.[62] But, as Mark Osteen argues, 'ironically, in dropping out of the commonwealth [...] Sachs more firmly attaches himself to the leviathans of personal and political affiliation'.[63] When Sachs entrusts his secret first to Aaron and then to their mutual friend Maria, a performance artist, it is as if the novel's core characters 'comprise a kind of secret society' in which 'shared confidences yield a measure of freedom from the larger state'.[64] Osteen goes on to argue (in terms that closely echo Allen's definition of 'ethical reciprocity') that 'the intertwined lives in Auster's *Leviathan* [...] establish bonds that limit individual autonomy and give it meaning'. Like the American Trilogy, *Leviathan* explores the kinds of affiliation that endure even for those who attempt to throw off what Nathan calls the 'agitating entanglements' of the social world.

Throughout the novel, these bonds are articulated through often oblique acts of generosity. Aaron forms a close friendship with Sachs's wife, Fanny, and when Sachs is away in California for a few months – conducting a secret affair, Fanny suspects – they sleep together. On one level, Aaron recognises that Fanny is using him to get back at Sachs, part of 'the quid pro quo that turns the victim into the one who victimizes, the act that puts the scales back in balance' (86). But on another, he wonders whether a different 'economy of justice' might be at work (86). After a joyless marriage, Aaron is separated from his wife, Delia, but is considering reconciling for the sake of their son. His love affair with Fanny, however, allows him to recognise that this would be a terrible mistake, and he comes to believe that Fanny 'did what she did to prevent me from going back to Delia'. If so, Fanny's actions were not vengeful, but a 'pure and luminous gesture of self-sacrifice'. 'Is such a thing possible?', Aaron wonders, 'Can a person actually go that far for the sake of someone else?' (89).

What are the limits of our generosity towards each other, and how will we know a gift when we receive it? Maria's performance art also poses these questions. There is a clear parallel between Aaron's narrative task in *Leviathan* – in which he tries to 'pick up the pieces' of Sachs's life – and one of Maria's performances, in which she attempts to create a 'portrait *in absentia*' of a stranger through the contacts in his 'little black address book' which she finds on the pavement, a portrait 'pieced together from everything he was not' (67). But another of Maria's projects seems to speak more ambiguously to Aaron's narrative, and to the novel's broader exploration of exchange and generosity. 'Since the age of fourteen', Aaron writes, Maria 'had saved all the birthday presents that had ever been given to her'. This provides the inspiration for 'the long-term project of dressing Mr L. [...] a stranger she had once met at a party':

> without announcing her intentions to anyone, she took it upon herself to improve his wardrobe. Every year at Christmas she would send him an anonymous gift – a tie, a sweater, an elegant shirt – and because Mr L. moved in roughly the same social circles that she did, she would run into him every now and again, noting with pleasure the dramatic changes [...] For the fact was that Mr L. always wore the clothes Maria sent him [...] he never caught on that she was responsible for those Christmas packages. (60–61)

'Maria wasn't hungry for the sorts of attachments most people seem to want', Aaron notes, and her performance pieces all explore the interstice between intimacy and surveillance (59).[65] Her project with Mr L. seems to be another version of Fanny's ambiguous generosity, and to recall Fanshawe's 'truly moral act' in *The Locked Room*, in which the gift and secrecy are similarly entwined. The novel suggests that it is these 'sorts of attachments', these odd alliances of obscure beneficence and obligation, that finally define a social world.

Maria's artworks also of course resemble Sachs's Phantom project, which Auster describes in an interview as 'political performance art'; Sachs's incognito bombing campaign is another version of Maria's 'anonymous gift[s]'.[66] But before he turns to terror, and before he considers writing an 'elegy' for Dimaggio, Sachs hopes to atone for the murder in another way: by giving Dimaggio's widow, Lillian Stern, the money he found in Dimaggio's car:

> Not just the money – but the money as a token of everything he had to give, his entire soul. The alchemy of retribution demanded it [...] That was the inner law [...] By handing the money over to Lilian Stern, he would be putting himself in her hands. (167)

Fanshawe's gift had been 'a piece of magic' in which 'the one thing had been turned into another', and Sachs hopes for a similar alchemical transformation. The money, he says, 'isn't about goodness. It's about justice' (207). Although he is dismissive of Lillian's pop-philosophy books on 'reincarnation' that he finds scattered on her coffee table, Sachs longs for a kind of redemption (209). But Lillian – who, as a former sex worker, is used to men trying to pay her off – is sceptical. 'No one gives away money for nothing', she says, 'I'll be in your debt, won't I? [...] Once I take your money, you'll feel that you own me' (177). Sachs insists that Lillian will get the money 'free and clear' (180). But although he had always envisaged 'giving the money to her in one go [...] a quick, dream-like gesture', when he sees the squalor in which Lillian lives, and her neglect for her daughter, he reconsiders (177). Instead, he decides to give her the money in thousand-dollar instalments, an arrangement that leads them into a brief and disastrous affair, and seals Sachs's own transformation into the Phantom. Not for the first or last time in his fiction, Auster is drawn to money's promise of crystallising the vicissitudes of generosity and indebtedness that underpin all personal and social relations. Here as elsewhere in his work, he explores the possibilities and dangers of imagining money as a kind of gift, one that might redistribute justice, but just as easily entrench inequality.

Like *The Locked Room*, the novel follows the contours of a detective plot, but it is 'the disintegration of liberalism in American culture during the Reagan era', Dustin Iler notes, that 'emerges as the mystery at the heart of *Leviathan*':

> In attempting to imagine the future of the U.S. after the Cold War [...] the novel fixates on a fear of relentless conservatism while yearning for the production of an alternative politics, one encompassing the spectrum from nostalgia for the New Left to radical anarchism.[67]

When the narrator of *The Locked Room* is tasked with writing Fanshawe's biography, Sophie wonders whether he might write something 'more personal [...] The story of your friendship. It could be as much about you as about him' (248). *Leviathan* is also the story of a friendship, Aaron recognising that his attempt to write about Sachs will inevitably also be about the web of social relations of which he was a part. 'One thing leads to another', he writes, 'every story overlaps with every other story [...] As much as Sachs himself, I'm the place where everything begins' (51). Varvogli argues that Aaron's 'search for his friend' represents a 'quest for meaning: not a universal, all-encompassing pattern, but something on a smaller and more personal scale'.[68] But, as in Roth's American Trilogy, this 'personal scale' is connected to a larger quest for political meaning in the novel. 'Everything is connected', Aaron writes, a phrase DeLillo adopts in *Underworld* (1997); but, if it is an insight that resonates with the logic of postmodern paranoia, it might also articulate a 'yearning for the production of an alternative politics' (51).[69] The 'concentric circles' and 'weird networks' of friends at the centre of *Leviathan* do not amount to a coherent vision of citizenship opposing Reaganite 'selfishness' (73).[70] But they do suggest a desire for a different kind of civic life, the novel's exploration of exchange and generosity echoing Allen's concept of 'ethical reciprocity'. Aaron's narrative of his friendship with Sachs therefore refutes even as it explores the postmodern nihilism which surrenders to terrorism the novel's ability to critique society. Aaron's own novels 'strike a deep chord' in the 'souls' of his readers, he notes, recalling Mauss's definition of the gift as a 'tie between souls'.[71] 'All of a sudden', he writes, 'they imagine [...] that you're the only friend they have in the world' (4).

The Blue Team

Oracle Night (2004) is the most recent of the three 'stories about male friendship' Auster identifies in his letter to Coetzee in *Here and Now*.[72] The novel develops the earlier books' exploration of the ethic of generosity and of the ability of fiction to forge intimacies and imagine community. In an interview, Auster notes that an 'edginess' characterises the relationship between the narrator Sidney Orr and the older, more successful John Trause, suggesting that, because of their difference in age, there is something of the 'master–apprentice' dynamic to the friendship between the two writers.[73] Mark Brown argues that *Oracle Night* depicts 'the destructive power of families, but also the redemptive power of friendship', and that 'Sidney's friendship with Trause is one of genuine kindness and mutual benefit'.[74] Auster, however, suggests that there is also an element of 'competition' in their relationship, centred on the blue Portuguese notebooks they both use.[75] Like *The Locked Room*, the novel is about writerly rivalry, the blue notebooks recalling the red notebook Fanshawe gives to the narrator at the end of the earlier novel.[76] But *Oracle Night* is not as narrowly about the anxiety of influence. It is rarely noted that the novel is a historical fiction, set in the early 1980s, and, while its political context is more opaque than *Leviathan*'s, *Oracle Night* is similarly concerned with the connection between friendship and citizenship.

After realising that he and John have both been drawn to the same blue notebooks, Sidney thinks back to his childhood summers spent at Camp Pontiac, 'named after the Indian chief' (43). The kids are divided into two groups – the Red Team and the White Team – and compete against each other in a range of sports. 'After a while', Sidney tells his wife, Grace, 'a third team was formed [...] the Blue Team':

> [It was] a kind of secret society, a brotherhood of kindred souls [...] [It] represented a human ideal, a tight-knit association of tolerant and sympathetic individuals, the dream of a perfect society [...] A Blue Team member had to be curious, a reader of books [...] a lover of justice. A Blue Team member would give you the shirt off his back [...] but he would much rather slip a ten-dollar bill into your pocket when you weren't looking. (43–45)

Overcoming America's historical racial divide symbolised by the Red and the White teams, Sidney's Blue Team resembles a mythic, romantic frontier vision of community defined by an ethic of generosity and liberal values.[77] Understandably, Grace mocks the Blue Team as 'silly boy's stuff' – 'I'll bet you and your friends had a secret handshake', she teases – but Sidney is not so quick to dismiss it: 'When I think about it now, I don't find it silly at all' (46, 43). Ruth Levitas also takes the Blue Team seriously in her analysis of 'the presence in contemporary culture of an existential quest for utopia'.[78] Partly inspired by *Oracle Night*, Levitas calls this quest 'looking for the blue', because the colour evokes a mixture of hope and despair that she associates with the contemporary utopian imagination.

I examine this utopian impulse in detail in the next chapter; here, I want only to note that Auster connects male friendship to a broader (and vaguer) 'dream of a perfect society', one defined by a code of generosity in which money might be a kind of gift.

In early draft material for the novel, Auster makes repeated reference to the 'Hotel Existence', an idea that would end up in another novel he was working on at the time, and that represents another version of the utopian Blue Team.[79] *The Brooklyn Follies* (2005) focuses on the elderly Nathan Glass and his nephew Tom Wood.[80] Their friendship is not easily classifiable; as Nathan says, they belong to the 'post-family, post-student, post-past age of Glass and Wood', gathering around them an eclectic group of misfits and oddballs (*BF* 22). The Hotel Existence is Tom's name for an imagined community where they might all live together, 'a place where a man goes to when life in the real world is no longer possible' – a 'little utopia' (106). As Mark Brown observes, this exact phrase is used earlier in the novel to describe works by Poe and Thoreau, and 'the implication is that literature and society can create spaces of "community" and "utopia"'.[81] In fact, I would suggest that Auster suggests it is *only* through literature that such a community can be imagined. The Blue Team, after all, is formed not only of 'lovers of justice' but also 'lovers of books', and Auster suggests that those two passions are interconnected.

Central to the appeal that the Blue Team still holds for Sidney in *Oracle Night* is the idea that 'you don't have to explain your principles. They're immediately understood by how you act'. But, as Grace points out, 'People don't always act the same way [...] Good people do bad things, Sid' (*ON* 46). As my earlier discussion of the gift suggests, distinguishing between a good and a bad act might not be so straightforward, and Sidney's own relationship with John bears this out. Recovering from a near-fatal illness, Sidney is struggling to pay his medical bills. He tries to earn a quick buck selling a film treatment, but, when it doesn't pan out, John offers him one of his own early unfinished stories that he suggests Sidney might work up into something sellable:

> It's an odd piece, not at all like my other work [...] I guess I'd call it a political parable. It's set in an imaginary country in the eighteen

thirties, but it's really about the early nineteen fifties. McCarthy, HUAC, the Red Scare – all the sinister things that were going on then. The idea is that governments always need enemies. (143)

Sidney is 'tongue-tied with gratitude', marvelling at John's readiness to 'go beyond the normal bounds of friendship [...] selflessly, without any thought of profiting from what he'd done' (145). But, when he reads it, Sidney suspects that 'Trause gave me that story for highly complex reasons' (193). It is a political parable, but it is also 'a story about a marital triangle (a wife running off with her husband's best friend)'. These two narratives also overlap in *Leviathan*, and, more so than in Roth's fiction, friendship between men in Auster's novels is often triangulated through relationships with women. John and Grace have always been close, and, despite the story having been written thirty years earlier, Sidney interprets it as 'about the woman we both loved – my wife'. John is telling him something about their friendship and his own marriage, Sidney reflects, 'in the finely nuanced codes and metaphors of fiction' (193).

John's story cautions of the duplicity of fiction, of how it can contain a 'veiled, cryptic form of revenge', as Sidney puts it, even as it appears to offer friendship – or, how it can turn members of the Blue Team into Cold War enemies (195). As in *The Locked Room* and *Leviathan*, then, Auster portrays an ambiguous textual exchange between male friends (and their wives) in which generosity and retribution seem to coalesce. Near the end of the novel, however, John sends Sidney something else: a letter. He writes that offering the story had simply been a way 'to earn you some money, so I've cut to the chase and written you this check'. The enclosed cheque is for the exact sum of Sidney's medical bills. John offers Sidney another currency in which to conduct their friendship. Money, unlike fiction, cuts to the chase. And unlike the story, the money can stand, John writes, as 'a gift, free and clear' (195).

Counterfeit money

Sidney never has the chance to thank John for his 'supreme generosity' because the older writer dies suddenly from a pulmonary embolism: 'the little bomb had finally gone off inside him, and my friend was dead at fifty-six' (196). *Oracle Night* is also a work of mourning, then, the 'little bomb' in John confirming a link back to *Leviathan* and to Sachs, who had also tried to offer Lillian money as a gift 'free and clear' (*L* 101). Like Sachs, John's aim in switching fiction for money is to clarify the intent and value of his gift. But one of the implications of the substitution is that money might be more similar to language than either man would wish. This, in fact, has become a commonplace of literary-economic criticism. The breach between sign and signified theorised by post-structuralist linguistic theory, the argument goes, is akin to that of the disassociation of money's face value from its material worth. The separation of the credit system from the gold standard, and the advent of paper (and electronic) money, has meant that the market economy 'float[s] on financial simulacra, subordinating "intrinsic" value to speculation, opinion, imagination'.[82] Money, in other words, became fictitious, and so (like texts) forgeable.[83] Even in the nineteenth century, 'understanding the relationship between substance and sign was complicated by the known existence of counterfeit notes', which divided into two kinds: illegal copies of legitimate so-called 'ghost moneys', and the fabrication of 'phantom bank notes'.[84] 'Ghosts, counterfeit ghosts, and phantoms [...] passed all alike', Marc Shell explains, haunting the market economy and undermining the primacy and verifiability of 'real' money.[85]

In *Here and Now*, Auster's and Coetzee's letters drift from discussing friendship to money, Coetzee looking to post-structuralism for an analogy for the arbitrary nature of financial markets. Discussing the 2008 credit crash, he suggests that 'the numbers [...] are mere signs, no less than the letter a, b, c [...] the numbers reflect no reality' (*HN* 19). In reply, Auster begins by agreeing that 'the supreme fiction of our world is money. What is money but worthless pieces of paper?' (22). But he goes on to point out that, despite its abstract nature, the crash 'is producing tangible results'. Money might be a 'fiction', Auster writes, but fictions 'affect reality'. He recognises along with Coetzee that the economy operates on 'collective belief', but he is not quite so willing to dismiss the power of that 'faith' (22).

Auster's letter echoes his reflections on his 'flawed, enigmatic', and 'contradictory' 'relationship with money' in his memoir *Hand* to Mouth (1997).[86] He suggests that this ambivalence is the product of his parents' opposing perspectives on money, their views representing 'two moral philosophies [...] in eternal conflict'. 'Like so many Americans before her and since', his mother 'cultivated shopping as a means of self-expression [...] to enter a store was to engage in an alchemical process [...] with magical, transformative powers' (HM 155). His father, meanwhile, was 'tight', resenting his wife's extravagant spending (155). But, in an earlier memoir, *The Invention of Solitude* (1982), Auster writes that his father also 'dreamed all his life of becoming a millionaire':

> It was not so much the money itself he wanted, but what it represented: [...] a way of making himself untouchable. Having money means more than being able to buy things: it means that the world need never affect you. Money in the sense of protection, then, not pleasure.[87]

I argue that, in his fiction, Auster develops a third 'moral philosophy' of money, closer though not identical to his mother's. If money is 'protection' for the father, for the son it will be a means of opening himself to the risk and responsibility of other people. In *Hand to Mouth*, Auster portrays his political education as beginning in a rejection of the 'orthodox view' of 'American capitalism' that money was a 'good to be valued above all others' (156). Yet he also notes that 'money talked, and to the degree that you listened to it and followed its argument, you would learn to speak the language of life' (157). Money, then, provides a compelling vocabulary that the novelist can hardly ignore. Auster's fiction listens out for the ways in which money might be made to speak of forms of generosity and indebtedness that are not simply financial, and how it might form social ties whose 'value' is of a different order from that accounted for in the market.

A number of critics have noted that the motif of receiving an inheritance features prominently in Auster's work, connecting this to the author's own description of how his literary career was made possible by some money left to him when his father died.[88] Pascal Bruckner writes of Auster's inheritance that 'the son would never stop repaying the debt, would never finish reimbursing the deceased, in prose, for this fearsome gift'.[89] It has been a short step to link this motif to the idea of literary influence, and to read the numerous filial relations involving an inheritance in his work as part of Auster's negotiation with his literary forefathers. But, as Mark Brown attests, 'conventions of genealogy' are frequently 'usurped' in Auster's fiction, and 'paternity [...] and the privileges it conventionally confers, such as inheritance, are lost as soon as they are acquired'.[90] Instead of filial relationships, Auster's fiction often imagines friendships between men formed through alternative circulations of money, imbued not with the burden of inheritance but with something like his mother's understanding of money's 'alchemical' potential.

For Lewis Hyde, the gift must be kept in constant circulation, its movement tracing an 'anarchic' and 'decentralised cohesiveness' antithetical to capitalism's substantiation of property rights and economic self-interest.[91] In *Hand to Mouth*, Auster recounts an anecdote about the recirculation of an inheritance that captures something of this countercultural spirit. The novelist H. L. Humes was one of the 'bevy of friends' Auster gathered around him in New York in the late 1960s.[92] Humes inherited $15,000 upon the death of his father and, 'rather than squander the money on himself', decided to 'give it away' with the instruction to 'get it circulating' (*HM* 178). Through this random exchange of money, Humes hoped to 'bring down the system' and 'strike a blow to capitalism' (179). His project therefore resembles the political performance art of Sachs and Maria. Auster has subsequently kept the anecdote circulating in his fiction. In *The Locked Room*, the narrator thinks of Humes while reading Fanshawe's notebooks (255). A version of the experiment also occurs in *Moon Palace* (1989). The narrator Fogg is working as a manservant to the elderly eccentric Offing, who proposes they carry out Humes's scheme in order to 'repay an outstanding debt'.[93] In each of its iterations, the anecdote tells the story of the redistribution of a father's wealth into a different set of relationships: the inheritance is turned into a kind of gift.

The recirculation of an inheritance is also at the centre of *The Music of Chance* (1990), described by Auster in an interview as a 'parable about political power', recalling Trause's 'political parable' in *Oracle Night*.[94] The protagonist, Jim Nashe, receives an unexpected windfall after the death of his long-absent father, and heads out on an aimless cross-country road trip. Disillusioned and directionless, he has already torn through most of his inheritance when he comes across Pozzi, a drifter-gambler ambling forlornly along the roadside. Pozzi recalls how, after being told as a boy by his mother that his dad had died in Vietnam, he was incredulous when, aged eight, a Cadillac rolled up to his house and the driver introduced himself as his father. Little Pozzi is taken for a ride and handed a hundred-dollar bill by the man. 'After six months', Pozzi tells Nashe, 'I got it into my head that the money was fake, that it was a counterfeit bill [...] I remember thinking that if the money was fake, then the guy who gave it to me couldn't be my father'.[95] But the banknote is genuine, and Pozzi accepts that the man is his father, although this conflicts with his understanding that 'fathers don't go away. They live with their families' (41). It is therefore unclear what the banknote's authenticity has guaranteed. By the little boy's logic, it has confirmed the man's claim to paternity, and yet it has also revealed him to be a 'fake' father in the sorts of ways that matter most. 'If this guy is really my father', Pozzi wonders, 'then why doesn't he come back and see me? At least he could write a letter or something' (41). For both Pozzi and Nashe, the money given to them by their fathers has been a kind of counterfeit gift, an exchange emptied of its affective value and yet imposing a relation of indebtedness; they know their fathers have tried to buy them off.

Nashe is struck by 'the curious correspondence' in their circumstances: 'the early abandonment, the unexpected gift of money, the abiding anger' (45). 'Once a man begins to recognise himself in another', Nashe notes, 'he can no longer look on that person as a stranger. Like it or not, a bond is formed' (45). The 'unexpected gift' of money creates an equally unexpected friendship, and the relationship between the two men continues to be articulated via a redistribution of inheritance. Nashe agrees to stump up the rest of his cash as a stake for Pozzi in a poker match with millionaire odd-couple Flower and Stone. Pozzi loses Nashe's money, but the bet – a speculative circulation of money that is the antithesis of inheritance – brings them together. Nashe goes the 'full distance for Pozzi [...] pushing past any reasonable limit', and in the process gains 'a friend': 'That friend now seemed prepared to do anything for him' (115).

But Auster also explores 'the extent to which money controls and coerces', Tom Woods observes.[96] Flower and Stone's wealth is the product of an 'unexpected gift of money' – a lottery win – but they use their fortune to exert authority. In the course of the poker match, Pozzi not only loses Nashe's stake but accrues an additional debt that they are unable to pay. To recompense Flower and Stone, the four come to an agreement that Nashe and Pozzi will work for the millionaires as employees to build a vast (and seemingly purposeless) stone wall within the grounds of their mansion, and so their relationship 'as employees is formalised in contract', Mark Brown argues.[97] The central chapters wherein Nashe and Pozzi are set to work are based on Auster's early play *Laurel and Hardy Go to Heaven* which, like *The Music of Chance*, owes much to *Waiting for Godot*. But Beckett's influence is also felt in the kind of double-act dynamic that develops between Nashe and Pozzi, who fit the mould of the Beckettian 'pseudo-couple' as defined by Fredric Jameson:

> The pseudo-couple is masculine [... and] might be understood as a kind of compensation formation, a curious structural halfway house in the history of the subject, between its construction in bourgeois individualism and its destruction in late capitalism. The partners of the pseudo-couple [are not] independent subjects in their own right [...] and find themselves thereby obliged to lean on one another in a simulation of psychic unity.[98]

There is much here that speaks to Nashe and Pozzi's relationship. Jameson's image of the 'curious structural halfway house' is oddly literalised in the useless wall the pair are building across Flower and Stone's meadow, and 'compensation formation' is resonant in regard to a relation formed through money. Jameson of course also makes this link to financial economy by suggesting that the pseudo-couple relationship is, as Sarah Cole puts it, 'a way to ward off the centrifugal spin into late-capitalist monadism'.[99] Paradoxically, Auster's 'parable of political power' suggests that if the pseudo-couple offers only a 'simulation of psychic unity' – if it is, in effect, a kind of counterfeit friendship – such relationships might nonetheless retain a 'true value' in a culture in which practices of citizenship and democratic participation have themselves been reduced to mere simulacra.

The indeterminacy of the authentic and the counterfeit, the real and the fake, is also at the heart of *Smoke*, the 1995 film Auster wrote and co-directed with Wayne Wang.[100] The film centres on a group of men who gather in Auggie's humdrum corner store tobacconist, the Brooklyn Cigar Company.[101] As Mark Brown notes, Auster expresses the 'solidarity' and 'friendship' between the men 'through money':

> On the face of it this seems like a restatement of the values and ethos of the system of international finance capital, as encoded in the Manhattan skyline across the East River. However, Auster treats the circulation of money as an act that contradicts the 'money relations' of New York's global finance center, by suspending the accrual of profit.[102]

As in Auster's fiction, the movement of money in *Smoke* traces a structure of feeling in which informal, often haphazard forms of affiliation and community manifest. As opposed to the rule of profit in mercantile Manhattan, what emerges in Brooklyn is a 'jurisprudence of generosity'.[103] In the next chapter, I explore Auster's localist politics further. Here, I want to focus on the way 'money becomes the material symbol of the growing affinity between the characters' in *Smoke*, 'as bad money is made good, and a theft is transformed into a gift'.[104] As a favour to his loyal customer Paul (a novelist and the film's protagonist), Auggie gives a job to Rashid, an African American kid from Harlem looking for work and a place to live. While Rashid is minding the store, the backroom floods, destroying $5000 of Cuban cigars Auggie has illegally imported. Rashid is fired. Later, in a conversation with Paul, it transpires that Rashid left Harlem after getting mixed up in a robbery in which he accidentally went off with the heist money – also $5000. Paul suggests that he can use the money 'to make things right with Auggie [...] Better to keep your friends than worry about your enemies'. When Rashid wonders what he'll do without the cash, Paul reassures him, 'You've got friends now, remember?' (*S* 103).

Within this network of friendship, cultural divisions seem to dissolve like smoke: Auggie's store is a classless, race-blind, male clubhouse, another version of the Blue Team, or the Hotel Existence. But *Smoke* is aware that it risks offering an idealised portrait of neighbourhood life, and crucially complicates its own patterning of debt and repayment in a way that undermines its apparent sentimentality. At the start of the film, Paul begins to tell an anecdote about Sir Walter Raleigh to the guys hanging out at Auggie's counter. 'I used to smoke Raleigh cigarettes', Jerry, one of the regulars, pipes up, 'they came with a free gift coupon in every pack' (26).[105] 'That's the man', Paul says, before telling them how Raleigh made a bet with Queen Elizabeth that he could weigh the smoke in a cigar. 'I admit it's strange', Paul says, as Jerry and the guys express puzzlement, 'almost like weighing someone's soul'. He explains how Raleigh took an unsmoked cigar, weighed it, then smoked it, carefully tapping the ash into a 'balance pan'. The difference between the two, Paul says with a smile, was 'the weight of the smoke' (27).

The anecdote is the story of a bet and the calculation of the apparently inestimable. Raleigh's method is clever, but it misses something of the essence of smoking, hence the apt comparison to weighing a soul.[106] Like Pozzi's story of the authentic banknote given to him by his fake father, Raleigh seems to value the wrong thing. His attempt to 'balance' the scales does little justice to tobacco's real worth – and anyway, what mattered most to Jerry about his Raleigh cigarettes was the 'free gift'. In the next scene, Paul is walking absent-mindedly into the road when Rashid saves him from an oncoming truck. 'I owe you something', Paul tells him afterwards, insisting that. 'It's a law of the universe [...] You have to let me do something for you to put the scales back in balance' (31). Recalling the image of Raleigh's balancing pan, Paul raises the question of what he could offer that would adequately recompense Rashid for saving his life. Mark Brown is right to suggest that friendships take shape in the film through a series of 'mutual obligations'.[107] But, in this opening sequence, *Smoke* also elaborates a more complex conception of exchange in which forms of excess and surplus unsettle the 'balance' of reciprocity.

As Michael Kaplan notes, *Smoke* shares much of its central imagery with Baudelaire's short story 'Counterfeit Money' (1869); in both, male friendship is linked to smoking, to money, and to the idea of the gift.[108] In Baudelaire's tale, two male friends are walking back from the tobacconist when one gives a coin to a beggar. The friend tells his companion that he gave away a counterfeit coin.[109] In his reading of the story, Derrida asks how the fact of the money being fake changes the act of the gift, before wondering whether the friend's confession, rather than his coin, is the 'real' counterfeit. If this were so, Derrida suggests, the story might be a commentary on Baudelaire's text itself – dedicated to a friend – and of the confidence game between authors and readers inherent to fiction.[110]

Smoke is more directly an adaptation of Auster's short story 'Auggie Wren's Christmas Story', commissioned and published by the *New York Times* on Christmas Day, 1990 – the year of *The Music of Chance*'s publication and of Auster's first full draft of *Leviathan*.[111] *Smoke*'s co-director Wayne Wang says that he was drawn to the story's 'complex world of reality and fiction, truth and lies, giving and taking', while Auster comments in an interview that 'Everything gets turned upside down in "Auggie Wren". What's stealing? What's giving? What's lying? What's telling the truth?'[112] The main thread of the story is a tale told by Auggie to Paul, who is in search of a Christmas story free from the 'unpleasant associations [...] of hypocritical mush and treacle'.[113] Auggie offers to tell him a good story if Paul buys him lunch, guaranteeing that 'every word is true'. The story Auggie tells is a convoluted one of good deeds and deception which has at its centre a scene in which he takes a camera – that was likely already stolen – from the house of an elderly, blind, African American woman who mistakes him – or pretends to mistake him – for her grandson, and with whom Auggie ends up having Christmas lunch. Auggie tells a version of the story to Paul in the final sequence of *Smoke*. Like the opening Walter Raleigh anecdote, the story offers a commentary on the film's broader exploration of forms of morally ambiguous exchange. When Auggie finishes telling his story, a 'wicked grin' spreads across his face, and Paul wonders whether he's been had, and whether Auggie was just blowing smoke:

> Paul: Bullshit is a real talent, Auggie [...] I'd say you were among the masters.
> Auggie: What do you mean?
> Paul: I mean, it's a good story.
> Auggie: Shit. If you can't share your secrets with your friends, what kind of friend are you? (*S* 139)

But what exactly is the secret being shared? The confession of the theft that is the subject of the story, or that the story itself is a 'fake', a fiction? The question is akin to that posed by the 'confession' of the friend in Baudelaire's story: if Auggie's story is a counterfeit like the friend's coin, is it any less valuable? What has Auggie given to Paul, in other words, and what has he given away about their friendship? The secret of Auggie's story – and, he suggests, the secret of friendship – might lie in this very indeterminacy. In *Smoke*, Auster therefore returns to the 'zone of not-knowing' that he suggested to Coetzee in *Here and Now* defines male friendship. Rather than a 'transparent' relation, as Coetzee argues, friendship here is obscured in a cloud of smoke, as mysterious as Sachs's relationship with Aaron – who, like Auggie, promises to 'give [a] true story', and who, like Paul, shares a cigar with a friend telling a very tall tale of stolen money and assumed identities.

Throughout his first letter to Coetzee, Auster quotes from his own translation of the notebooks of the French essayist Joseph Joubert, picking out Joubert's gobbets on friendship: 'He must not only cultivate his friends, but cultivate his friendships within himself [...] We always lose the friendship of those who lose our esteem.'[114] But there is one line of Joubert's on friendship that Auster translates but does not quote back to Coetzee: 'A person who is never duped cannot be a friend'.[115] 'Getting people right is not what life is about anyway', Nathan writes in *American Pastoral*, 'It's getting them wrong that is living'.[115] In Auster's fiction, getting people wrong is similarly a part of living, even if his work also entertains Sidney's utopian fantasy, in *Oracle Night*, of a more 'transparent' form of social exchange, in which 'you don't have to explain your principles. They're immediately understood by how you act.' One of money's allures is that it speaks to just this fantasy of transparency. It can provide an objective index of value that rationalises exchange. You know what you're getting with money, and what is owed to whom, even if prices fluctuate; it cuts to the chase. In imagining money as a gift, Auster not only reveals this fantasy to be a kind of counterfeit but explores how all social relations, all projects of community, are 'haunted' by the phantom spectres of value, indebtedness, and authenticity. Mauss writes that much of 'our morality and our lives themselves are [...] permeated with [the] atmosphere of the gift, where obligation and liberty intermingle'.[117] Auster shows that even our closest relationships are imbricated in this ambivalent exchange of freedom and control. The paper trail I have traced between friends in Auster's work – the letters, the manuscripts, the novels, the postcards, the cheques, the cash – reproduces this quandary of reciprocity, of corresponding with another, showing generosity to be an act of ultimately unaccountable risk. Friendships for Auster are chance encounters: speculative relations, freighted with the potential of the unforeseen.

Notes

1 For an overview, see Mark Osteen (ed.), *The Question of the Gift: Essays Across Disciplines* (New York: Routledge, 2002).
2 Lewis Hyde, *The Gift: Creativity and the Artist in the Modern World* [1983] (New York: Vintage, 2007), 58, 154.
3 Paul Auster, 'Kafka's Letters' (1977), in *The Art of Hunger: Essays, Prefaces, Interviews* [1992] (New York: Penguin, 1997), pp. 134–139 (135–136).
4 Paul Auster and J. M. Coetzee, *Here and Now: Letters, 2008–2011* (London: Faber and Faber, 2013), 219. Subsequent references are given in the text as *HN* and in parentheses. Both writers have included their own names in their novels: see, for example, Auster's *The New York Trilogy* (1987) and Coetzee's *Boyhood* (1997). Auster has explored the epistolary form before, in *In the Country of Last Things* (London: Faber and Faber, 1987). On postmodern experimentations with epistolarity, see Sunka Simon, *Mail-Orders: The Fiction of Letters in Postmodern Culture* (Albany: State University of New York Press, 2002).
5 Martin Riker, 'Pen Pals', *New York Times*, 17 March 2013.
6 Amanda Wilcox, *The Gift of Correspondence in Classical Rome: Friendship in Cicero's* Ad Familiares *and Seneca's* Moral Epistles (Madison: University of Wisconsin Press, 2012), 14, 8.
7 Kathy Eden, *The Renaissance Rediscovery of Intimacy* (Chicago: University of Chicago Press, 2012), 50; Lisa Jardine, *Reading Shakespeare Historically* (London: Routledge, 1996), 80. See also Lorna Hutson, *The Usurer's Daughter: Male Friendship and Fictions of Women in Sixteenth-Century England* (London: Routledge, 1994), 1–15, 52–87; Alan Bray, *The Friend* (Chicago: University of Chicago Press, 2003), 159–164.

8 Elizabeth Hewitt, *Correspondence and American Literature, 1770–1865* (Cambridge: Cambridge University Press, 2004), 189, n. 8. Emphasis in original; William Decker, *Epistolary Practices: Letter-Writing in America Before Telecommunications* (Chapel Hill: University of North Carolina Press, 1998), 47.
9 Hewitt, *Correspondence and American Literature*, 56–57.
10 Decker, *Epistolary Practices*, 116.
11 Ralph Waldo Emerson, 'Friendship' (1841), in *The Essential Writings of Ralph Waldo Emerson*, ed. Brooks Atkinson (New York: Modern Library Classics, 2000), pp. 201–215 (202).
12 Hewitt, *Correspondence and American Literature*, 3; Emerson, 'Friendship', 211.
13 On Lamb and Coleridge's textually mediated friendship, see Felicity James, *Charles Lamb, Coleridge and Wordsworth: Reading Friendship in the 1790s* (Basingstoke: Palgrave Macmillan, 2008), 43–47.
14 Jacques Derrida, *The Post Card: From Socrates to Freud and Beyond*, trans. Alan Bass (Chicago: University of Chicago Press, 1987), 48. See also Janet Altman, *Epistolarity: Approaches to a Form* (Columbus: Ohio State University Press, 1982), 193–194.
15 Wayne Booth, *The Company We Keep: An Ethics of Reading* (Chicago: University of Chicago Press, 1988), 173.
16 Booth, *The Company We Keep*, 163; Martha Nussbaum, *Love's Knowledge: Essays on Philosophy and Literature* (Oxford: Oxford University Press, 1990), 148, 230. See also Nussbaum, 'Reading for Life', *Yale Journal of Law & the Humanities*, 1:1 (1989), pp. 165–180; 'Exactly and Responsibly: A Defence of Ethical Criticism', *Philosophy and Literature*, 22:2 (1998), pp. 343–365; Wayne Booth, 'Why Banning Ethical Criticism Is a Serious Mistake', *Philosophy and Literature*, 22:2 (1998), pp. 366–393.
17 Dorothy Hale,'Fiction as Restriction: Self-Binding in New Ethical Theories of the Novel', *Narrative*, 15:2 (2007), pp. 187–206 (195). See Lionel Trilling, 'Manners, Morals, and the Novel', *Kenyon Review*, 10 (1948), pp. 11–27 (22).
18 Dorothy Hale, 'Aesthetics and the New Ethics: Theorizing the Novel in the Twenty-First Century', *PMLA*, 124:3 (2009), pp. 896–905 (897); Nussbaum, *Love's Knowledge*, 231.
19 Hale, 'Fiction as Restriction', 190.
20 See Lawrence Buell, 'In Pursuit of Ethics', *PMLA*, 114:1 (1999), pp. 7–19 (13–15). Hale writes that 'the reader's apprehension through literature of an alterity that exceeds comprehension is connected in

new ethical theory to the positioning of the reader not as friend but as judge'. 'Fiction as Restriction', 195.
21 Hale, 'Aesthetics and the New Ethics', 899.
22 Booth, *The Company We Keep*, 175, n. 8.
23 Marcel Mauss, *The Gift: The Form and Reason for Exchange in Archaic Societies* [1925], trans. W. D. Halls (London: Routledge, 1990), 59; Gerald Moore, *Politics of the Gift: Exchanges in Poststructuralism* (Edinburgh: Edinburgh University Press, 2011), 3.
24 Hyde, *The Gift*, xiv.
25 Lee Konstantinou, 'Lewis Hyde's Double Economy', *ASAP/Journal*, 1:1 (January 2016), pp. 123–149 (127–128).
26 See Jeffrey Severs, *David Foster Wallace's Balancing Books: Fictions of Value* (New York: Columbia University Press, 2017), 88–123; Zadie Smith, 'The Difficult Gifts of David Foster Wallace', in *Changing My Mind: Occasional Essays* (London: Penguin, 2009), pp. 257–300. Jonathan Lethem, 'The Ecstasy of Influence' (2007), in *The Ecstasy of Influence: Nonfictions, etc.* (New York: Vintage, 2012), pp. 93–120.
27 Konstantinou, 'Lewis Hyde's Double Economy', 134, 139.
28 See Adam Kelly, 'David Foster Wallace and the New Sincerity in American Fiction', in David Hering (ed.), *Consider David Foster Wallace: Critical Essays* (Austin: Sideshow Media Group Press, 2010), pp. 131–146.
29 Adam Kelly, 'David Foster Wallace and New Sincerity Aesthetics: A Reply to Edward Jackson and Joel Nicholson-Roberts', *Orbit: A Journal of American Literature*, 5:4 (2017), pp. 1–32 (17).
30 Vanessa Smith, *Intimate Strangers: Friendship, Exchange and Pacific Encounters* (Cambridge: Cambridge University Press, 2010), 113.
31 Jacques Derrida, *Given Time: 1. Counterfeit Money*, trans. Peggy Kamuf (Chicago: University of Chicago Press, 1992), 12, 14.
32 Kelly, 'David Foster Wallace and the New Sincerity in American Fiction', 146.
33 See Mauss, *The Gift*, 28–32.
34 Derrida, *Given Time*, 12.
35 Emerson, 'Gifts' (1844), in *The Essential Writings of Ralph Waldo Emerson*, pp. 360–364 (361).
36 'Dedicating the work is a public act that the reader is [...] called on to witness [...] and this proclamation [serves] as a theme or commentary [...] The dedicatee is always in some way responsible for the work that is dedicated to him and to which he brings [...] a little of his support and therefore participation'. Gérard Genette, *Paratexts:*

Thresholds of Interpretation, trans. Jane Lewin (Cambridge: Cambridge University Press, 1997), 136.
37 Paul Auster, *Leviathan* (London: Faber and Faber, 1992). Subsequent references are given in the text as *L* and in parentheses.
38 See Ryan Simmons, 'What Is a Terrorist? Contemporary Authorship, the Unabomber, and *Mao II*', *Modern Fiction Studies*, 45:3 (Fall 1999), pp. 675–695.
39 See Steven Alford, 'Chance in Contemporary Narrative: The Example of Paul Auster', *Lit: Literature Interpretation Theory*, 11:1 (2000), pp. 59–82.
40 Given *Leviathan*'s titular allusion to *Moby-Dick*, this scene also brings to mind Melville's friendship with Hawthorne, and the latter's recollection of their 'talk about time and eternity […] that lasted pretty deep into the night […] we smoked cigars even within the sacred precincts of the sitting room' Nathanial Hawthorne, *The American Notebooks*, ed. Claude Simpson (Columbus: Ohio State University Press, 1972), 448. Auster wrote an introduction to Hawthorne's *Twenty Days with Julian and Little Bunny by Papa* (New York: NYRB Classics, 2003), and frequently alludes to his work. See William Marling, 'Paul Auster and the American Romantics', *Lit: Literature Interpretation Theory*, 7:4 (1997), pp. 301–310.
41 Aliki Varvogli, *The World that Is the Book: Paul Auster's Fiction* (Liverpool: Liverpool University Press, 2001), 123.
42 Paul Auster, *The New York Trilogy* [1987] (London: Faber and Faber, 2005). Subsequent references are given in the text in parentheses.
43 Alex Segal, 'Secrecy and the Gift: Paul Auster's *The Locked Room*', *Critique: Studies in Contemporary Fiction*, 39:3 (1998), pp. 239–257.
44 Segal, 'Secrecy and the Gift', 240.
45 Mark Osteen, 'Phantoms of Liberty: The Secret Lives of *Leviathan*', *Review of Contemporary Fiction*, 14:1 (Spring 1994), p. 87.
46 Varvogli, *The World that Is the Book*, 123; Mark Brown, *Paul Auster* (Manchester: Manchester University Press, 2007), 160.
47 See Adam Kelly, *American Fiction in Transition: Observer-Hero Narrative, the 1990s, and Postmodernism* (London: Bloomsbury, 2013), 53.
48 Dustin Iler, 'Suicide and the Afterlife of the Cold War: Accident, Intentionality, and Periodicity in Paul Auster's *Leviathan* and Jeffrey Eugenides's *The Virgin Suicides*', *Modern Fiction Studies*, 63:4 (Winter 2017), pp. 737–758 (740).
49 Iler, 'Suicide and the Afterlife of the Cold War', 741.

50 Lauren Berlant, *The Queen of America Goes to Washington City: Essays on Sex and Citizenship* (Durham, NC: Duke University Press, 1997), 3.
51 Berlant, *The Queen of America Goes to Washington City*, 3.
52 Auster and Siegumfeldt, *A Life in Words*, 167–168.
53 Berlant *The Queen of America Goes to Washington City*, 177–178.
54 Lauren Berlant, *The Anatomy of National Fantasy: Hawthorne, Utopia, and Everyday Life* (Chicago: Chicago University Press, 1991), 23.
55 Emerson, 'Politics' (1844), in *The Essential Writings of Ralph Waldo Emerson*, pp. 378–389 (382).
56 Hewitt, *Correspondence and American Literature*, 53.
57 Auster and Siegumfeldt, *A Life in Words*, 169.
58 Danielle Allen, *Talking to Strangers: Anxieties of Citizenship since Brown v. Board of Education* (Chicago: University of Chicago Press, 2004), 78.
59 Allen, *Talking to Strangers*, 82. On connections between Hobbes's *Leviathan* and Reaganism, see Michael Rogin, *Ronald Reagan, the Movie: and Other Episodes in Political Demonology* (Berkeley: University of California Press, 1987), 283–300.
60 Allen, *Talking to Strangers*, 97, 138.
61 Allen, *Talking to Strangers*, 132–133.
62 Brown, *Paul Auster*, 90, 87.
63 Osteen, 'Phantoms of Liberty', 87.
64 Osteen, 'Phantoms of Liberty', 87.
65 Maria is closely based on the performance artist Sophie Calle, with whom Auster has collaborated. See Sophie Calle, *Double Game* [1999] (London: Violette Editions, 2007); *The Address Book* [1983] (Los Angeles: Giglio Press, 2012); Auster and Calle, 'Gotham Handbook' (1994), in Auster, *Collected Prose* (London: Faber and Faber, 2003), pp. 283–292. Maria's birthday project is a version of Calle's 'The Birthday Ceremony' (1980–1993).
66 Auster and Siegumfeldt, *A Life in Words*, 170.
67 Iler, 'Suicide and the Afterlife of the Cold War', 242.
68 Varvogli, *The World that is the Book*, 147.
69 See Peter Knight, 'Everything Is Connected: *Underworld*'s Secret History of Paranoia', *Modern Fiction Studies*, 45:3 (Fall 1999), pp. 811–832.
70 Auster also uses the phrase 'concentric circles' in *Here and Now*, 6.
71 Mauss, *The Gift*, 59.
72 Paul Auster, *Oracle Night* (London: Faber and Faber, 2004). Subsequent references are given in the text as *ON* and in parentheses.

73 Auster and Siegumfeldt, *A Life in Words*, 224.
74 Brown, *Paul Auster*, 96.
75 Auster and Siegumfeldt, *A Life in Words*, 224.
76 See Auster, *New York Trilogy*, 294.
77 On the presence of Native Americans in Auster's fiction, and the influence of the myth-and-symbol school on his early work, see Alys Moody, 'Eden of Exiles: The Ethnicities of Paul Auster's Aesthetics', *American Literary History*, 28:1 (Spring 2016), pp. 69–93.
78 Ruth Levitas, 'Looking for the Blue: The Necessity of Utopia', *Journal of Political Ideologies*, 12:3 (2007), pp. 289–306 (290).
79 See Paul Auster, 'Oracle Night Drafts', Box 23, Folder 1, The Paul Auster Collection of Papers, 1999–2006 (bulk 2000–2005), The Henry W. and Albert A. Berg Collection, The New York Public Library.
80 Paul Auster, *The Brooklyn Follies* (London: Faber and Faber, 2005). Subsequent references are given in the text as *BF* and in parentheses. 'It is hard not to think of Roth when we read Auster', Michael Schmidt notes, observing that Nathan Glass 'calls to mind Roth's Nathan Zuckerman'. *The Novel: A Biography* (Cambridge, MA: Belknap Press, 2014), 1099.
81 Brown, *Paul Auster*, 96.
82 Sandra Sherman, 'Book Review: *Writing and the Rise of Finance: Capital Satires of the Early Eighteenth Century*', *Eighteenth-Century Studies*, 31:1 (Fall 1997), pp. 144–145 (144).
83 See Nicky Marsh, *Money, Speculation and Finance in Contemporary British Fiction* (London: Continuum, 2007), 1–24.
84 Marc Shell, *Money, Language and Thought* (Baltimore: Johns Hopkins University Press, 1982), 14. See also John Chown, *A History of Money: From AD 800* (London: Routledge, 1994), 17–22.
85 Shell, *Money, Language and Thought*, 7.
86 Paul Auster, *Hand to Mouth* (1997), in *Collected Prose* (London: Faber and Faber, 2003), pp. 151–240 (153). Subsequent references are given in the text as *HM* and in parentheses.
87 Paul Auster, *The Invention of Solitude* (1982), in *Collected Prose*, pp. 1–150 (47).
88 See Martin, *Paul Auster's Postmodernity*, 41; Carsten Springer, *A Paul Auster Sourcebook* (Frankfurt: Peter Lang, 2001), 16.
89 Pascal Bruckner, 'Paul Auster, or The Heir Intestate', in Dennis Barone (ed.), *Beyond the Red Notebook: Essays on Paul Auster* (Philadelphia: University of Pennsylvania Press, 1995), pp. 27–33 (27).
90 Brown, *Paul Auster*, 80.

91 Lewis Hyde, *The Gift*, xvii.
92 William Marling, *Gatekeepers: The Emergence of World Literature and the 1960s* (Oxford: Oxford University Press, 2016), 75. Humes co-founded the *Paris Review*.
93 Paul Auster, *Moon Palace* (London: Faber and Faber, 1989), 198.
94 Mary Morris, 'A Conversation with Paul Auster', in James Hutchison (ed.), *Conversations with Paul Auster* (Jackson: University Press of Mississippi, 2013), pp. 163–179 (166).
95 Paul Auster, *The Music of Chance* (London: Faber and Faber, 1990), 41. Subsequent references are given in the text as *MC* and in parentheses.
96 Tom Woods, '*The Music of Chance*: Aleatorical (Dis)harmonies within "The City of the World"', in Dennis Barone (ed.), *Beyond the Red Notebook: Essays on Paul Auster* (Philadelphia: University of Pennsylvania Press, 1995), pp. 27–33 (27).
97 Brown, *Paul Auster*, 137.
98 Fredric Jameson, *Fables of Aggression: Wyndham Lewis, the Modernist as Fascist* (Berkeley: University of California Press, 1979), 59. In an essay on Beckett's *Mercier and Camier* (1970), Auster writes, 'Like Flaubert's Bouvard and Pécuchet, like Laurel and Hardy, like the other "pseudo couples" in Beckett's work, [Mercier and Camier] are not so much separate characters as two elements of a tandem reality, and neither one could exist without the other. The purpose of their journey is never stated, and their destination is unclear.' 'From Cakes to Stones: A Note on Beckett's French' [1975], in *Collected Prose*, pp. 346–350 (346).
99 Sarah Cole, *Modernism, Male Friendship, and the First World War* (Cambridge: Cambridge University Press, 2003), 5.
100 On a similar theme, see James Peacock, 'Faking It or Making It? Forgery, Real Lives and the True Fake in *The Brooklyn Follies*', in Stefania Ciocia and Jesús González (eds), *The Invention of Illusions: International Perspectives on Paul Auster* (Newcastle-upon-Tyne: Cambridge Scholars Press, 2011), pp. 75–96.
101 Paul Auster, *Smoke* (1995), in *Collected Screenplays* (London: Faber and Faber, 2010), pp. 21–140. Subsequent references are given in the text as *S* and in parentheses.
102 Brown, *Paul Auster*, 176.
103 Karin van Marle, 'Laughter, Refusal, Friendship: Thoughts on a "Jurisprudence of Generosity"', *Stellenbosch Law Review*, 18 (2007), pp. 194–206 (204–205).
104 Chris Darke, *Light Readings: Film Criticism and Screen Arts* (London: Wallflower, 2000), 40.

105 Walter Raleigh is alluded to throughout Auster's fiction. As far back as his student days at Columbia in the late 1960s, he was planning a novel called *The Death of Sir Walter Raleigh*, which was to feature a fictionalised version of H. L. Humes. An essay of the same title appeared in 1975. See Marling, *Gatekeepers*, 81–86. Raleigh is also associated with interracial male friendship in *Mr. Vertigo* (London: Faber and Faber, 1994), through the protagonist Walt's relationship with Aesop. Walt describes how Aesop transformed his life: 'I'm not just referring to my prejudices, the old witchcraft of never looking past the color of a person's skin, but to the fact of friendship itself' (37). Unsurprisingly given his name, Aesop has a rich store of magical tales, and Walt's favourites are those 'about my namesake, Sir Walter Raleigh' (43).
106 The comparison also echoes Sachs's effort to give Lillian money 'as a token of everything he had to give, his entire soul'. *Leviathan*, 167.
107 Brown, *Paul Auster*, 176.
108 Michael Kaplan, *Friendship Fictions: The Rhetoric of Citizenship in the Liberal Imaginary* (Tuscaloosa: University of Alabama Press, 2010), 183. Mark Brown suggests that 'Auster's urban representations have been richly influenced by [...] Baudelaire'. Brown, *Paul Auster*, 8.
109 Charles Baudelaire, 'Counterfeit Money' (1869), in Jacques Derrida, *Given Time*, pp. 72–78.
110 Derrida, *Given Time*, 116.
111 See Auster, '*Leviathan*: Drafts', Box 3, Folder 3, The Paul Auster Collection of Papers, 1987–2001 (bulk 1995–1999).
112 John Blades, 'City of Smoke and Dreams', *Chicago Tribune*, 5 November 1995; Auster, 'The Making of *Smoke*' (1995), in *Collected Screenplays*, pp. 3–17 (3).
113 Paul Auster, 'Auggie Wren's Christmas Story' (1990), in *Collected Screenplays*, pp. 141–147 (143).
114 Auster and Coetzee, *Here and Now*, 6; Joseph Joubert, *The Notebooks of Joseph Joubert,* trans. Paul Auster (New York: New York Review of Books, 2005), 132.
115 Joubert, *The Notebooks of Joseph Joubert*, 113.
116 Roth, *American Pastoral*, 35.
117 Mauss, *The Gift*, 65.

3

Broken utopias: Michael Chabon's *Telegraph Avenue* (2012) and Jonathan Lethem's *The Fortress of Solitude* (2003)

'You'll never get it if you don't slow down'

Before turning to the work of Michael Chabon and Jonathan Lethem, I want to spend a little longer in Auggie's tobacconist, where I concluded the previous chapter. In *Smoke*, Auster portrays the Brooklyn Cigar Company as a focal point for a model of community. Auggie's corner store is the block's local spot where men go to 'shoot the breeze', creating a loose network of overlapping neighbourhood affinities that cohere into a ramshackle sociality.[1] In the previous chapter, I explored how money moves differently around Auggie's store from how it does in Manhattan, its flow tracing a structure of feeling in which the working up and off of debts indexes emotional ties as well as financial obligations. From its opening shot of a Brooklyn-bound subway train crossing the East River, with the downtown Manhattan skyline behind, the film suggests how the two boroughs constitute one another spatially and temporally. Imagined as local and rooted, and as a 'place' characterised by face-to-face relations, neighbourhood Brooklyn defines itself in relation and distinction to the globalised, corporatised 'space' of the financial centre looming large across the water.[2] Time is money in the city, but in Brooklyn, at least during the 'slow hours' at Auggie's, it is spent a little differently – savoured like a good smoke, or wasted just 'hanging out' (21).

Paul starts dating a woman whose doctoral thesis is entitled 'Visions of Utopia in Nineteenth-Century American Fiction', and the film consciously situates its narrative in this tradition, while

Broken utopias 121

Figure 1 Auggie's Photographs. Photo Credit K. C. Bailey (still photographer), *Smoke*, Dir. Wayne Wang, Pers. Harvey Keitel, William Hurt (New York: Miramax Films, 1995).

also acknowledging the proximity of a certain naive optimism to its depiction of Brooklyn bonhomie. *Smoke* conjures its own, partial vision of an alternative way of life, and, to glimpse it, one has to follow Auggie's advice to Paul as they view his collection of photographs (Figure 1). Taken at the same time each morning from the same position across the street, the four thousand photos all depict Auggie's storefront. As Paul leafs through the albums, Auggie cautions that 'You'll never get it if you don't slow down, my friend'. 'But they're all the same', Paul laughs. 'They're all the same', Auggie says, 'but each one is different from every other one' (43–44). As a 'record' of his 'little spot', Auggie's photos constitute the history of a sense of place unfolding day by day, and *Smoke* is similarly attuned to the gradual, uneven ways in which neighbourhood life takes shape. The slow work of negotiating difference in similitude might be another name for the work of friendship; it is no coincidence that as we watch Auggie and Paul looking through the photographs, we are also watching the formation of their relationship.

Smoke's evocation of the leisurely pace of life on the block does have an air of nostalgia. There is a similarity between the portrayal of the loose solidarities forming in Auggie's corner-store hangout and a raft of popular social commentary from the 1980s and 1990s that mourned the disappearance of local communities. The store resembles the kind of 'third place' – beyond the home and the workplace – that Ray Oldenburg celebrated as 'central to the political processes of a democracy'.[3] Christopher Lasch similarly suggested that 'the decline of participatory democracy may be directly related to the disappearance of third places', while Robert Putnam took the decline of another form of third-place sociality – the bowling league – as emblematic of a wider crisis in American civic society.[4] Decrying the decline of civic life, many of these elegiac critiques were socially conservative in their emphasis on religion, morality, and 'family values'. But, their attention to small-scale social networks was contiguous with a broader, more politically diverse analysis of liberal individualism. Many of these critiques looked to forms of friendship to model the kinds of revitalised affiliations they had in mind. In his communitarian analysis of Rawlsian deontology, for example, Michael Sandel evokes an Aristotelian idea of civic friendship to stress the importance of 'constituent attachments' in civic life.[5] In Chantal Mouffe's very different 'project of radical and plural democracy', a conception of the 'friend/enemy divide' derived from the work of Carl Schmitt and Michael Oakeshott's notion of *societas* suggests a 'grammar' for an iteration of citizenship combining liberal pluralism and participatory democracy.[6] As I suggested in my discussion of communitarianism in Roth's work, the appeal to civic friendship here is multifaceted. On the one hand, friendship protects and promotes important liberal democratic values, such as individual rights, justice, and pluralism. But on the other, civic friendship challenges the liberal dichotomy of the private and public spheres by suggesting that political affiliations should be shaped by, rather than separate from, personal relations. The kinds of political community imagined vary considerably but, in each account, it is suggested friendship might help to solve the crisis of citizenship in late twentieth-century liberalism.

The rough-and-ready local community that takes shape in and around Auggie's store may appear to offer a version of 'third place' sociability, while the film's portrayal of easy camaraderie between 'counter guys' seems to be in dialogue with communitarian descriptions of civil society. But, through the central relationship between Paul and Rashid, *Smoke* suggests a more complex politics of friendship, attuned to broader anxieties about race and representation in 1990s America. Their friendship recalls the archetype of interracial male bonding in nineteenth-century American literature analysed by Leslie Fiedler, but also the kind of black–white 'bromance' that was a Hollywood trope by the 1990s.[7] In the same year as *Smoke*, Benjamin DeMott argued that the 'friendship orthodoxy' of the interracial buddy film 'miniaturizes, personalizes, and moralizes the large and complex dilemmas of race, removing them from the public sphere' and reducing them to a matter of personal relations.[8] Such diminution and displacement is indicative of what Lauren Berlant calls the 'downsizing' and 'privatization of citizenship' in late twentieth-century liberalism, wherein the 1960s leftist-feminist principle, 'the personal is the political', is contorted into 'the political is the personal'.[9] In this schema, the 'political public sphere' is reduced to an 'intimate public sphere', and citizenship to a 'scene of private acts'.[10] DeMott similarly argues that the friendship orthodoxy pervasive in popular culture renders racism 'one-dimensional – lacking, that is, in institutional, historical, or political ramifications', a problem solved at the level of 'private attitudes and emotions'.[11] DeMott's and Berlant's critiques are something of a corrective to more hopeful 1990s evocations of civic friendship: they caution that friendship might not so much inform the political as displace it altogether, and that friendship's mediation of the private and public spheres might be more ambiguous than communitarian readings acknowledge.[12]

Smoke is attuned to this vexed politics. During a discussion of the racial divide between neighbourhood Brooklyn and the Projects, Rashid concludes that 'Black is black and white is white and never the twain shall meet'. Paul counters, 'It looks like they've met in this apartment'. Rashid, deadpan, replies, 'Let's not get too idealistic' (79). If Hollywood's sentimental friendships de-historicise the complexities of race relations, Rashid's allusion to Rudyard Kipling inserts an awareness of the legacies of imperialism and racism into his relationship with Paul.[13] Similarly, Rashid's real name – Thomas Jefferson Cole – at once raises and problematises the prospect of their friendship as neatly symbolic of post-civil rights interracial harmony.[14] *Smoke* thus reflexively critiques and distances itself from the popular Hollywood bromance while not, I would suggest, disavowing the political possibilities of friendship *per se*. If, in eschewing what DeMott calls the 'moral fantasy' of the friendship orthodoxy, Auster cautions against becoming 'too idealistic', his portrayal of the community formed around Auggie's store gestures toward the idea that an *unorthodox* conception of friendship might yield a different register of political potentiality.

Post-utopian utopianism

In elucidating this different register, I turn back to Derrida's *The Politics of Friendship* (1997) and his suggestion that Aristotelian civic republicanism renders citizenship a militaristic form of fraternity, resulting in an exclusionary and repressive kind of political community.[15] In this regard, Derrida's analysis shares an affinity with the work of Jean-Luc Nancy and Maurice Blanchot, who also sought to defamiliarise the idea of an 'organic' or 'natural' community constituted by a universalised brotherhood, and who instead outlined a conception of community as 'inoperative' and 'unavowable'.[16] We might expect Derrida to do away with the idea of friendship altogether in his theorisation of 'democratic subjectivity'. But in fact, in tracing the integral yet contested role friendship plays within the history of democratic thought, Derrida gestures towards what he calls a 'democracy to come' – a precarious form of political community akin to those imagined by Nancy and Blanchot.[17] Derrida suggests that the elegiac apostrophe that frames his study – 'O my friends, there is no friend' – encapsulates the simultaneity of friendship's political possibility and impossibility, and so marks an opening into thinking of friendship as 'never a given of the present', but as instead belonging to the 'future anterior', a temporality of 'waiting, promise', but also of loss.[18] Consequently, the temporality of friendship becomes a way for Derrida to figure the oddly retrospective futurity of democracy, a tentative future that is always conditional, precarious, and shadowed by failure.

In placing *The Politics of Friendship* alongside communitarian accounts of civic friendship, I suggested in my Introduction that we might read Derrida's critique as yet another 1990s commentary on the transformation of citizenship. But we can also historicise Derrida's conception of a 'democracy to come' as one among a number of attempts, by a range of thinkers on the Left, to reconceive a valence of hope for contemporary progressive politics and imagine a kind of idealism that is not, in Rashid's phrase, 'too idealistic'. Ash Amin and Nigel Thrift diagnose a dwindling 'capacity to visualise the future' in contemporary leftist thought, arguing that 'the utopian impulse has all but disappeared' from progressive politics.[19] This 'waning of the utopian' can be traced back to the 'political failures' of 'the sixties' that inform Marianne DeKoven's understanding of the 'postmodern moment' as 'post-sixties and post-utopian', as pointed up in my discussion of Sachs's politics in *Leviathan*, and my reading of *Subtle Bodies*.[20] Yet DeKoven discerns a recalcitrant or 'residual' utopianism stretching into the late twentieth century: 'the intensely utopian sixties structure of feeling' does 'persist in postmodernity', she writes, but is now 'in every way "limited"': muted, partial, local' – a 'qualified hope', checked and marked by the failures and disappointments of an earlier era.[21] Lauren Berlant elaborates a version of this limited utopianism – or what DeKoven elsewhere calls 'post-utopian utopianism' – and imagines it informing a certain kind of historicism. Asking 'What does it mean to be accused of being '68 in the 1990s?', Berlant suggests that 'refusing to learn the lessons of history, refusing to relinquish utopian practice' might enable the theorisation of 'social change in the present tense, but a present tense different from what we can now imagine for pragmatic [...] politics'. Part of the task of 'embracing utopian logics', she argues, is to recognise the centrality of 'waste, failure, loss' to the project of imagining transformation.[22] Berlant's 'utopian historicity' thus responds to Jameson's argument that the attenuation of utopian thinking in postmodernity is a result of a 'weakening of historicity'; she proposes a form of historical inquiry that might recapture a sense of the future from the ruins of the past.[23] And there is an affinity, I suggest, between the complex temporal order of Berlant's 'politics of futurity' and the 'future anterior', the strange time of friendship defining Derrida's 'democracy to come'.

Imagining a future steeped in the past, Berlant's historicism envisions what might be called a politics of anachronism.[24] Put another way, what emerges in her essay – as in much recent work on 'queer time' – is a form of historical imagination characterised by a kind of emancipatory waywardness. As Pamela Thurschwell suggests:

> Queer theorists have set themselves the task of uncovering historical alternatives to the teleological stories of heteropatriarchy which dominate our understanding of history, engaging with a 'not yet' approach to the history of sexuality and culture that looks backwards, and sideways, to imagine different, more utopian [...] presents than the [...] ones we currently inhabit.[25]

Thurschwell's summary is helpful in situating the 'temporal turn' in queer theory within a broader tradition of Marxist utopian historicism. Indeed, much recent work on queer time is indebted to Ernst Bloch's critical idealism, which sought to 'reintroduce the openness of the future into the past [...] restoring the dimension of potentiality to mere actuality'.[26] For example, Bloch's theorisation of the 'not-yet-conscious' – a 'futurity embedded in the past and present, which may or may not emerge' – informs José Esteban Muñoz's account of 'critical utopianism'.[27] Understanding 'hope as a hermeneutic', Muñoz describes a practice of reading texts for their 'anticipatory illuminations' of the utopian, for 'a mode of being and feeling that was then not quite there but is nonetheless an opening'.[28] It is also Muñoz who unpacks a concept I have been borrowing from Giorgio Agamben, and which also sutures Berlant's Blochian historicism – 'potentiality':

> Unlike a possibility, a thing that simply might happen, a potentiality is a certain mode of nonbeing that is eminent [sic], a thing that is present but not actually existing in the present tense [...] Bloch would posit that such utopian feelings can and regularly will be disappointed. They are nonetheless indispensable to the act of imagining transformation.[29]

Attuned to potentialities, the forms of utopian historicism that I have been describing hazard not only anachronism but nostalgia too; they risk resembling a romance of what might have been. Yet, in entwining the past and future in uncanny configurations, and in being open to what Leela Gandhi calls 'the risky arrival of the not quite, not yet', they also adumbrate a complex and conflicted form of political affect at once knowing and naive, elegiac, and optimistic, one which tries to reread the past for its missed futurities.[30]

This chapter focuses on two novels – Jonathan Lethem's *The Fortress of Solitude* (2003), and, firstly, Michael Chabon's *Telegraph Avenue* (2012) – that trace versions of this post-utopian utopianism, and, like *Smoke*, approach ideas of citizenship and community through the figure of interracial male friendship. I use DeKoven's ungainly term 'post-utopian utopianism', not least because it recalls another inelegant yet useful critical label, one sometimes used to describe Lethem's and Chabon's work, and which I discussed in my Introduction: 'post-postmodernism'.[31] In their uneasy periodisation of the contemporary, both terms gesture towards my broader claim about the historical imagination of these novels. Their utopian historicism is akin to Linda Hutcheon's 'historiographic metafiction', but, in their exploration of the utopian potentiality of forms of temporal disorder, drag, and delay, of nostalgia and anachronism, they also substantiate a political perspective that corresponds with the contemporary theoretical accounts of utopia, hope, and futurity I have been outlining.[32] Chapter 1 was also concerned with the forms of historical imagination available to contemporary fiction, but Chabon's and Lethem's work returns to the radicalism of the past in a manner distinct from Roth's revisionary cultural pluralism. Both novels look back to the 1960s and their legacy, investing in the figure of interracial male friendship something of the decade's utopian promise of a realignment of the personal and the political, while at the same time refracting contemporary debates regarding citizenship and communitarianism. But these friendships also come to symbolise the precarity, contradictions, and limitations of that hope, and of remaining utopian in post-utopian times.

Brokeland Creole

Like *Smoke*, *Telegraph Avenue* centres on an independent store. 'Brokeland Records' represents another 'protopolitical' third place wherein local community takes shape, a 'neighborhood institution', as one character puts it.[33] Like Auster's cigar store, Chabon's record shop is 'full of time-wasting' and 'male conversation', from which a casual interracial sociability emerges, forged in the image of the seemingly unlikely friendship between the store's owners, Archy and Nat

(*TA* 473). Troy Patterson has queried what he views as the novel's 'naïve outlook' towards race relations, suggesting that its 'chin-up optimism' can be explained by a phrase 'at the end of the About the Author note: "he lives in Berkeley"'.³⁴ But Chabon locates his novel elsewhere. As Matt Feeney observes, '"Telegraph Avenue" usually denotes the "Cal Berkeley" terminus [of that] famous street [...] where all that stuff happened in the Sixties', that 'frisky, clamorous thoroughfare', as Michiko Kakutani describes it, 'identified since the 1960s with the counterculture and community'.³⁵ The novel is in fact set just a little further along the road: 'Brokeland' is the name in the book for the neighbourhood straddling 'the ragged fault where the urban plates of Berkeley and Oakland subducted' (*TA* 47), and so the novel's title is 'a sly misdirection', marking a certain critical as well as geographical distance from 'hippie-progressive Berkeley'.³⁶ Archy and Nat's relationship is therefore pitched in the borderland between historically white Berkeley and historically black Oakland, and the novel is steeped in each city's history of radical politics. The title offers the first indication that the portrayal of race and place will be less 'naïve' than Patterson suggests, and that its 'optimism' is more reflexive than he assumes. Furthermore, Patterson reads Archy and Nat's friendship as a black–white relationship, obscuring Nat's Jewish identity, and the novel's broader interest in the history of Jewish American and African American solidarity.

In an essay published alongside the novel, Chabon reveals that *Telegraph Avenue* was not begun in Berkeley at all, but in 'Los Angeles on October 3 1995', the day of O. J. Simpson's acquittal.³⁷ Watching footage of African Americans celebrating the verdict on television, Chabon recalls being struck by the fact that his 'astonishment' at their jubilation 'indexed directly to the absence of black people in my life'. The Simpson trial was one of a handful of events that revealed 'the importance of the 1960s to the public life of the 1990s' in America, especially in regard to the question of race, and Chabon also veers back in time to make sense of his own reaction to the Simpson episode.³⁸ In 'the Fall of 1969', Chabon writes, his family moved to the 'planned community' of Columbia, Maryland, an integrated new city that aspired 'to make life better in America' by affording 'white people and black people the chance to engage in the radical activity of living next door to one another'.³⁹ Designed by James Rouse – who amassed his fortune building shopping malls – Columbia was a 'Great Society [...] dream', and its model of racially mixed community life was intended to be replicated across the country.[40] But Columbia remained an isolated experiment, and an example of some of the contradictions of the period's spatial politics. Funded through a public–private partnership, Rouse's vision of 'post-urban' city life was unambiguously a for-profit venture.[41] Designed as a series of 'villages' encompassing pseudo-public spaces largely set aside for shops and restaurants – and a grand Rouse mall – Columbia resembled a 'bourgeois utopia', an uneasy mix of well-meaning liberal planning and corporate land speculation.[42]

The timing of the Chabons' move to Columbia resonates symbolically, the 'Fall of 1969' suggesting something of the fading idealism the end of the decade came to mark; elsewhere he describes growing up 'in the broken Utopias of Columbia and the 1970s'.[43] As a child, however, Columbia seemed a 'City of the Future [...] avowedly utopian in its aims', and a place where 'a young Jewish boy' could 'feel connected' to 'black history'.[44] In 1990s Los Angeles, 'capital of the eternal American present', Chabon realises he has lost a connection not only to African American culture but to the concept of the future. It is only when he moves to the East Bay area that he again picks up a 'trace' of the utopian. Describing the 'D.I.Y. Fourierists and urban foragers' whose 'cranky attachment to their own individual development' is matched 'only by their yearning for fellowship', Chabon satirises the fate of post-'60s Berkeley hippiedom.[45] But among the 'ashrams' and 'dojos', 'on the Oakland side', he finds his own 'would-be utopia'. At the counter of a used-record store run by 'a big black dude' and 'a little white guy', Chabon comes across a group of customers 'theorising, opining [...] Hanging together':

> I didn't kid myself that these guys were united in perfect brotherhood. They had not bound up the nation's racial wounds or invented a better America [...] They were just shooting the breeze, passing the time [...] In a little pocket of a big world, for a little hour.[46]

'Kid myself' draws attention to how the essay delineates two developmental narratives. Entwining Chabon's passage from childhood to adulthood with the course of American history since the late

1960s, it highlights how both are normatively marked as transitions from innocence to maturity, from youthful idealism to mature compromise. In this scene, however – in which adult men indulge in a passion of their adolescence – Chabon conjures something unassimilable to this familiar teleology. 'Little hour', 'shooting the breeze', 'hanging together', 'passing the time' – phrases that recall the 'slow hours' passed at Auggie's store – trace a mode of temporal suspension and disjuncture that is at once prospective and retrospective, utopian and nostalgic, in the way Elizabeth Freeman describes 'the mutually disruptive energy of moments that are not yet past and yet are not entirely present either'.[47] The scene's vision of interracial friendship is anachronistic, like the men's shared love of vinyl, yet anticipatory. In another essay, Chabon had suggested that, over the course of his life, 'the idea of the future [...] came itself to feel like something historical'.[48] In chronicling his journey from Columbia to Berkeley, Chabon records a version of this dwindling sense of futurity, but also suggests how the past might be reread for its utopian impulse. In this portrait of a 'little pocket of a big world', Chabon offers – as Auster does through Auggie's photographs – a local picture that invokes, even as it repudiates, a national context. Through the figure of interracial male friendship, Chabon gestures to a kind of historical imagination that might restore the idea of the future.

'It is the nature of utopia', Chabon remarks in the O. J. essay, 'to go out of business', and, as *Telegraph Avenue* opens, it seems Brokeland Records is destined to close. The central duo of the novel, set in 2004, are mired in a less recent past. Connoisseurs of early 1970s jazz-funk fusion, Archy and Nat are self-appointed wardens of the 'Brokeland Creole sound', the signature style, back in the day, of their elderly musical guru, Cochise Jones. Brokeland Creole, Archy explains towards the end of the novel, was:

> Not just white boys playing black music, like always, or even black dudes playing in a white style, but really, like, this moment, this one moment, lasted four, five years, when the styles and the players were mixing it all up. (502)

'Creole' becomes Archy and Nat's unofficial credo, 'sort of a, what, an *ideal*' that the pair 'always had in mind for this store' even if it is a vision they can see only in retrospect: Archy here is delivering Cochise's eulogy, the store is set to shut, and Carole King's 'It's Too Late' plays in the background (504). But if Archy's analysis is elegiac, it nevertheless reads 'this moment' of music history for its potentiality, and provides a way of reading Brokeland's ephemeral, improvisatory arrangement of race relations. Cochise 'liked to play against your expectations of a song, to light the gloomy heart of a ballad with a Latin tempo [...] root out the hidden mournfulness, the ache of longing, in an up-tempo pop tune'; the novel's historical imagination is similarly attuned to hidden rhythms, time-signatures, and syncopations that deviate and disorganise the steady beat of linear history (375).[49]

At the centre of the book is another kind of 'record keeping': like Auggie's photography project, Archy and Nat's vinyl collection indexes a form of historicism. As a business venture, their store is a disaster, but they are less interested in turning a profit than in a kind of cultural stewardship, Archy noting that Nat acts as if they are 'not a couple of secondary-market retailers trying to stay afloat but guardians of some ancient greatness that must never be tainted' (45). Collecting the ephemera of another age, they create a world in which history accrues unevenly and where the past lingers longer than expected. Their store becomes a site of 'temporal drag': 'a *productive* obstacle to progress, a usefully distorting pull backwards, and a necessary pressure upon the present tense'.[50] Elizabeth Freeman develops the concept of 'temporal drag' to reconsider 'the interesting threat that the genuine past-ness of the past sometimes makes to the political present'.[51] Archy and Nat's record collecting similarly gestures towards the novel's broader exploration of the political potential of an unorthodox historicism. They practise a form of 'dissident materiality' – Scott Herring's term for 'when a person's stuff questions, problematizes, or refutes [...] the normative orderliness of what counts for everyday material life'.[52] We hear, for example, an echo of utopian historicity as conceptualised by Muñoz and Berlant in the way that, as he 'sift[s] through' the latest batch of records to arrive at the store, Nat is at once 'hopeless and hopeful', because 'each disc' is 'potentially something great', even if the chances of such a discovery are slight (9). *Telegraph Avenue* similarly explores modes of reading the past that are not straightforwardly nostalgic, but that might yield a kind of precarious hope for the future.

Archy Stallings, as his name suggests, is practised in putting off the inevitable, and as the novel opens he is struggling to keep step with two processes of seemingly unalterable progress. Archy and Nat's relationship is mirrored by the partnership of their wives, Gwen and Aviva, who run a midwifery practice. Gwen herself is pregnant with their first child and the 'imminence of paternity' is hanging heavy over Archy; as in *Subtle Bodies*, the time of male friendship is contrasted to the time of family life (8). Imminent, too, is the closure of Brokeland Records, its fate sealed when Gibson Goode – star quarterback-turned-businessman, and 'the fifth richest black man in America' – decides to open his 'Dogpile' media megastore, with dedicated vinyl department, just down the block (13). Brokeland Records, Archy and Nat acknowledge, is the 'last of its kind', a 'holdout [...] in the path of the great wave of late-modern capitalism' (44, 146). 'I've been fucking off, fucking up, and fucking around for too long', Archy resolves, 'I need insurance, a paycheck, all that straight-life bullshit' (469).

The men's partnership is also refigured in the friendship between Nat's son, Julie, and Titus, who it eventually transpires is Archy's son from a previous relationship. The boys' friendship is sometimes sexual, Julie describing himself as 'twenty-five minutes to gay o'clock', while Titus is 'straight-up-noon straight' (119). The 'queer time' of the boys' friendship suggests an alternative temporal arrangement to the 'straight time' of family and capitalism weighing Archy down:

> A white boy rode flatfoot on a skateboard, towed along, hand to shoulder, by a black boy pedaling a brakeless fixed-gear bike [...] The white boy uncoupled the cars of their little train [...] the black boy gripped his T-shirt at the hem and scissored it over his head. He lingered inside the shirt, in no kind of hurry [...] In a moment, maybe, the black boy would tug the T-shirt the rest of the way off [...] But for now, the kid on the skateboard just coasted along behind the blind daredevil, drafting. (1)

The 'brakeless fixed-gear bike' suggests, like 'the imminence of paternity' and 'the wave of late-modern capitalism', a form of immutable progress. But the passage also draws out a quite different temporal logic. Its focus on moments of delay – 'lingered', 'no kind of hurry' – seems to precipitate a move into the conditional future tense – 'In a moment, maybe, the black boy would' – before a return to the present tense – 'But for now' – and then the past – 'the kid [...] just coasted' – which itself is rendered obliquely conditional, or provisional we might say, in that final word, 'drafting'. Chabon here explores the sense of potentiality evoked by a shiftingly pervious and 'unhinged' temporality.[53] This alternative sense of time can open up into a realm of fantasy in the novel. Rolling 'through the nighttime summer streets of South Berkeley and West Oakland', Julie and Titus travel 'through the wildly ramifying multiverse of their mutual imagination' (120). This expands into virtual reality, too, when they team up to roam the Marvel Comic Universe online.[54] But while *Telegraph Avenue* sometimes pitches into the alternative universes and mythic landscapes that have always been a part of Chabon's genre-bending fictional world, the historical imagination of the novel is embedded in a particular place and shaped by a local past.[55] In his history of postwar Oakland, Robert Self argues:

> The long corridor from West Oakland north through South Berkeley [...] between San Pablo and Telegraph avenues, formed one of the most vibrant political landscapes anywhere in the nation in this period [...] Beginning in 1964 and continuing through the early 1970s, this corridor was home to some of the most creative and inspired political projects on the American scene. The flatlands were no utopia of racial egalitarianism [...] but they nonetheless formed a physical world where political milieus intersected: Berkeley emerged as the center of the white New Left in the East Bay (and nationally), while [...] North Oakland emerged as the center of African-American radicalism.[56]

Archy and Nat's relationship is freighted with the legacies of this region's radicalism, saturated with the political style of the late 1960s and early 1970s as much as by the period's fashion and music. The twinned local histories of the New Left and Black Power are interwoven with a broader exploration of the politics of the men's interracial friendship. Asked in interview about the book's treatment of racial diversity, Chabon replied 'some things are globally impossible but locally possible. And I think that's kind of what the record store represents.'[57] The novel, though, provides a more complex answer to the question of 'scale' than Chabon's distinction between the 'local' and the 'global' allows, problematising the historical moment sketched by Self, a moment which produced competing and often contradictory cultural and political geographies, and a shifting sense of how the scales of the personal, local, national, and international measured up and intersected.

'drop a little lore and history on the man'

Berkeley was 'synonymous with student protest' in the 1960s, imagined as a 'prototype of the national student rebellion' forming the main strand of the New Left movement.[58] A diverse programme of dissent formed around overlapping issues of civil rights, gender equality, freedom of assembly, and the anti-war movement, taking shape in the collective action of groups founded in the town, such as the Peace/Rights Organizing Committee, the Free Speech Movement – 'born near the corner of Bancroft and Telegraph' – and prominent campus chapters of national organisations, including Students for a Democratic Society.[59] As important as individual causes were, equally significant was the style of political engagement: to coin a New Left slogan, 'The Issue is not the issue'.[60] The forms of protest that emerged in the period were less 'about' specific policy agendas than they were 'expressions of a radical and utopian upsurge' in the younger generation.[61] Nonconformist and anti-establishment, Berkeley student activists engaged in a 'prefigurative politics' of 'utopian, spontaneous and participatory' democratic assembly.[62] Their commitment to 'practice the future in the present' took form in local, grassroots 'communities of equality' that were imagined – in their spontaneity and emphasis on face-to-face relationships – as opposing a bureaucratised, de-personalising state machinery, variously figured by the university, the military, and the government.[63]

This style of political engagement reflected the role Berkeley radicals saw themselves and their town playing within a national revolutionary struggle: 'setting examples, pointing the way forward, elucidating the possibilities for the New Left in America'.[64] But, as Anthony Ashbolt notes, a 'radical movement [seeking] wide-ranging social change in a country [like] the United States must have a twin focus: the local or regional and the national'. What was required was 'an alertness to the general and particular'.[65] This dialectical understanding of scale became increasingly obfuscated, the movement risking a provincialism in its political ambition, 'spawning perceptions of the possibilities for revolution in one town, even one street' – and one street in particular, with groups such as the Telegraph Avenue Liberation Front imagining Tel Ave as a 'utopian enclave', and a 'liberated territory'.[66]

The New Left's conception of social protest emerged in dialogue with the political struggle developing at the other end of Telegraph Avenue. The Black Panthers were founded in Oakland in 1966, and, like the counterculture taking shape around the university in Berkeley, their political critique was 'grounded in urban space'.[67] The party's 'famous alchemy' combined 'revolutionary socialism' and black nationalism with what the co-founder Huey Newton referred to as the 'brothers on the block'.[68] The Panthers adapted the internationalist rhetoric of anti-imperialist struggle, applying a 'colonial analogy to the American ghetto' and marking out a subjugated 'black territory' across America.[69] This 'nation within a nation' was to be defended by an armed militia, the Panthers finding justification for armed resistance in Frantz Fanon's *The Wretched of the Earth* (1961), which stressed the inevitability of violence in the anti-colonial struggle.[70] Despite its internationalist framing, 'the heart of the movement would be a politics and an expanded analysis of Oakland as a colonized space': the Panthers, in other words, stayed local.[71] While struggles over ghetto neighbourhoods often took the form of armed protest against police brutality, they were also elaborated in projects like the popular free breakfast programme for schoolchildren.[72] This 'communitarian approach adapted neatly to some New Left thinking about community' and elucidated a similar spatial politics to that which was emerging over in Berkeley.[73] 'The Panthers hoped to achieve a kind of revolutionary utopia', Self writes, imagining Oakland as 'the starting line in a revolutionary race':

Anticolonial political struggle in Oakland would yield a 'people's city', an example of rearranged political, social and economic priorities that would supply an example to the remaining 'colonized world'. It was simultaneously a practical, because specific to Oakland, and ambitiously utopian notion.[74]

By the mid-1970s, however, this utopianism had waned as the New Left and black nationalism at either end of Telegraph Avenue began to move further apart. The localist orientation that had always been important to the New Left's conceptualisation of politics became more pronounced, as activists 'learned the art of making do' in smaller, neighbourhood-based projects with modest, 'reformist' aims, leading to what Michael Walzer describes as 'the pastoral retreat of the New Left'.[75] Membership of the Black Panther Party, meanwhile, peaked in 1970, with increasing militarism and infighting leading to the party's marginalisation and diminishing influence. This isolationist splintering of the counterculture was replayed nationally, undoing the pluralistic coalition politics of the early civil rights struggle that had sought to ferment solidarity across class and racial lines.

A prominent casualty of this rupture in progressive politics was the always 'fractious brotherhood' between Jewish and African Americans.[76] Although Eric Sundquist is right to suggest that 'the civil rights alliance, said to tie the two groups together from the early years of the NAACP forward, was surely never as strong as some of its more idealistic proponents claimed at the time or later', and that the familiar narrative of a 'golden age' of black–Jewish collaboration is therefore overstated, the early twentieth century had seen a variety of successful projects of political coalition, notably within the labour movement.[77] 'But while genuinely felt, the claim of black and Jewish kinship through suffering, made by both blacks and Jews, also obscured racial and class differences between the two communities', differences that became starker in the postwar period, when Jewish Americans became increasingly affluent and socially mobile in comparison to African Americans.[78] 'The class tensions between most blacks and Jews that had long threatened their political collaboration intensified with the mass action' while, for many Jewish American liberals and progressives alike, 'the rise of Black Power exploded the myth that Jews and blacks shared common histories or destinies'.[79]

Telegraph Avenue, then, looks back ambivalently to the late 1960s and early 1970s, not for a model for contemporary utopia but as a period in which 'concrete utopian imagining' was still viable and vital, and the 'scale' and 'location' of political action still fluid and contested.[80] The novel reads the political history of the period in much the same way as Archy reads its musical history, as 'this one moment, lasted four, five years, when the styles and the players were mixing it all up' – a moment, then, not of fixed perfection but of experimental potentiality. Its utopian historicism finds its most prominent figuration in Archy and Nat's friendship, which is freighted with a 1960s hope for the realignment of the personal and the political, and a 1970s sense of the shortcomings of radical politics. Having 'grown up in the black part of Richmond with a black stepmother, black friends, [...] and culture heroes who, barring a few Jewish exceptions, were almost exclusively black', Nat's background blurs the boundaries of African and Jewish American experience and cultural expression, their friendship refracting the long and difficult history of black–Jewish political solidarity (255). If Berkeley students engaged in a utopian 'prefigurative politics' to 'practice the future in the present' in their personal relationships, Archy and Nat's friendship figures a politics of a more convoluted temporal order, a 'post-utopian utopianism' unevenly binding the past and future.

'Hope unfulfilled, not yet betrayed'

The East Bay area's political history resonates throughout the novel. One subplot chronicles a shady episode from the past of Luther Stallings, ageing blaxploitation star and estranged father of Archy. In 1973, Luther was the getaway driver in a Panther shooting gone wrong in downtown Oakland. His accomplice was Chan Flowers; fast forward to 2004, and 'Chan the Man' is a power-broker councilman taking bribes, a living reminder of how near at hand Oakland's radical past remains to the novel's present. It is Chan who, after a kickback or two, approves Goode's plan to open a 'Dogpile' media megastore in Brokeland. The fact that Goode is black not only upends the usual dynamic of powerful versus powerless at play in the familiar gentrification script, in which a national chain runs a local store out of town, but raises the question of who exactly in Brokeland is an out-of-towner, and what constitutes the local community.[81] Goode grew up in Los Angeles, but was born in Oakland, making him 'a semi-local product', as Garnet Singletary, Brokeland Records's landlord, puts it to Nat. 'Like [...] if you was to put you and Archy together. Half local, half out of town' (43). 'Half and half', Nat responds, picking up on Singletary's sly allusion to the mixture of racial and spatial politics underwriting Goode's arrival. Indeed, Goode's 'Dogpile Thang' is not just a business venture. His 'imperial longings' are 'married to a sense of social purpose', and he maintains that 'the main idea of a Thang was not to make money but to restore, at a stroke, the commercial heart of a black neighborhood' (14). 'Imperial' recalls the internal colonialism thesis that informed black nationalism but now refers ironically to Goode's 'one-hundred-percent black-owned' business empire, with 'black neighborhood' echoing the localist focus of the Panther movement. In this way, Goode's project is framed by the spatial politics of the city's radical history and its vexed contestation of the scales of the local, national, and international.

The connection between Goode and Oakland's political history is developed aboard the 'Dogpile blimp', when the media mogul offers Archy a job managing his 'Cochise Jones Memorial Beats Department' (312). Cruising at one thousand feet, the scene aboard the airship elaborates another perspective towards the question of scale and the politics of space and race. Playing to Archy's vanity, Goode recounts his version of their first meeting, back when they were a couple of young comic-book nerds. Goode claims Archy

> [w]as peeling off all these sophisticated interpretations. Inner meanings. In *Luke Cage*. Talking about the American penal system as portrayed in Marvel Comics. Referencing all kinds of heavy reading materials. Eleven, twelve years old, telling me what, like, Frantz Fanon has to say about the possibility of black superheroes in a white superpower structure and whatnot. (303)

Archy knows Goode is bullshitting him, because even now he has 'only a vague idea of who Frantz Fanon was, and apart from the redoubtable Black Panther [...] had never taken particular interest in the skin color of the comic book superheroes he loved' (304). These allusions to Marvel's early black superheroes – *The Black Panther* and *Luke Cage* appeared in 1966 and 1972 respectively – coupled with the reference to Fanon, return readers to the cultural politics of Oakland's radical past.[82] But Goode's crude postcolonial cultural criticism is a clumsy attempt to play upon a feeling of racial solidarity. We see this worked through later in the scene when the blimp flies over Port Chicago, infamous for the 1944 munitions explosion that killed 320 navy serviceman, the vast majority of whom were African American:

> 'Fireball was three miles wide,' Goode said. 'Air was filled with burning Negroes falling out of the sky. Only thing they ever did wrong was try too hard and work too fast to fight somebody else's war.'
> 'It was their war,' Archy said. (315)[83]

In this 'history lesson', Goode adopts a simplified Fanonism of the kind espoused by the Black Panthers, for whom Fanon was inspirational not only in condoning revolutionary violence but in his emphasis upon the importance of a black national culture and consciousness. But Archy and Nat's 'creole' ideal points to a very different conception of cultural pluralism. As Goode attempts to persuade him to join the Dogpile 'mission', Archy can't avoid the feeling that he is 'stepping out on Nat' (304). He thinks back to the beginning of their friendship, and how they 'fell through the circular portals of Nat's record collection, one after another, flat-out tumbled awestruck arm in arm like that team of chrononaut dwarfs in *Time Bandits*, through those magic wormholes in the fabric of reality' (308). The 'time' of the men's friendship opens up into a fantasy world much like that in which Julie and Titus sometimes travel together. But this alternative temporality also offers a serious rebuttal to Goode's 'history lesson', Archy and Nat's friendship affording a different figuration of democratic affiliation, one attuned, but not subject, to fixed racial identities.

Goode's version of 'neighborhood revitalization' also comes into conflict with Nat's vision of Brokeland (374). When Chan tells him that the Dogpile store will be a 'real boon for the community', Nat gets riled:

> 'You know, Councilman, I don't know why, but I was under the impression that this place right ... here' – and Nat pounded the counter, *Right! Here!* – 'was a community! But I guess I was wrong'. (55, emphasis in original)

Nat responds by forming a protest group that bears all the hallmarks of the 'pastoral retreat of the New Left'. 'Conserve Oakland's Character against Homogenization, Impact, and Stress on the Environment' – or 'COCHISE' for short – is made up of a 'motley gathering of freaky Caucasians united [...] only by a reflexive willingness if not compulsion to oppose pretty much anything new that came along', a preservationist instinct symptomatic of the reactionary turn taken by post-1960s leftism (257, 266). Describing COCHISE's membership, Chabon offers a satire of Berkeley's contemporary progressive politics, depicting Claude Rapf, an 'urban planner', and 'the lady who owned the new-wave knitting store' standing beside 'two of the ageing Juddhists who had recently opened a meditation center called Neshama' (261).

But Nat's effort to save the store is also connected to a broader history of radical politics and a longer tradition of utopian thinking. At Cochise's funeral, the funky scion of Brokeland Creole, much to everyone's surprise, is discovered to have been a member of a Marxist library housed further up Telegraph Avenue. As the 'flutyvoiced old Marxist librarian' puts it in his eulogy for Mr Jones, Cochise understood 'the interactions of base and superstructure, the way ultimately, class struggle underpinned all the racism in America' (495). In naming his protest group after Cochise, then, Nat (unwittingly) connects the record store to an Old Left conception of class-based politics and its tradition of revolutionary utopianism, in contradistinction both to contemporary Berkeley progressivism and to the black nationalism invoked by Goode – who had also tried, like Nat, to play on Cochise's good name in his effort to win Archy round.

Chabon complicates this political genealogy further by way of Nat's family history. Nat is 'saddled with the especial uselessness of the third-generation socialist, one of the lonely grandsons of Eugene

V. Debs, stood up by Utopia' (155). Five-time Presidential candidate of the Socialist Party of America in the early twentieth century, Debs came to national prominence in 1894 for leading the American Railway Union out in a mass boycott of the Pullman Palace Car Company – one of the country's biggest railroad car manufacturers – in protest over pay cuts.[84] The Pullman Company is alluded to throughout *Telegraph Avenue*, in part because of Oakland's role as the West Coast headquarters of the Brotherhood of the Sleeping Car Porters, the first African American workers' union in the country when formed in 1925.[85] As Eric Sundquist notes, 'the Jewish left, including labor leader affiliated with the Communist Party, advocated on behalf of black rights and black labor' throughout the 1930s and 1940s, 'supporting A. Philip Randolph and the Brotherhood of Sleeping Car Porters, among others'.[86] The Brotherhood 'drew upon the memories of slavery and emancipation to connect the union's challenge to the Pullman Company to the larger quest for first-class citizenship in the broader political arena'.[87] Luther Stallings spins a funk-fusion version of this history to his grandson Titus. 'Oakland, California', Luther announces, 'End of the dream. End of the motherfucking line [...] Everything got started for us, minute the white man wanted to get some sleep on the train':

> The discourse had been riding this particular local for most of the past fifteen, twenty minutes [...] something about how white folks back in the day, needing to catch their beauty sleep as they traveled West subjugating and conquering, turned to a man named Pullman. And this one white dude, Joe, no, George Pullman [...] not out of any kind of wanting to do the right thing but only because he was cheap [...] started hiring up free black men [...] [Luther] evoked the nightly scene, vigilant black men studying the sonorous nocturnal rumblings of wealthy sleepers in the sleeper cars [... travelling towards] the far shore of the American Dream [...] all because the word 'America' was actually a broken-down version of 'Amenthe-Ra', the Land of the West in Ancient Egypt, where you went when you died [... in] a westbound boat like those that had freighted the sorrows of the Pullman porters' African ancestors, even though [...] the death journey to Amenthe-Ra was only a kind of sleep, in fact a dream – not Dream as in 'I Have a Dream' [... although] you had to wonder why Dr. King [...] had chosen to couch his message using a term

so central to the Secret History of the Black Man in California, the language of the Pullman Porter. (423–425)

Luther's history maps a national (and international) context, even as his train of thought stays on a 'local' track. The 'westward' journey of the Pullman's white passengers echoes the expansionist frontier movement of America's early colonial period but also picks up the discourse of postcolonialism shaping the Panthers' rhetoric; Luther's allusion to ancient Egypt has a flavour of the Afrocentrism of Black Power too. In connecting the 'language of the Pullman Porter' to Martin Luther King's rhetoric, Luther grounds his history of early twentieth-century Oakland in the civil rights struggle, even as he looks back to a longer history of racial subjugation and resistance, including the Underground Railroad. Finally, Luther connects this history, told to his grandson, back to Archy's record shop. 'This building you're in', he tells Titus, 'it was a train barn. You see that line there in the cement, crack like a big circle going all the way around. That's where the turntable is. Big old concrete turntable, spinning the music of dreams' (426–427). Brokeland Records, then, is another station stop on this journey and the tracks seem to lead from Archy and Nat to Julie and Titus, too. Taking cues from Luther's funk-fusion historicism, we might connect his 'secret history' of the railroad back to the novel's opening image of the two friends, riding in tandem, the boys forming a 'little train' as they cruise the streets of Brokeland (1).

In connecting Nat to Debs, the novel follows the tracks laid by Luther, plotting a political history that unsettles periodisation. Reaching back beyond New Left counterculture protest to a tradition of Old Left utopianism and collectivist action, it traces a tangled weave of progressive politics that crisscross the colour line and blur the border between local and national. It enacts a kind of 'temporal drag' which works to 'complicate the idea of horizontal political generations or waves succeeding each other in progressive time'.[88] The novel's saturation in Berkeley's and Oakland's histories produces a 'stretched-out' contemporaneity in which Nat's socialist 'inheritance' belongs not so much to the past as to the 'not-yet'.[89] What emerges is, as Berlant suggests, a way of imagining 'social change in the present tense, but a present tense different from what we can now imagine for pragmatic [...] politics'.[90]

Something of this utopian desire is discernible during the inaugural meeting of COCHISE, when the past veers into the present in a Benjaminian flash:

> For a kinescoped instant Nat cut away in his imagination from the scene at Brokeland to an afternoon forty years earlier, men and boys, maybe Chan Flowers and Luther Stallings among them, jostling around a portable black-and-white to watch Cassius Clay take down the Big Bear. Nat wished intensely that this gathering could be that gathering, these people could be those, with all the years of ferment and innovation in the music and the life of black America ahead of them. Hope unfulfilled, not yet betrayed. (272–273)

As Matt Kavanagh suggests, Nat expresses 'a longing not so much for the past but for the possibilities foreclosed in the present'.[91] Nat gives voice to the kind of proleptic longing described by Svetlana Boym, 'not for the idealised past, but only for its many potentialities that have not been realised' – a nostalgia that is 'prospective rather than retrospective, a kind of future perfect with a twist'.[92] Linking Chan and Luther to the Clay versus Liston fight, the scene gestures at the way the novel frequently approaches the political via black popular culture, whether it be music, film, comic books, or boxing. Also watching the fight on 24 February 1964 – at ringside, rather than on television – was Malcolm X; it was in the post-match interview that the newly crowned world champion shed the name Clay and became Cassius X (and later Muhammad Ali), marking his first public acknowledgement of a long-rumoured affiliation with the Nation of Islam.[93] That a history of radical black nationalism should be invoked by COCHISE's decidedly white membership is indicative of the way in which the novel tries to give form to a 'creolised' political history in its exploration of race and community, one that draws upon the civic traditions either side of the Berkeley–Oakland line.

The audacity of hope

While I have situated Archy and Nat's friendship in relation to East Bay radical politics of the 1960s and 1970s and a broader history of leftist utopianism, their relationship also seems to echo discussions regarding race relations prompted by Obama's victory in 2008, and to reflect debates as to whether the election of the country's first black president might herald a 'post-racial' America.[94] Attica Locke has noted that 'Obama's presence – and his most famous catchphrase, "change" – seems to linger at the outer corners of this novel's soul'.[95] But it is the other refrain of Obama's candidacy that resounds more clearly in the book. 'Hope' was an evolving concept in Obama's political idiom, a hallmark of the 'utopian propensities' of the Senator's rhetoric, developed in *The Audacity of Hope* (2006) but also central to his speech at the Democratic National Convention two years earlier.[96] This optimism is what seems to have drawn Chabon himself to the Obama campaign, as he outlines in 'An Article of Hope' (2007):

> On the hustings Obama likes to toss around the word 'hope,' as if all of us knew what he meant by it [...] but hope is one of those things that slips, when you think of it, from your understanding. [...] Is it only a kind of reaching in the darkness for a light switch that may never be found, a temporizing, a bid in troubled circumstances to buy ourselves a little more time? Is hope, in other words, a kind of lie? I don't know. It might be.[97]

Chabon seems to call for 'hope in the dark', to borrow the title of Rebecca Solnit's 2004 book.[98] But in figuring hope as a kind of 'temporizing', Chabon also foreshadows *Telegraph Avenue*'s exploration of the forms of temporal delay, drag, and uneven progress through which a 'post-utopian utopianism' might emerge. He suggests his advocacy for Obama is, in part, explained by his 'coming of age' in the late 1960s and early 1970s in the 'semi-utopia of Columbia, Maryland'; since leaving Columbia, he 'lost [his] illusions about racial progress in America'. Obama rejuvenates Chabon's belief in racial equality because he believes the Senator's 'black identity' allows him to 'embod[y] and inherit [...] the most inspiring and terrible of our national narratives'.[99] Obama reaffirms for Chabon 'the one illusion that I have not lost: that America's history is [...] the responsibility of all its citizens, that our tragedies are common tragedies, and that the pride we take in the record of our national accomplishments ought to be only so great as the common blessings those accomplishments have bestowed'.

This is a familiar vision of national citizenship, based in a common history and figured symbolically in the 'intimate person' of the president.[100] But what is striking is how closely this description of the nation tallies with the description of 'the neighborhood' at the close of *Telegraph Avenue*: 'that space where common sorrow could be drowned in common passion' (624). Just as the essay links the 'semi-utopia' of Columbia to Obama's message of hope for America, *Telegraph Avenue* explores these competing scales of commonality and affiliation, querying the ways in which the local and the national align and diverge in the political imaginary's fantasies of citizenship and community.

At one point in the novel, Archy and Nat's soul-funk fusion band is booked to play a political fundraiser at which Obama, fresh from his DNC address, is due to speak.[101] The friends are grooving with particular fervour because Cochise Jones has just died, and the gig has become a tribute to their musical guru. The Senator for Illinois 'stop[s] in the doorway' to 'listen for a minute to the hired band [...] cooking their way with evident seriousness of intent through an instrumental cover of "Higher Ground"' (214). As he 'lingers', Obama taps his foot, 'bobbing his close-cropped head', and mentally 'fill[s] in the missing vocal line, lyrics that somehow managed to be at once hopeful and apocalyptic, perfectly in keeping with the mood of the hour politically, if there were anyone in the crowd to attend [...] He listened a while longer' (214). The political 'hour', and its precarious utopianism, seems here to belong to 1973, the year 'Higher Ground' was released, and the novel's present, the two eras ambiguously twinned. Stevie Wonder was one of the most prominent Motown artists to engage with the rise of Black Power, using his albums as a 'forum to engage issues of racial, economic and political inequalities', and 'Higher Ground' was part of a wave of 'black freedom music' that 'responded to this era of activism'.[102] Singing along to Wonder, Obama is not only situated within a legacy of radical black politics but brought into a kind of contemporaneity – a unison as well as a harmony – with that history. In the way in which he 'stop[s]', 'linger[s]', and 'listen[s] a while longer', Obama enacts the kind of 'temporizing' that underpins the novel's utopian historicism, allowing him, unlike the assembled guests, to hear in 'Higher Ground' a political potentiality that resonates for the present.[103] But, of course, this 'present' has receded: in setting the novel in 2004, and imagining Obama before he announces his candidacy, Chabon plays upon a dramatic irony that further complicates the moment's optimism. Again, the novel effects a kind of nostalgia for hope, for a time before the inevitable disappointment of Obama's presidency. That Obama will, ultimately, fail to deliver on his message of hope is signalled by a description of the Senator arriving at the fundraiser by 'catching a ride' on 'Gibson Goode's private airship' (218).

Chabon's bravura depiction of Obama confirmed for many reviewers *Telegraph Avenue*'s status as a 'big, serious, probing American novel' that spoke to a national context, even as it focused on a local story.[104] In bringing Obama into the orbit of Brokeland Records, the novel plays on the symbolic resonance of the President and his office to extend its analysis of national identity and belonging. Just as in *Smoke* Rashid's real name – Thomas Jefferson Cole – seems to raise and query the prospect of his relationship with Paul being read as neatly symbolic of national race relations, so the portrayal of the nation's first black President in *Telegraph Avenue* inflects the exploration of Archy and Nat's friendship as a figure for citizenship and interracial solidarity. While Benjamin DeMott argues that the 'friendship orthodoxy' removes 'the large and complex dilemmas of race […] from the public sphere', rendering racism 'one dimensional – lacking, that is, in institutional, historical, or political ramifications', Archy and Nat's friendship is deeply embedded in Brokeland's racial history, and informed by its shifting cultural and political geographies.[105] In my discussion of *Smoke*, I argued that the historicisation of Paul and Rashid's relationship worked to distinguish their friendship from buddy-film bonhomie, marking a conscious critical distance from Hollywood's sentimental depoliticisation of race. *Telegraph Avenue* goes much further. Aficionados of anachronism, Archy and Nat focalise the novel's exploration of the political potentiality of a certain kind of historical imagination. Freighted with the legacies of Berkeley's and Oakland's countercultural histories, and carrying a kind of afterglow of the era's hope for a realignment of the personal and political, their friendship substantiates a mode of historicism articulating a temporally wayward register of political desire in the novel – a 'post-utopian utopianism' in which the future is steeped in the past.

Seventies throwback

Published a year after *Telegraph Avenue*, Jonathan Lethem's ninth novel, *Dissident Gardens* (2013), is 'structured as a history of American radical leftism' told through the prism of a single family, the Angrush-Zimmers.[106] It opens in Sunnyside Gardens in Queens, New York, a Garden City-era planned housing complex, and 'the official Socialist Utopian Village of the outer boroughs'.[107] 'Forged by idealists', Sunnyside was 'sanctified' as a 'leftist laboratory' by Lewis Mumford, the influential urban planner and, for many years, author of the *New Yorker*'s 'Sky Line' column (*DG* 143). Socially egalitarian and planned around a shared commons, the Gardens were intended to foster a 'robust political life' among residents, Mumford said, 'with effective collective action'.[108] Lethem's novel is similarly concerned, as Benjamin Hollander notes in his review, with the 'politics of the polis emerging out of the Gardens' real and existential foundations'.[109]

As the book begins, however, the once dissident Gardens are transforming into 'a suburb of disappointment', and Rose Zimmer – family matriarch and 'one-woman embodiment of the Old Left' – is being kicked out of the Communist Party (27).[110] It opens very specifically in 'late Fall, 1955', just prior to the Hungarian Revolution and the Twentieth Congress, the twinned crises of the Soviet project that would change the course of Communism. Rose is at odds with the Party authorities, not because of a lapse of faith, but because she is 'too sensuous' an egalitarian: 'Bringing revolution to the Negros, fine. To have one particular black cop in her sheets, not so fine. Oh hypocrites!' (7). While her German-born husband, Albert, stays loyal to the cause – eventually returning to his native country to write Soviet revisionist history – Rose's affair with the policeman Douglas Lookins begins her disassociation from the Popular Front, and the evolution of her political praxis. Rose gradually 'replaces her husband's "Communism is twentieth-century Americanism" advocacy with her own "Sunnysideism is Late-Twentieth-Century

Communism"' community activism.[111] Her politics begin to converge with those of her daughter, Miriam, who inherits from her mother a 'second-generation cynicism toward collapsed gleaming visions of the future', and is, like Rose, 'a Bolshevik of the five senses' (29). Married to a folk-singer and living in a Greenwich Village commune, Miriam 'incarnates the New Left'.[112] Together, mother and daughter represent how a localist politics emerges through the 1960s and 1970s. The involvement of Miriam's son, Sergius, in the Occupy movement brings the novel's 'collective portrait' of American leftism up to date, delineating a 'post-sixties and post-utopian' contemporary moment struggling with the inheritance of the counterculture.[113] 'The sixties formed a seaweed gauze through which they all paddled', Lethem writes of Sergius's generation, 'browsing for opening enough to surface and breathe free' (311).

On the one hand, Lethem's decline-of-the-family novel tells a familiar story of the decline of the Left, a drift from ideology to identity politics, from internationalism to individualism. But on the other, *Dissident Gardens* is itself akin to the sort of work carried by Albert, a revisionist history, not dissimilar to the 1990s re-evaluations of the Popular Front surveyed in Chapter 1. Emphasising family resemblances between successive generations of leftists, Lethem portrays a contemporary political culture grounded in the ideals of a previous era, suggesting hope for the future of progressive politics. In Lee Konstantinou's reading, Lethem elaborates a 'postironic political commitment' indicative of a 'new sincerity' in contemporary fiction.[114] Konstantinou argues that the novel may be read as a 'postironic bildungsroman', which 'figures postirony as the end of a process of either individual or collective political maturation', closing 'with a culminating – tentative but unambiguous – renewal of postironic political engagement, a new political hope'.[115]

Nicholas Dames also discerns a political hopefulness in *Dissident Gardens*, but understands its historical imagination quite differently, positioning the novel as a 'Seventies Throwback Fiction', a sub-genre of contemporary literature that looks back to the earlier decade with 'complicated admiration and longing'.[116] In terms similar to my analysis of the utopian historicism of *Telegraph*

Avenue, Dames suggests that such novels attempt to 'transcend our knowing cynicism' by reconceptualising anachronism and nostalgia. Resisting the 'leftist dogma that insists that nostalgia can only vitiate and never strengthen a progressive politics', such novels draw out the 'radical possibilities' of nostalgia. What throwback fiction never 'quite gets over', Dames writes, are the 'temporary, ramshackle utopias' that seemed possible in the 1970s, even after the 'decline of sixties radicalism', and its grander utopian aspirations.[117] Dames reorientates Konstantinou's account of the novel's hopefulness, positing a more complex form of historical imagination and political desire. In contrast to Konstantinou's conception of the 'postironic bildungsroman' elaborating a process of political 'maturation', Dames exposes how throwback fictions move ambiguously between past and future. I want to keep both Konstantinou's and Dames's arguments in mind as I turn to another of Lethem's 'New York novels', *The Fortress of Solitude* (2003). More than *Dissident Gardens*, *The Fortress of Solitude* is pitched between the present and what Chabon called the 'Broken Utopia' of the 1970s, providing a different iteration of throwback fiction. This earlier, more autobiographical, novel is also more explicitly an experiment in the form of the *bildungsroman*, offering another test case for the emergence of 'postirony' in 'post-postmodern' fiction.

Dose

Like *Telegraph Avenue*, *The Fortress of Solitude* portrays a changing neighbourhood, and, like *Smoke*, is steeped in what Lethem calls Brooklyn's 'slow-motion gentrification'.[118] The first, long section chronicles the formative years of Dylan Ebdus, a white, Jewish kid growing up on a black and Puerto Rican block in the 1970s. The demographics of Dean Street are shifting as the narrative opens, with young white families moving in and renovating dilapidated brownstones. Overseeing this transformation is Isabel Vendle, an elderly middle-class woman also new to Brooklyn, intent on encouraging the ragged region of North Gowanus to reimagine itself as the neighbourhood of 'Boerum Hill':

Gowanus wouldn't do. Gowanus was a canal and a housing project. Isabel Vendle needed to distinguish her encampment [...] her new paradise, distinguish it from the canal, from Red Hook, Flatbush [...] she was explicating a link to the Heights, the Slope. So, *Boerum Hill*, though there wasn't any hill.[119]

'Hill' invents a topography and 'Boerum' fabricates a history: Vendle comes across the name in a 'leather-bound volume at the Brooklyn Historical Society', and reads that the Boerums were a 'Dutch family, farmers, landowners' who 'kept their wealth in Bedford-Stuyvesant, had actually come nowhere near Gowanus' (7). Nevertheless, the name change – like those of nearby areas such as 'Carroll Gardens' and 'Cobble Hill' – performs important cultural work. Suleiman Osman explains that, 'If Boerum and Carroll gave the "neighborhoods" an imagined aristocratic founding father, hill and garden symbolically delayered the industrial cityscape to reach Brooklyn's agrarian past'.[120] Conjuring a premodern pastoral idyll, this 'delayering' of the city was also a 'de-colouring'; attempting to rewrite the region's past, brownstoners like Vendle tried to erase its ethnic diversity.[121] The Boerums weren't just landowners, but slave owners too.[122]

The Fortress of Solitude captures just how broad a church the 'back to the city' movement of the 1960s and early 1970s was, and the range of political outlooks it encompassed. Vendle is less than impressed with her 'ragged first recruits' to the neighbourhood, the 'motley' mix of beatniks and 'hippies making communes little better than rooming houses' (8). Among them are Dylan's parents, Abraham, an avant-garde painter and filmmaker, and Rachel, a pot-smoking lefty and precursor to Miriam in *Dissident Gardens*. Vendle disapprovingly notes Rachel 'talking Spanish to the men on the crates on the corner. That wasn't going to solve anything.' But for Rachel, the street's ethnic diversity is not a problem to be solved but a local quality to be preserved. 'If someone asks you say you live in *Gowanus*', she tells Dylan, 'Boerum Hill is pretentious bullshit' (52, emphasis in original).

Historically, brownstoners of Rachel's political orientation 'described a mission to bring participatory democracy [...] and face-to-face communal life' to impoverished urban enclaves, and many leftists 'arrived in Boerum Hill with the idealism of the period', drawing inspiration from social movements of the 1960s.[123] But by the mid-1970s, the 'new localism' of the brownstoners resembled another iteration of the 'pastoral retreat' of the New Left that I traced in the political history of Berkeley, the town to which Dylan moves in the second half of the novel. Suspicious of 'universal social programs', the spatial politics of brownstoning took its cues not from Garden City projects of planners like Mumford (or James Rouse) but from the 'street ballet' of the ethnically diverse urban village described by Jane Jacobs in *The Death and Life of Great American Cities* (1961).[124] Celebrating the 'organic spontaneity' of face-to-face relations on the sidewalks of Hudson Street in Greenwich Village, Jacobs developed an evocative urban romanticism that appealed across the political spectrum. By the late 1970s, the new localism of New Left brownstoners 'dovetailed with a national conservative movement that was similarly hostile to government regulation and [...] planning'.[125] Both wings of the neighbourhood movement practised a highly organised preservationism that successfully campaigned against new building developments (including social housing) within brownstone Brooklyn, in the process pricing out many economically disadvantaged social groups from the area. 'Gentrification', Rachel tells Dylan, 'is a Nixon word', but she fails to recognise the role played by her brand of leftist localism in the transformation of the neighbourhood she thinks she is protecting (52).

The first part of the novel, narrated in the third person, offers an evocative portrait of Dean Street. While Dylan's home life is disjointed, life on the street is vivid and exuberant. At the heart is Dylan's intense friendship with Mingus Rude, son of the washed-up soul singer Barrett Rude Junior of 'The Subtle Distinctions', and Dylan's ticket to a world of music, comics, graffiti, and drugs. Mingus and his father live next door to Vendle but represent a very different Brooklyn, much more to Rachel's liking. She introduces the boys to one another – 'Rachel's last setup', before she leaves the family for good – and their friendship carries the optimism of her integrationist politics (54). Their relationship is formed in summer-long games of 'skully' played out on the street, and 'solidified on the walls, billboards, and train cars of Brooklyn as they share the graffiti tag "Dose"'.[126] The use of graffiti allows Dylan to 'lose his funkymusicwhiteboy geekdom in the illusion that he and his friend Mingus Rude are both Dose' (138). When Dylan comes into possession of a ring bestowing the power of flight (and later invisibility), he and Mingus merge again in another 'secret identity', becoming 'Aeroman', an ineffectual superhero who only 'works locally' (203). It is Arthur, the block's only other white kid, who unwittingly links the boys' superhero alter-ego with the other 'secret' they share, calling Aeroman's costume their 'homo suit'. Like Titus and Julie's relationship in *Telegraph Avenue*, Dylan and Mingus's friendship is sometimes sexual and, like their other secret identities, their experimentation allows a fantasy of merging subjectivities, rendering them 'sole and extraordinary' (211). But by the end of the novel's first part, their friendship is on the wane. When Rachel ups and leaves, Dylan's enchantment with the street dissipates: he attends a private high school, and starts saving to go to Camden, an expensive, 'experimental' college (383).[127] When he offers Mingus money to buy the magic ring, it seems to them both that he has 'asked to buy their friendship back' (285). Hurt, Mingus asks his old friend, 'what you got on you', a phrase that both know comes straight from the script of a street mugging, carrying 'the stony authority over white boys Mingus never exercised. Mingus had let him hear it: their difference, finally' (286).

The second half of the novel switches to Dylan's first-person narrative. Now in his mid-thirties and living in California, Dylan is a music journalist and self-confessed 'vinyl hawk'. His understanding of his childhood has become increasingly conflicted, 'rich with unresolved yearning' as he describes Barrett Rude Junior's voice in the liner notes he writes to a reissued CD box set of The Subtle Distinctions' back catalogue (296).[128] His narrative drifts through a number of comic set-pieces – such as his unsuccessful pitch to make an epic movie about The Prisonaires, a 1950s group of incarcerated black musicians – that highlight an uneasy appropriation of black cultural history. These scenes give credence to his girlfriend Abby's suggestion that Dylan is 'collecting [her] for the color of [her] skin', and that she amounts to another 'exhibit in the Ebdus collection of sad black folks', alongside his records and the talismanic objects of his childhood, including the magic ring (317). Abby also highlights

Dylan's equivocal relationship to his Jewish background. When he excitedly telephones to let her know that 'the reason the Four Tops never broke up is they all go to the same synagogue. They're Jewish. Isn't that kind of moving?', she notes that 'you always said that the fact that you happened to be Jewish was, like, the *least* defining thing about you' (459–460, emphasis in original). This gestures at how his friendship with Mingus is defined by a longer fraught political and cultural history of black–Jewish intimacy. As the novel progresses, Dylan attempts to reconnect directly with the vanished figures of his past: his mother, his father, and, finally, Mingus, 'the rejected idol of my entire you, my best friend', a quest that leads him to the prison in and out of which Mingus has spent the last eighteen years (44).

Dylan never quite gets out from under the shadow of his old Dean Street brownstone. As Abby tells him, 'Your childhood is some private sanctuary you live in all the time instead of here with me'. 'My childhood', Dylan replies, 'is the only part of my life that wasn't, uh, overwhelmed by my childhood'. He then pauses: 'Overwhelmed – or did I mean *ruined*?' (319, emphasis in original). Highlighting this moment, Samuel Cohen argues that the exchange constitutes 'the hinge between the time capsule of childhood' in the first part of the book and 'the narrative of the present' in the second, and that it provides 'a key descriptive term for one often-criticised aspect of the experience of reading the novel': the sense that the first half of the novel 'overwhelms' the second, and even that Dylan's adult first-person narrative 'ruins' the effect of the third-person narrative of his childhood.[129] Many reviewers make this point, focusing on the narrative's central 'split'. Ron Charles, for example, notes that 'the novel's structure begins to creak and break apart' after the narrative leaves Brooklyn, while John Leonard argues that 'everything goes wrong about two thirds of the way through'.[130] Godbey reads this structural break as symptomatic of the political failing of the novel, arguing that the sociological sweep of the Brooklyn section is left behind for the 'individualistic, identity-obsessed [...] heart of Dylan's story', the narrative effectively 'recasting the story of gentrification as the story of the alienation of a middle-class white man'.[131] Others have read it as a failure of character development. 'If this is a Bildungsroman', Adam Mars-Jones writes, 'it would be an advantage for Dylan Ebdus to actually grow up at some point', echoing James Wood's observation that 'in general we are engrossed in the prospect of the child as father to the man precisely in proportion to the development of the man, not just the persistence of the child'.[132] A disappointment with the failure of Dylan and the novel to 'grow up' in the expected way is connected to the other widely criticised element of the book: the 'immature' superhero fantasy thread which runs through the text, and which 'many readers seemed to have a hard time knowing what to do with in the context of an otherwise realistic book'.[133]

Cohen is one of few readers to argue that the feeling of 'a terrible fall' the novel effects with its change of time and place is 'part of a larger design'.[134] He suggests that the 'structural split' is crucial to how the text 'understands the relation between past and present', a preoccupation particularly prevalent in turn-of-the-century novels written after the 'end of history'.[135] Eventually, Cohen writes, 'Dylan stops jumping the gap' and 'leaving things out', and so 'begins to suture his life back together'. Part of this 'gap-filling work' is understanding his past in relation to 'family and community and history', and in particular to 'confront [his] guilt at having left Mingus behind'. Ultimately, Cohen argues, the 'lesson' Dylan learns, and 'the lesson this novel takes from seeing the past as ever-changing is the existence and importance of contingency. Things change, in unforeseen ways, and they always will.'[136] James Peacock concurs, suggesting that, in contrast to the 'idyllic vision of childhood utopian community' described in its first section, the second half of the novel 'reminds us of [...] the perpetuity of change'. While the novel 'acknowledges the nostalgic desire to romanticise communities of the past', it ultimately portrays the 'utopian past moment' as one that will inevitably 'evade capture'.[137] The novel's understanding of contingency means that it refuses the consolation of either nostalgia or closure by showing the work of historical sense-making to be ongoing, offering a 'vision of a world of unfixed positions, of possibility'.[138]

Cohen's reading usefully revises our understanding of *The Fortress of Solitude*'s structural split from a shortcoming to a central facet of the novel's historical imagination. And yet his argument that the book's hopefulness emerges from a lesson in historical contingency seems to inadequately account for the readerly, affective experience – recorded so insistently in the reviews above – of the novel's move away from 1970s Brooklyn. If we agree with Peacock that the novel does not simply hanker after a romanticised vision of neighbourhood life but instead interrogates and qualifies Dylan's idealisation of the Dean Street of his youth, we nevertheless have to find another vocabulary with which to describe the book's attachment to a past that seems to overwhelm it; or, to put it another way, to find a way to talk about how the novel can feel 'ruined' and hopeful at the same time.

Growing up adolescent

Cohen's analysis rests on his own historicisation, as it were, of the historical imagination of the novel. He argues that *The Fortress of Solitude*'s approach to history reflects that 'American optimism and faith in self-determination [...] were shaken' in the wake of 9/11. 'The happy future assumed to be around the bend after the U.S. found itself the only superpower', at the end of the Cold War, 'was harder to assume in such a radically contingent-feeling present'.[139] Rather than take the Cold War and 9/11 as historical touchstones, however, I read the novel within its 'post-sixties and post-utopian' setting, exploring how it is 'thrown back' to the 1970s in the long first half. In clarifying the novel's temporal shift, I also read it within the longer literary history of the *bildungsroman*, examining how the novel's structural break subverts generic expectations. The paradigmatic genre of development, the *bildungsroman* dramatises and produces a certain version of growing up, what Jed Esty calls a 'historically specific notion of becoming'.[140] The genre 'stabilises the protagonist's ageing process within and against the backdrop of the modern state', such that 'adulthood and nationhood' serve as 'mutually reinforcing versions of stable identity'.[141] In Esty's reading of the modernist *bildungsroman*, the protagonist's development into 'national-historical time' begins to unspool when the nation state itself begins to lose its coherence as a structure of belonging.[142] His analysis aligns with postcolonial responses to Benedict Anderson's conception of the 'old-fashioned novel' as a 'device' for the presentation and production of the 'empty, homogeneous time' of the nation.[143] Homi Bhabha suggests that this temporalisation does not account for the lived experience of time as 'disjunctive' and multiple, or for the realist novel's propensity to register 'competing orders of time'.[144] As I outlined in the first section of this chapter, recent queer theory has contributed to this critique by analysing how the institutionalisation of a 'linear, ordered, teleological' conception of time inscribes a form of heteronormativity – what Valerie Rohy terms 'the "straight time" of linear history', or what Lee Edelman calls 'reproductive futurism' – in which the structures of marriage, child rearing, and generational inheritance are folded into the time of the nation and its history.[145] Part of this work specifically challenges the developmental narrative in which the *bildungsroman* is invested. Jack Halberstam, for example, asks that we 'rethink the adult/youth binary' in order to 'disrupt conventional accounts of […] adulthood and maturity'.[146] Esty also argues that, as the temporal logic of the *bildungsroman* began to falter, the genre recorded this disruption in its portrayal of adolescence. Once thought to entail 'the telos of maturity', the 'trope of adolescence' came to 'refer both to the developmental process and its multiple site of failure and incompleteness'.[147] In queer theory, these 'sites of failure and incompleteness' have been imagined as sites of potential political hope. Halberstam, for example, suggests that 'failure allows us to escape the punishing norms that […] manage human development with the goal of delivering us from unruly childhoods to orderly and predictable adulthoods'.[148] In this schema, adolescence becomes a time in which the apparent certainties of growing up might be called into question. Pamela Thurschwell describes adolescence as a 'strange and uncanny temporal state' of suspension, an 'insecure cultural space' marked not only by an 'anticipatory relation to the future and a haunted relationship to the past, but also something less assimilable to teleological notions of time and progress'.[149] Not growing up in the expected ways, failing to fall into step with 'national' time, might suggest the possibility of other kinds of futurity, and other kinds of political community.

Telegraph Avenue is a novel in part about 'fucking off, fucking up, and fucking around' (*TA* 469), about not growing up in the right ways, and about forestalling inevitabilities. Lethem's reviewers similarly felt that *The Fortress of Solitude* was a novel in which adolescence lasted too long. Outgrowing itself, the Brooklyn section enacts a kind of arrested development upon the narrative, impeding the 'teleological process' expected of the *bildungsroman*.[150] I argue that it is Dylan's friendship with Mingus that is integral to the 'temporal drag' effected by the first part of the book, the novel forging a link between what Thurschwell calls the 'uncanny' temporality of adolescence and the time of friendship. Engaging with the generic expectations of the *bildungsroman*, *The Fortress of Solitude* explicates a different form of 'becoming', and, with it, a different form of historical imagination. The novel's hopefulness, its 'postironic' politics, is articulated not in a process of 'maturation', as Konstantinou suggests, but in the ways in which it fails to grow up.

Windows of time

In school, Dylan is taught 'how to tell time', and that 'a book report told the story of a book' (*FS* 32), but the novel itself teaches a less straightforward lesson about temporality and narrative. Dylan inherits from each of his parents a sense of untimeliness. Abraham's film, Lethem suggests in an interview, 'is more like a novel than the work of a painter or filmmaker', and, 'like *Fortress*, the film is a record of days on a given street – Dean Street'.[151] As a 'record', the film elaborates a form of historical imagination that the rest of the novel will explore and develop. Early in the book there is a scene much like the one in *Smoke* in which Auggie shows his photographs to Paul:

> 'That looks the same.' Dylan said, watching his father finish a frame, turn to the next.
> 'It changes very slightly.'
> 'I can't see.'
> 'You will in time'. (10)

'Progress', we learn, is an 'illusion': 'the stillness of the film was part of the project' (30). This sense of suspension stretches out on to the street itself: 'Time was indeed a series of days, and the film of the block's changing was as static as a series of hand-painted frames [...] Fifth grade was an abstract art, painted one frame at a time' (25, 64). When Rachel leaves the family to travel, eventually settling in a Californian commune, she keeps in infrequent contact with Dylan through a series of postcards, which she signs 'Running Crab'. Cryptic, lyrical, and carrying a trace of Beat poeticism, her messages force Dylan to read carefully, for 'the stories embedded in the words like puns, waiting' (95). The missives continue sporadically, such that, after a while, Dylan trusts that there is 'no urgency to the Running Crab postcards [...] nothing in any way timely' (169). Both the film and the postcards intertextually elaborate temporal modes resistant to linearity, their nonconformity chiming with Abraham and Rachel's countercultural politics. Running Crab's sideways cross-country shuttle and Abraham's 'incomprehensible progress' become twinned images of a hopefulness in retreat, of the kind of dwindling utopian desire that Dames suggests is longed for and mourned in throwback fiction.

This political affect – a post-utopian utopianism – is manifest most clearly in the boys' relationship. Dylan's friendship with Mingus exists in brief 'windows of time', a phrase used repeatedly in the first half of the book in connection to their relationship (69, 79). Like Chabon's sense of the interracial 'fellowship' within an Oakland record store forming a 'little pocket of a big world, for a little hour', these windows open up a provisional form of temporal disjuncture in the novel that is also a time of hope:

> The two boys on the walkway apparently standing still: they were moving faster than the cars.
> Nineteen seventy-five.
> Dylan Ebdus and Mingus Rude in the spring of 1975, walking home along Dean Street studying marker tags in black and purple ink [...] Dylan and Mingus together and alone, in windows of time [...] White kid, black kid, Captain America and Falcon, Iron Fist and Luke Cage. In windows of time [...] Dylan Ebdus and Mingus Rude like figures stepping through mists of silence every few weeks to read a comic book or fool around with tags in ballpoint, dry runs, rehearsals for something else. (78–79)

Much of this recalls Chabon's evocation of Titus and Julie's friendship: the 'unhinged' temporality shifting between past and present;

the allusion to early black comic book superheroes; the sense of futurity gestured to in 'rehearsals', echoing the provisionality of the final word of *Telegraph Avenue*'s opening vignette, 'drafting'. Something of this waywardness comes to define the two secret identities the boys share, 'Dose' and then 'Aeroman', each of which appears to offer a brief transcendence of the racial divide and material reality of the street. Reading the novel as a conventional *bildungsroman*, Peacock suggests that 'graffiti writing [...] exerts the strongest emotional pull on Dylan and thus constitutes the greatest obstacle to his maturation'.[152] The novel's exegeses on tagging form part of Dylan's effort, Peacock writes, to 'remediate childhood experience through the figure of ekphrasis' so as to 'at least attempt, in deeply ambiguous ways, to move on from them'. Because 'graffiti is racially inscribed for Dylan', this process of ekphrasis makes painfully legible the unsurmountable social divide separating him from Mingus. For Peacock, graffiti is therefore a form of trauma writing, betokening 'loss, division, betrayal and social injustice'.[153]

But when Dylan and Mingus first team up, 'Dose' seems to briefly symbolise something different. Graffiti might well be an 'obstacle to [Dylan's] maturation', but obstacles, Elizabeth Freeman tells us, can be 'productive', and ekphrasis is one of the ways the novel explores this potential. 'The figure of ekphrasis belies the more familiar story about modern time, its relationship to nationalism, and the theory of modern literature that the figure of print encapsulates'.[154] Instead of the homogeneity of national time, Lloyd Pratt argues, ekphrasis makes visible 'two different orders of time': 'the linear time of progress and an experience of simple duration'.[155] Like Abraham's film, the novel's other prominent example of ekphrasis, graffiti conjures an alternative temporality that disrupts the 'flow' of narrative time, and, in so doing, posits a different sense of 'progress' from that in which the *bildungsroman* genre is invested. Rather than the process of 'gap filling work' that Cohen argues defines the novel's historicism, the figure of ekphrasis suggests that it is in the text's moments of temporal discontinuity, its windows of time, that its historical imagination takes shape.

Another of these windows opens with the boys' second secret identity, Aeroman, and the ring which briefly grants their alter-ego superhero the power of flight. The ring 'enacts the story' of Dylan's 'fusion' with Mingus, briefly allowing them 'to resist, even defy, what are presented as the logics of nature and culture', including the logic of race.[156] While Michiko Kakutani dismisses the superhero narrative as 'cutesy pyrotechnics' – a holdover from Lethem's more explicit experiments with genre fiction earlier in his career – the ring can also be read as part of the novel's political project of imagining another form of belonging.[157] As A. O. Scott suggests in his review, Aeroman is 'a sign of utopian possibility' in the novel, just as the boys' friendship itself represents 'a shred perhaps of utopian symbolism'.[158] Like graffiti, the ring elaborates a different form of time in the book. Kakutani complains that the superhero scenes amount to 'awkward interludes' in the narrative, but this is precisely their purpose: their 'awkwardness' exemplifies the 'in-between time' of adolescence, giving shape to what Kathryn Bond Stockton calls 'the unruly contours of growing that don't bespeak continuance'.[159] In an essay, Lethem draws attention to the novel's 'formal discontinuity', arguing that *The Fortress of Solitude* 'wrenches its own "realism" [...] into crisis' by 'insisting on uncanny events' which work to disrupt the conventional developmental narrative of the *bildungsroman*.[160] This 'uncanniness' doesn't just belong to the novel's unexpected elements of 'magic realism', but also to the boys' friendship itself. Dylan and Mingus are 'that uncanny sporadic pair, their solidarity a befuddlement to passerby' (137), and, when Mingus reads aloud to him from an issue of *Black Panther*, Dylan feels himself 'permeated by some ray of attention, moved so that he felt an uncanny warmth in the half of his chest that was turned toward Mingus' (55–56).

Like *Telegraph Avenue*, *The Fortress of Solitude* forges a connection between friendship, comic books, and superheroes. But though both books frame friendship as a form of potential fantasy, in neither novel is it a form of escapism. Aeroman's powers, after all, extend only a few blocks from Dean Street, and the ring is given to Dylan by a local homeless African American man. A symbol of the possibility of transcending the socio-economic realities of the street, the ring also emblematises the intransigence of these material conditions. 'Dose' and the figure of ekphrasis similarly seem to briefly gesture to a different form of race relations, but the boys' moniker also makes legible the institutional apparatus ultimately structuring life on the street. We see this most clearly when, during a solo flight, Mingus tags the prison:

> Four letters: D, O, S, E.
> The tag was a cry, a claim, an undeniable thing. The looming jail which no one mentioned or looked at and the trail of dripping paint that covered the city's every public surface and which no one mentioned or looked at: two invisible things had rendered one another visible, at least for one day. (274)

In *Smoke*, Paul and Rashid's friendship allows Auster to reflect upon the racial divide between neighbourhood Brooklyn and the Projects; through Dylan's friendship with Mingus, *The Fortress of Solitude* engages with the diverse cultural geography of the 'the grid of zones, the huddled brownstone streets between prison and projects' (222). Their relationship thus focalises the novel's interrogation of the localist politics of Dylan's parents, and the dwindling, qualified utopianism of 1970s leftism. Near the end of the story, Dylan reflects upon the records that led him to become a music journalist. In particular, he describes how Brian Eno's *Another Green World* 'conjure[s] and dwell[s] in' a 'middle space [...] a bohemian demimonde, a hippie dream' (509), which he likens to Dean Street when his parents first moved there:

> It was the same space the communists and gays and painters of celluloid imagined they'd found in Gowanus, only to be unwitting wedges for realtors, a racial wrecking ball. A gentrification was the scar left by a dream, Utopia the show which always closed on opening night. (510)

Like 'third place', 'middle space' captures the conflicted sense of scale organising the localist politics of the 'back to the city' movement, in which political action is located between the private and the public – an ambiguation that the concept of civic friendship also risks. 'Middle' is a useful temporal, as well as spatial, term in analysing the novel's politics. It gestures to *The Fortress of Solitude*'s preoccupation with times of transition – Dean Street on the cusp of gentrification, the 'in-between-time' of adolescence – and to how the novel looks back to the 1970s as a time of utopian possibility, however provisional and temporary. Like the 'windows of time' in which Mingus and Dylan's friendship exists, middle spaces 'open and close like a glance' in the novel (510). But, as Michael Warner writes in his study of 'counterpublics', 'the direction of our glance can constitute our social world'.[161] By exploring the potential of the *bildungsroman* to articulate non-teleological forms of development and progress, and by elongating the 'awkward' time of adolescence, *The Fortress of Solitude* attempts to keep these 'collapsing' middle spaces open a little longer, and to direct and fix our attention towards them, so as to see them anew.

In both *Telegraph Avenue* and *The Fortress of Solitude*, it is finally the novel, not the neighbourhood, in which these utopian middle spaces become most vividly imaginable. Reflecting on his parents' politics, Dylan wonders whether 'Abraham had the better idea, to try and carve the middle space on a daily basis, alone in his room' (510). Abraham's asceticism cautions that art might only be a renunciation of the political. But Lethem and Chabon also suggest that the middle space of reading might constitute a site of 'postironic' political engagement, a 'place' for the articulation of the collective contemporary feeling that I have been calling post-utopian utopianism.[162] In Anderson's conception of the nineteenth-century novel, fiction represents national time as 'empty' and 'homogenous', allowing readers to imagine their 'simultaneity' with other citizens, and so to conceive of themselves as members of a national public sphere.[163] These post-postmodern novels elaborate a form of what we might call, following Ernst Bloch, 'nonsynchronous time', in which the contemporary 'moment' emerges as fractured and multiple, unevenly steeped in the past.[164] In this way, the novels gesture to a different kind of civic belonging, attuned to Blanchot's and Nancy's sense of community as ultimately 'unavowable', in which the time of friendship is a Derridean one of retrospect futurity. 'The nonsynchronous is not synonymous with backwardness', but is 'something new that emerges in the articulation and contradictions between different temporalities'.[165] In their portrayals of untimely interracial male friendship, these oversized neighbourhood novels explore the scale of intimacy and affiliation that structure a community and a civic imaginary. These national stories are attuned to the fluxes of local time, as they search for the American futures embedded in the regional histories of Brooklyn and Brokeland.

Notes

1 Paul Auster, *Smoke* (1995), in *Collected Screenplays* (London: Faber and Faber, 2010), pp. 21–140 (21). Subsequent references are given in the text in parentheses.
2 On the literary histories of Brooklyn and Manhattan, see James Peacock, *Brooklyn Fictions: The Contemporary Urban Community in a Global Age* (London: Bloomsbury, 2015), 12–40. My argument here about New York's boroughs maps on to Miranda Joseph's broader analysis of how the concepts of community and capital are symbiotically constituted in the liberal imaginary. See Joseph, *Against the Romance of Community* (Minneapolis: University of Minnesota Press, 2002), 1–29.
3 Ray Oldenburg, *The Great Good Place: Cafes, Coffee Shops, Community Centers, Beauty Parlours, General Stores, Bars, Hangouts, and How They Get You Through the Day* (New York: Paragon House, 1989), 67.
4 Christopher Lasch, *The Revolt of the Elites and the Betrayal of Democracy* (New York: Norton, 1996), 122–123; Robert Putnam, *Bowling Alone: The Collapse and Revival of American Community* (New York: Simon & Schuster, 2000).
5 Michael Sandel, *Liberalism and the Limits of Justice* (Cambridge: Cambridge University Press, 1982), 182. See John Rawls, *A Theory of Justice* (Oxford: Oxford University Press, 1971).
6 Chantal Mouffe, 'Democratic Citizenship and the Political Community', in Chantal Mouffe (ed.), *Dimensions of Radical Democracy: Pluralism, Citizenship, and Community* (London: Verso, 1992), pp. 225–239 (234).
7 Christopher Looby notes 'the subsequent reinvention' of Fiedler's archetype 'in countless artefacts of American popular culture', listing a number of 1990s 'buddy narratives'. Looby, '"Innocent Homosexuality": The Fiedler Thesis in Retrospect', in Gerald Graff and James Phelan (eds), *Adventures of Huckleberry Finn: A Case Study in Critical Controversy* (Boston: Bedford Books, 1995), pp. 535–550 (536).
8 Benjamin DeMott, *The Trouble with Friendship: Why Americans Can't Think Straight About Race* (New Haven: Yale University Press, 1995), 27.
9 Lauren Berlant, *The Queen of America Goes to Washington City: Essays on Sex and Citizenship* (Durham, NC: Duke University Press, 1997), 4–5, 177–178.

10 Berlant, *The Queen of America Goes to Washington City*, 4, 178.
11 DeMott, *The Trouble with Friendship*, 22.
12 For an elaboration of this argument, see Sharon Monteith, *Advancing Sisterhood?: Interracial Friendships in Contemporary Southern Fiction* (Athens, GA: University of Georgia Press, 2000).
13 Rashid's allusion is to 'The Ballad of East and West' (1889). The ballad's opening line, 'Oh, East is East, and West is West, and never the twain shall meet', has, Peter Howarth notes, 'become a shorthand summary of the imperial racism that Kipling's poetics supposedly promote' (607). However, the stanza continues, 'But there is neither East nor West, Border, nor Breed, nor Birth/When two strong men stand face to face, though they come from the ends of the earth!'. The poem tells the story of the mutual respect between the brigand-chief Kamal and the Colonel's son following a horse chase, and offers their heroic friendship as an example of racial equality. The parallel to Rashid and Paul's relationship is thus in one sense comic; but it also links Paul to a troubling colonial history and a suspect romanticisation of interracial friendship. See Howarth, 'Rudyard Kipling Plays the Empire', in Matthew Bevis (ed.), *The Oxford Handbook of Victorian Poetry* (Oxford: Oxford University Press, 2013), pp. 605–617 (606–607); Harry Ricketts, '"Nine and sixty ways": Kipling, Ventriloquist Poet', in Howard Booth (ed.), *The Cambridge Companion to Rudyard Kipling* (Cambridge: Cambridge University Press, 2011), pp. 111–125 (114–115).
14 Michael Kaplan notes that Rashid's real name 'invokes the highly conflicted entry of African people into the colonial and national history of America and eventually into U.S. citizenship'. Kaplan, *Friendship Fictions: The Rhetoric of Citizenship in the Liberal Imaginary* (Tuscaloosa: University of Alabama Press, 2010), 157–158, 172–173.
15 Jacques Derrida, *The Politics of Friendship*, trans. George Collins [French, 1994; English, 1997] (London: Verso, 2005), 1–26, 75–112.
16 Jean-Luc Nancy, *The Inoperative Community*, trans. Peter Connor, Lisa Garbus, Michael Holland, and Simona Sawhney (Minneapolis: University of Minnesota Press, 1991); Maurice Blanchot, *The Unavowable Community*, trans. Pierre Joris (Barrytown: Station Hill Press, 1988). For an overview, see Irving Goh, *The Reject: Community, Politics, and Religion after the Subject* (New York: Fordham University Press, 2014), 24–97.
17 Derrida, *The Politics of Friendship*, 104.

18 Derrida, *The Politics of Friendship*, 236. See also Antonio Calcagno, *Badiou and Derrida: Politics, Events and Their Time* (London: Continuum, 2007), 11–60.
19 Ash Amin and Nigel Thrift, *Arts of the Political: New Openings for the Left* (Durham, NC: Duke University Press, 2013), 80.
20 Fredric Jameson, *Valences of the Dialectic* (New York: Verso, 2009), 413; Jameson, *Postmodernism, or, The Cultural Logic of Late Capitalism* (Durham, NC: Duke University Press, 1991), xvi; Marianne DeKoven, *Utopia Limited: The Sixties and the Emergence of the Postmodern* (Durham, NC: Duke University Press, 2004), 25.
21 DeKoven, *Utopia Limited*, 290, 25; Mitchum Huehls, *Qualified Hope: A Postmodern Politics of Time* (Columbus: Ohio State University Press, 2009). On the idea of the 'residual cultural element', see Raymond Williams, *Marxism and Literature* (Oxford: Oxford University Press, 1977), 121–127.
22 Lauren Berlant, ''68, or Something', *Critical Inquiry*, 21:1 (1994), pp. 124–155 (126–127).
23 Berlant, ''68, or Something', 132, 128; Jameson, *Valences of the Dialectic*, 214.
24 This formulation is inspired by a question posed by Pamela Thurschwell: 'can anachronism signify a politics, or is [the] desire for an impossibly different world, one which is past, simply a capitulation to the impossibility of a politics?'. Thurschwell, 'The Ghost Worlds of Modern Adolescence', in Maria del Pilar Blanco and Esther Peeren (eds), *Popular Ghosts: The Haunted Spaces of Everyday Culture* (London: Continuum, 2010), 239–250 (246).
25 Pamela Thurschwell, 'Bringing Nanda Forward, or Acting Your Age in *The Awkward Age*', *Critical Quarterly*, 58:2 (2016), pp. 72–90 (73).
26 Slavoj Zizek, 'Preface: Bloch's Ontology of Not-Yet-Being', in Peter Thompson and Slavoj Zizek (eds), *The Privatization of Hope: Ernst Bloch and the Future of Utopia* (Durham, NC: Duke University Press, 2013), pp. xv–xx (xviii). See Ernst Bloch, *The Utopian Function of Art and Literature: Selected Essays*, trans. Jack Zipes and Frank Mecklenburg (Cambridge, MA: MIT Press, 1988).
27 Thurschwell, 'Bringing Nanda Forward', 87, n. 6; José Esteban Muñoz, *Cruising Utopia: The Then and There of Queer Futurity* (New York: New York University Press, 2009).
28 Muñoz, *Cruising Utopia*, 4, 9.
29 Muñoz, *Cruising Utopia*, 9; Giorgio Agamben, *Potentialities: Collected Essays in Philosophy*, trans. Daniel Heller-Roazen (Stanford: Stanford University Press, 1999), 177–184.

30 Leela Gandhi, 'Friendship and Postmodern Utopianism', *Culture Studies Review*, 9:1 (May 2003), pp. 12–22 (19–20).
31 See Andrew Hoberek, 'Introduction: After Postmodernism', *Twentieth-Century Literature*, 53:3 (Fall, 2007), pp. 233–247 (235–239).
32 See Linda Hutcheon, *A Poetics of Postmodernism: History, Theory, Fiction* (New York: Routledge, 1988).
33 Christopher Lasch, *The Revolt of the Elites*, 123; Michael Chabon, *Telegraph Avenue* (London: Fourth Estate, 2012), 271. Further references will appear in the text as *TA* in parentheses. Brokeland Records is perhaps intended to recall Cody's, the famous independent bookstore on Telegraph Avenue in the 1960s. See Jesse McKinley, 'In Berkeley, a Store's End Clouds a Street's Future', *New York Times*, 18 June 2006.
34 Troy Patterson, 'Archy and Nat's Last Stand', *Slate*, 7 September 2012.
35 Matt Feeney, 'Michael Chabon's Oakland', *The New Yorker*, 26 September 2012; Michiko Kakutani, 'Battling Progress and Other Demons: *Telegraph Avenue* by Michael Chabon', *New York Times*, 3 September 2012.
36 Feeney, 'Michael Chabon's Oakland'; Carolyn Kellog, 'Review: Michael Chabon Joyfully Sets Down on "Telegraph Avenue"', *Los Angeles Times*, 9 September 2012.
37 Michael Chabon, 'O. J. Simpson, Racial Utopia and the Moment that Inspired My Novel', *New York Times Magazine*, 27 September 2012. In the late 1970s and 1980s, O. J. Simpson was well-known as an NFL Hall of Fame running back, actor, and popular public figure. In 1994, he was charged with the murder of his ex-wife and her friend. The subsequent criminal trial, which acquitted Simpson, became a flashpoint for racial tensions in Los Angeles, where Simpson lived, and across the country.
38 Samuel Cohen, *After the End of History: American Fiction in the 1990s* (Iowa City: University of Iowa Press, 2009), 11.
39 Chabon, 'O. J. Simpson'.
40 Chabon, 'Fountain City', *McSweeney's*, 36 (December 2010), pp. i–112 (iii). See Ann Forsyth, *Reforming Suburbia: The Planned Communities of Irvine, Columbia, and The Woodlands* (Berkeley: University of California Press, 2005), 107–161. On race relations in Columbia, see Nicholas Bloom, *Suburban Alchemy: 1960s New Towns and the Transformation of the American Dream* (Columbus: Ohio State University Press, 2001), 184–207. Rouse is cited in the Acknowledgements of *Telegraph Avenue* as 'dreamer of the original Brokeland' (628).

41 See Nicholas Bloom, *Merchant of Illusion: James Rouse, America's Salesman of the Businessman's Utopia* (Columbus: Ohio State University Press, 2004), 126–150.
42 Robert Fishman, *Bourgeois Utopias: The Rise and Fall of Suburbia* (New York: Basic Books, 1987), 202.
43 Chabon, 'Fountain City', iii.
44 Chabon, 'O. J. Simpson'.
45 Chabon is also connecting Berkeley's radicalism to a longer tradition of American utopianism. See James Gilbert, 'New Left: Old America', *Social Text*, no. 9–10 (1984), pp. 244–247.
46 Chabon, 'O. J. Simpson'.
47 Elizabeth Freeman, 'Packing History, Count(er)ing Generations', *New Literary History*, 31:4 (Fall 2000), pp. 727–744 (742).
48 Michael Chabon, 'The Future Will Have to Wait', *The Long Now Foundation*, 22, January 2006.
49 Cochise's musical style tallies with Michaeline Crichlow's description of 'Creolization' as a 'historicized process of selective creation and cultural struggle' alert to 'the plural uneven temporalities and spaces that constitute nation-states' and subjects' histories'. Crichlow, *Globalization and the Post-Creole Imagination: Notes on Fleeing the Plantation* (Durham, NC: Duke University Press, 2009), 1.
50 Elizabeth Freeman, *Time Binds: Queer Temporalities, Queer Histories* (Durham, NC: Duke University Press, 2010), 64. Emphasis in original.
51 Freeman, *Time Binds*, 63.
52 Scott Herring, 'Material Deviance: Theorizing Queer Objecthood', *Postmodern Culture*, 21:2 (January 2011), n.p.
53 Cindy Weinstein analyses 'temporally unhinged' texts that are 'incapable of keeping discrete past, present, future, and conditional'. *Time, Tense, and American Literature: When Is Now?* (Cambridge: Cambridge University Press, 2015), 2.
54 On comic books in Chabon's fiction, see Stephen Hock, 'Comix Remix; or, The Strange Case of Mr. Chabon', in Jesse Kavaldo and Bob Batchelor (eds), *Michael Chabon's America: Magical Words, Secret Worlds, and Sacred Spaces* (Lanham: Rowman & Littlefield, 2014), pp. 81–97.
55 On Chabon's interest in genre fiction, see Jesse Kavaldo, 'Real Maps of Imaginary Places; or, Michael Chabon, Shadowtail', in *Michael Chabon's America*, pp. 1–17.
56 Robert Self, *American Babylon: Race and the Struggle for Postwar Oakland* (Princeton: Princeton University Press, 2003), 223.

57 Michael Mechanic, 'Michael Chabon's Vinyl Draft', *Mother Jones*, September/October 2012.
58 Terry Anderson, *The Movement and the Sixties: Protest in America from Greensboro to Wounded Knee* (New York: Oxford University Press, 1995), 89; Robert Cohen, 'The Many Meanings of the FSM', in Robert Cohen and Reginald Zelnik (eds), *The Free Speech Movement: Reflections on Berkeley in the 1960s* (Berkeley: University of California Press, 2002), pp. 1–55 (4).
59 Self, *American Babylon*, 223. For a sense of the political climate on campus, see Jo Freeman, *At Berkeley in the Sixties: The Education of an Activist, 1961–1965* (Bloomington: Indiana University Press, 2004).
60 Cited in Wini Breines, *Community and Organization in the New Left* (New Brunswick: Rutgers University Press, 1989), 20.
61 Breines, *Community*, xiv.
62 Wini Breines, 'Community and Organization: The New Left and Michels' "Iron Law"', *Social Problems*, 27:4 (April 1980), pp. 419–429 (427).
63 Flora Cornish et al., 'Rethinking Prefigurative Politics', *Journal of Social and Political Psychology*, 4:1 (2016), pp. 114–127 (121); Breines, *Community*, 27.
64 Anthony Ashbolt, *A Cultural History of the Radical Sixties in the San Francisco Bay Area* (London: Pickering & Chatto, 2013), 27.
65 Ashbolt, *A Cultural History of the Radical Sixties*, 69.
66 Ashbolt, *A Cultural History of the Radical Sixties*, 7. Ashbolt quotes a member of the TALF who acknowledged, in 1969, that, 'As Telegraph Ave has come more and more to be under a state of siege, a tendency to overlocalize our problems has plagued us' (152).
67 Self, *American Babylon*, 2.
68 Robert Self, '"To Plan Our Liberation": Black Power and the Politics of Place in Oakland, California, 1965–1977', *Journal of Urban History*, 27:6 (September 2000), pp. 759–792 (769).
69 Self, *American Babylon*, 226.
70 On Fanon and the Panthers, see Self, *American Babylon*, 222–229; Donna Jean Murch, *Living for the City: Migration, Education, and the Rise of the Black Panther Party in Oakland, California* (Chapel Hill: University of North Carolina Press, 2010), 133–134.
71 Self, *American Babylon*, 229.
72 See Dean Robinson, *Black Nationalism in American Politics and Thought* (Cambridge: Cambridge University Press, 2001), 59; David Hillard, *The Black Panther Party: Service to the People Programs*

Broken utopias 169

(Albuquerque: University of New Mexico Press, 2008), 30–35; Murch, *Living for the City*, 171–180.
73 Ashbolt, *A Cultural History of the Radical Sixties*, 124.
74 Self, '"To Plan Our Liberation"', 770.
75 Michael Walzer, '"The Pastoral Retreat of the New Left"', *Dissent*, Fall 1979, pp. 406–411.
76 Eric Sundquist, *Strangers in the Land: Blacks, Jews, Post-Holocaust America* (Cambridge, MA: Belknap Press, 2005), 2.
77 Sundquist, *Strangers in the Land*, 4.
78 Cheryl Lynn Greenberg, *Troubling the Waters: Black-Jewish Relations in the American Century* (Princeton: Princeton University Press, 2006), 12.
79 Greenberg, *Troubling the Waters*, 13; Marc Dollinger, *Quest for Inclusion: Jews and Liberalism in Modern America* (Princeton: Princeton University Press, 2000), 192.
80 Berlant, "68, or Something', 125.
81 Michiko Kakutani noted the similarity between the novel's plot and that of Nora Ephron's 1998 movie *You've Got Mail*, in which a national chain runs a local bookstore out of business. Kakutani, 'Battling Progress and Other Demons'.
82 The association of Fanon and superheroes is an allusion to Fanon's *Black Skin, White Masks* (1952).
83 See Robert Allen, *The Port Chicago Mutiny: The Story of the Largest Mass Mutiny Trial in U.S. Naval History* (Berkeley: Heyday Books, 1993).
84 See Nick Salvatore, *Eugene V. Debs: Citizen and Socialist* (Urbana: University of Illinois Press, 1982), 127–128.
85 See Robert Allen, *Brotherhood of Sleeping Car Porters: C. L. Dellums and the Fight for Fair Treatment and Civil Rights* (London: Routledge, 2015).
86 Sundquist, *Strangers in the Land*, 31.
87 Beth Tompkins Bates, *Pullman Porters and the Rise of Protest Politics in Black America, 1925–1945* (Chapel Hill: University of North Carolina Press, 2001), 5.
88 Freeman, *Time Binds*, 65.
89 Lauren Berlant, *Cruel Optimism* (Durham, NC: Duke University Press, 2011), 5, 258–263.
90 Berlant, "68, or Something', 126.
91 Matt Kavanagh, '"Hope Unfulfilled, Not Yet Betrayed": Michael Chabon's Nostalgia for the Future', in Jesse Kavaldo and Bob Batchelor (eds), *Michael Chabon's America: Magical Words, Secret*

Worlds, and Sacred Spaces (Lanham: Rowman & Littlefield, 2014), pp. 235–255 (237).

92 Svetlana Boym, *The Future of Nostalgia* (New York: Basic Books, 2001), 168.

93 See Kasia Boddy, *Boxing: A Cultural History* (London: Reaktion Books, 2008), 327–330.

94 See Mark Ledwidge, Kevern Verney, and Inderjeet Parmar (eds), *Barack Obama and the Myth of a Post-Racial America* (London: Routledge, 2013).

95 Attica Locke, 'Telegraph Avenue by Michael Chabon – Review', *The Guardian*, 5 September 2012.

96 Mark Ferrara, *Barack Obama and the Rhetoric of Hope* (Jefferson: McFarland, 2013), 13. In 2004, Obama asked the DNC, 'Do we participate in a politics of cynicism, or do we participate in a politics of hope?'

97 Michael Chabon, 'An Article of Hope' (2007). See also Chabon, 'Obama vs. the Phobocracy', *Washington Post*, 4 February 2008; Chabon, 'Obama & the Conquest of Denver', *New York Review of Books*, 9 October 2008.

98 Rebecca Solnit, *Hope in the Dark: Untold Histories, Wild Possibilities* (Chicago: Haymarket Books, 2004).

99 Chabon, 'An Article of Hope'.

100 Sean McCann, *A Pinnacle of Feeling: American Literature and Presidential Government* (Princeton: Princeton University Press, 2008), 4.

101 On depictions of Democratic Party figures in twentieth-century fiction, and the Party's long-standing association with African American music, see Michael Szalay, *Hip Figures: A Literary History of the Democratic Party* (Stanford: Stanford University Press, 2012).

102 Yohuru Williams, *Rethinking the Black Freedom Movement* (New York: Routledge, 2016), 99; Portia Maultsby, 'African American Musical Cultures', in Ellen Koskoff (ed.), *Music Cultures in the United States: An Introduction* (New York: Routledge, 2005), pp. 185–242 (237).

103 My argument echoes Daphne Brooks's account of 'sonic critical memory' in Brooks, '"Bring the Pain": Post-Soul Memory, Neo-Soul Affect, and Lauryn Hill in the Black Public Sphere', in Nicholas Cook and Richard Pettengill (eds), *Taking It to the Bridge: Music as Performance* (Ann Arbor: University of Michigan Press, 2013), pp. 180–203 (190).

104 Locke, 'Telegraph Avenue by Michael Chabon – Review'. John Freeman

wrote of Chabon 'imagining the Great American Novel'. 'Telegraph Avenue by Michael Chabon', *Boston Globe*, 1 September 2012.
105 DeMott, *The Trouble with Friendship*, 27.
106 Marco Roth, 'I Don't Want Your Revolution', *London Review of Books*, 36:4 (20 February 2014), pp. 24–25 (24).
107 Jonathan Lethem, *Dissident Gardens* (New York: Doubleday, 2013), 14. Subsequent references are given in the text as *DG* and in parentheses.
108 Lewis Mumford, *The Culture of Cities* (New York: Harcourt, Brace and Co., 1938), 484.
109 Benjamin Hollander, 'The Long View Back to the Gardens: Politics as Dissident Polis in Jonathan Lethem's *Dissident Gardens*', *The Brooklyn Rail*, 18 December 2014.
110 Lee Konstantinou, 'Outerborough Destiny: Jonathan Lethem's *Dissident Gardens*', *Los Angeles Review of Books*, September 8, 2013.
111 Stacey Olster, *The Cambridge Introduction to Contemporary American Fiction* (Cambridge: Cambridge University Press, 2017), 89.
112 Hal Parker, 'Jonathan Lethem's *Dissident Gardens*', *The American Reader*, 1:9 (November 2013).
113 Konstantinou, 'Outerborough Destiny'.
114 Lee Konstantinou, *Cool Characters: Irony and American Fiction* (Cambridge, MA: Harvard University Press, 2016), 275.
115 Konstantinou, *Cool Characters*, 275, 281.
116 Nicholas Dames, 'Seventies Throwback Fiction: A Decade in Review', *n+1*, 21 (Winter 2014).
117 Dames also includes Norman Rush's *Subtle Bodies*.
118 Jonathan Lethem, 'L. J. Davis' (2009), in *The Ecstasy of Influence: Nonfictions, etc.* (New York: Vintage, 2012), pp. 406–409 (406).
119 Jonathan Lethem, *The Fortress of Solitude* (London: Faber and Faber, 2003), 7. Subsequent references are given in the text as *FS* and in parentheses. Vendle is based on Helen Buckler, who coined the name Boerum Hill. See Suleiman Osman, *The Invention of Brownstone Brooklyn: Gentrification and the Search for Authenticity in Postwar New York* (Oxford: Oxford University Press, 2011), 197–198.
120 Osman, *The Invention of Brownstone Brooklyn*, 199.
121 Osman, *The Invention of Brownstone Brooklyn*, 199.
122 See Marc Linder and Lawrence Zacharias, *Of Cabbages and Kings County: Agriculture and the Formation of Modern Brooklyn* (Iowa City: University of Iowa Press, 1999), 86.
123 Osman, *The Invention of Brownstone Brooklyn*, 209, 8, 16.

124 Osman, *The Invention of Brownstone Brooklyn*, 14. See Jane Jacobs, *The Death and Life of Great American Cities* (New York: Vintage, 1961), 4–25. Jacobs called Mumford's *The Culture of Cities* 'a morbid and biased catalogue of ills' (10). Mumford responded in a review of Jacobs's book, 'Mother Jacobs' Home Remedies', *The New Yorker*, 1, December 1962, pp. 148–179.
125 Osman, *The Invention of Brownstone Brooklyn*, 14.
126 Matthew Mullins, *Postmodernism in Pieces: Materializing the Social in U.S. Fiction* (Oxford: Oxford University Press, 2016), 87.
127 Camden is based on Bennington College, which Lethem attended for a year before dropping out; his contemporaries included Donna Tartt and Brett Easton Ellis.
128 These liner notes constitute a short section between the two halves of the narrative. As such, Lethem suggests, the novel as a whole 'spatially mimic[s] the shape of a two-CD box set enshrining a soul group's career and breakup'. Lethem, 'Writing and the Neighbor Arts', in *The Ecstasy of Influence*, pp. 205–206 (205).
129 Cohen, *After the End of History*, 177.
130 Ron Charles, 'There Goes the Neighborhood', *Christian Science Monitor*, 11 September 2003; John Leonard, 'Welcome to New Dork', *New York Review of Books*, 7 April 2005.
131 Godbey, 'Gentrification', 146. See also Elizabeth Gunport, 'Gentrified Fiction', *n+1*, 2 November 2009.
132 Adam Mars-Jones, 'It's All in the Detail. Unfortunately …', *The Observer*, 11 January 2004; James Wood, 'Spaldeen Dreams', *The New Republic*, 13 October 2003.
133 Cohen, *After the End of History*, 175.
134 Wood, 'Spaldeen Dreams'; Cohen, *After the End of History*, 175.
135 See Cohen, *After the End of History*, 7–15. Cohen, *After the End of History*, 180–181.
136 Cohen, *After the End of History*, 180–181.
137 James Peacock, *Jonathan Lethem* (Manchester: Manchester University Press, 2012), 121.
138 Cohen, *After the End of History*, 185.
139 Cohen, *After the End of History*, 170.
140 Jed Esty, *Unseasonable Youth: Modernism, Colonialism, and the Fiction of Development* (Oxford: Oxford University Press, 2012), 5.
141 Esty, *Unseasonable Youth*, 39.
142 See Mikhail Bakhtin, *Speech Genres and Other Late Essays*, trans. Vern McGee (Austin: University of Texas Press, 1986), 25.

143 Benedict Anderson, *Imagined Communities: Reflections on the Origin and Spread of Nationalism* [1983] (London: Verso, 2006), 26.
144 Homi Bhabha, *The Location of Culture* (London: Routledge, 1994), 177; Lloyd Pratt, *Archives of American Time: Literature and Modernity in the Nineteenth Century* (Philadelphia: University of Pennsylvania Press, 2010), 8.
145 Dana Luciano, *Arranging Grief: Sacred Time and the Body in Nineteenth-Century America* (New York: New York University Press, 2007), 2; Valerie Rohy, *Anachronism and Its Others: Sexuality, Race, Temporality* (Albany: State University of New York Press, 2009), xii; Lee Edelman, *No Future: Queer Theory and the Death Drive* (Durham, NC: Duke University Press, 2004), 5.
146 Jack Halberstam, *In a Queer Time and Place: Transgender Bodies, Subcultural Lives* (New York: New York University Press, 2005), 2.
147 Esty, *Unseasonable Youth*, 36.
148 Jack Halberstam, *The Queer Art of Failure* (Durham, NC: Duke University Press, 2011), 3.
149 Thurschwell, ,The Ghost Worlds of Adolescence', 239–240.
150 Kenneth Millard, *Coming of Age in Contemporary American Fiction* (Edinburgh: Edinburgh University Press, 2007), 5.
151 Lorin Stein, 'The Art of Fiction No. 177: Jonathan Lethem', in Jaime Clarke (ed.), *Conversations with Jonathan Lethem* (Jackson: University of Mississippi Press, 2011), pp. 46–68 (65).
152 Peacock, *Jonathan Lethem*, 117.
153 Peacock, *Jonathan Lethem*, 127–128.
154 Pratt, *Archives of American Time*, 27.
155 Pratt, *Archives of American Time*, 54.
156 Mullins, *Postmodernism in Pieces*, 97.
157 Michiko Kakutani, 'White Kid, in a Black World', *New York Times*, 16 September 2003. On Lethem's experiments in genre fiction, see Peacock, *Jonathan Lethem*, 1–18.
158 A. O. Scott, 'When Dylan Met Mingus', *New York Times Book Review*, 21 September 2003; Lethem, *Fortress of Solitude*, 241.
159 Kakutani, 'White Kid, in a Black World'; Kathryn Boyd Stockton, *The Queer Child, or Growing Sideways in the Twentieth Century* (Durham, NC: Duke University Press, 2009), 13.
160 Jonathan Lethem, 'My Disappointment Critic/On Bad Faith', in *The Ecstasy of Influence*, pp. 384–389 (387).
161 Michael Warner, *Publics and Counterpublics* (New York: Zone Books, 2005), 89.

162 See Daniel Punday, *Writing at the Limit: The Novel in the New Media Ecology* (Lincoln: University of Nebraska Press, 2012), 232–234.
163 Anderson, *Imagined Communities*, 25.
164 See Bloch, 'Nonsynchronism and the Obligation to Its Dialectics', *New German Critique*, 11 [German, 1932] (Spring 1977), pp. 22–38. Lethem alludes to Bloch's theory of nonsynchronism in a different context in 'Diary', *London Review of Books*, 38:24 (15 December 2016), pp. 38–40.
165 Steffen Jensen and Finn Stepputat, 'Notes on Securitization and Temporality', in Martin Holbraad and Morten Axel Pederson (eds), *Times of Security: Ethnographies of Fear, Protest and the Future* (New York: Routledge, 2013), pp. 213–222 (222).

4

The borders of friendship: Dinaw Mengestu's *The Beautiful Things that Heaven Bears* (2007) and Teju Cole's *Open City* (2011)

This chapter begins in another corner store in a gentrifying neighbourhood. Logan Circle Market is a struggling grocery in a predominately African American district of Washington, DC, run by Sepha Stephanos, an Ethiopian immigrant and the narrator of Dinaw Mengestu's debut novel, *The Beautiful Things that Heaven Bears* (2007).[1] Despite there being little sign of business picking up any time soon – a WholeFoods is set to open down the street – Sepha's store appears to be another 'third place' like the Brooklyn Cigar Company, Brokeland Records, or the chalk-lined sidewalks of Dean Street, a place where diverse worlds intersect.[2] The previous chapter considered the sometimes sentimental, often nostalgic yet always hopeful, portrayals of civic life and community that took shape around these 'would-be utopias'. I focused on portrayals of interracial male friendship – and specifically between Jewish and African American characters – exploring how local solidarities offer an always imperfect model for national citizenship, while revealing the ways in which these relationships become freighted with the difficult legacies of 1960s radical politics. Setting out from the 'narrow, shabby, and brightly lit' aisles of Sepha's quiet store, where decades-old calendars and a fading out-of-date map of Africa hang on the walls, this chapter offers a contrasting account of race, friendship, and belonging in contemporary American fiction (3). Concentrating on works by Mengestu and Teju Cole – two writers belonging to a generation heralded as representing an 'African literary renaissance' – this chapter elaborates a multifaceted understanding of black identity in America by bringing into focus the diverse histories and geographies of African migration to the US.[3]

I complicate the account of citizenship put forward thus far. While previous chapters analyse the contemporary American novel's preoccupation with the interplay of personal friendship, local community, and national politics in imagining civic life, Mengestu's and Cole's fictions consider forms of belonging beyond the nation state. While cosmopolitan in outlook, these global fictions are not paeans to transnational mobility. In stories of refugees and poor new arrivals to America, and immigrant narrators whose relationships are difficult to parse or sentimentalise, they bring to light traumatic realities of globalisation: statelessness, rootlessness, and psychic dislocation. A crucial continuity with previous chapters is that Mengestu and Cole privilege male friendship as a figure through which to mediate and imagine the possibilities for, and limits of, cross-cultural connection and transnational belonging.

African, American

With Chris Abani, Chimamanda Ngozi Adichie, and Ike Oguine, among others, Mengestu and Cole belong to a cohort of authors that Louis Chude-Sokei describes as 'newly Black Americans' whose work explores the experience of black African immigrants in the US.[4] Challenging a hegemonic conception of American 'black' identity, these fictions of African migration 'map the restless psychology of newly mobile contemporary global subjects', and dramatise the 'struggle' of recent African immigrants to 'understand themselves as racial subjects in the United States'.[5] Charting the myriad routes and flows of migration and movement that characterise globalisation, these texts reflect recent critical work on the 'transnational origins of national literatures', revealing the 'citizenship' of American fiction to be multiple and varied.[6] Accordingly, African migration fiction is often celebrated for its exploration of cosmopolitan mobility and interconnection. In a *New York Times* piece discussing the 'flowering of African writing', for example, Manthia Diawara suggests that the work of Mengestu, Cole, and others is 'more about being a citizen of the world' than of any one place.[7] Just as frequently, however, these works are caricatured and criticised for abandoning incisive postcolonial critique in favour of the 'afropolitan' travails of middle-class intellectuals and upwardly mobile young professionals.[8] As read and reviewed, these fictions seem to occupy a space 'at the critical and theoretical crossroads where African-American, immigrant, and postcolonial literary studies meet'.[9] Dramatising narratives of 'being American, but newly and reluctantly American; being black and African, but not African-American, the texts examined in this chapter refute 'a linear path toward immigrant assimilation in the U.S.' in favour of an expansive diasporic sensibility, requiring 'more complex scales of comparison and analysis sufficient to navigate local, regional, and global formations' of identity.[10] As writers, Mengestu and Cole reflect on their plural identities, either claimed or conferred. Mengestu drily notes that he is described as 'an immigrant writer, or an African writer, or an Ethiopian-American writer, and occasionally an American writer according to the whims and needs of my interpreters'.[11] Contending that 'citizenship is an act of imagination', Cole similarly observes that he writes 'from multiple positions' as 'an African, a black man living in America', and 'an American'.[12] Citing Paul Gilroy's *Black Atlantic* (1993), Cole explains how he has 'sought to understand the interconnected networks of trade and atrocities that formed the histories of the cities I've known and visited', a comparativist perspective he develops in *Open City* (2011), which explores not only the links between the history and culture of Africa and the Americas that are Gilroy's focus but also connections between the Holocaust and colonialism.[13]

In Mengestu's and Cole's fiction these larger histories of persecution and multiple debates about black identity in America are negotiated through small-scale encounters between individuals whose position in their adopted country is marginal and potentially precarious. While Sepha's store is located near the geographic centre of his neighbourhood – in sight of the statue of the Civil War general John Logan for whom the Circle is named and in whose shadow the novel plays out – he is a peripheral figure in the community. When he opened his store a decade ago, Sepha recalls, Logan Circle was 'still predominately poor, black, cheap, and sunk in a depression', and thus was part of the neighbourhood's appeal to him (35). 'The circle', he writes, was 'proof that wealth and power were not immutable, and America was not always so great after all' (16). Now, the neighbourhood is slowly gentrifying, as white middle-class professionals – like Judith, with whom Sepha will have a fleeting romantic relationship – move in and renovate the dilapidated, 'tragic' brownstones bordering the circle (15). Sepha's store, however, remains in a state of steady decay, 'eggs rotting in the back of the refrigerator' and a 'thick layer of dust' gathering on the paper towels (70). I argued that *Telegraph Avenue*'s Brokeland Records is a kind of time capsule in which nostalgia holds utopian propensities, but Sepha's ossifying store more closely resembles a time *warp*. 'I love the things that are timeless', he writes, like 'rolls of tape, White-Out, hair gel [...] the things that endure and survive' (71).

Endurance and survival seem to be all that Sepha craves. Far from fulfilling the stereotype of immigrant ambition, he recoils from aspiration; as Stephanie Li suggests, moving to a poor African American neighbourhood allows Sepha to use 'the low expectations attached to blackness to his advantage', and to effectively 'pass' as African American.[14] Refusing a 'recognizable narrative of immigrant hope', Sepha seems 'melancholically suspended in a strange geography' where his Ethiopian past blurs into his American present.[15] As he walks DC streets, he is struck by the city's 'resemblance' to his home country's capital, Addis Ababa; looking at a mural of Frederick Douglass, he notes the 'striking resemblance' to 'the pictures of Haile Selassie that used to adorn the walls of the capitol' (173, 176). In a survey of trends in contemporary world literature, Bruce Robbins highlights an 'underlying schema' common in much recent fiction about immigration: 'Step one: atrocity in a foreign country. Step two: escape to the U.S.'[16] Sepha's story refutes this redemptive teleology. He states plainly that 'I did not come to America to find a better life', but rather 'running and screaming with the ghosts of an old one firmly attached to my back' (41). Specifically, Sepha is haunted by his father's violent death during the Ethiopian Red Terror of the late 1970s. In his seventeen years in America, he has not sought prosperity or any 'grand narrative'; rather, his goal has been 'to persist unnoticed through the days' (147, 41).

However, as Rob Nixon notes, the 'deeply felt pain' in the novel is 'offset by the solace of friendship', and, though Sepha cuts an isolated figure, he is not without connections.[17] The novel opens with a closely observed portrait of his friendship with two other African immigrants, Kenneth and Joseph. The trio meet shortly after their arrival in America, while working together at a hotel in DC. Since then, they have drifted into lives of moderate comfort and quiet disappointment: Kenneth is an engineer, but his work goes largely unappreciated in his office; Joseph works as a waiter in an upmarket restaurant but is a frustrated poet who drinks too much. Their lives are structured around routines, rituals, and habits – what Sepha calls 'small daily reassurances' – which include regular after-hours drinking sessions in the back of Sepha's store (2). With their 'beer wrapped in brown bags, in homage to the men doing the same on the corner', they appear a marginal and transitory group, both unwilling and unable to shed their status as outsiders (15). That Kenneth's nickname at the hotel is 'Ken the Kenyan' and Joseph's is 'Joe from the Congo' is indicative of how their immigrant identities are quickly essentialised in their new country. While they often talk of life and work in America, 'inevitably, predictably', Sepha writes, 'our conversations find their way home' (9). From their plastic stools in the store, the men draw a political history of their continent through a game they often play, in which one friend calls out the name of an African dictator, and the others identify the relevant conflict, and locate it on the decades-old map of Africa taped to the wall. The borders and names have changed since it was made, but 'maps, like pictures and journals, have a built-in nostalgic quality that can never render them completely obsolete' (7). The game requires a 'terrible, exhausted expertise' which for Caren Irr 'underscores the theme of melancholic repetition' defining the novel.[18] But the game is also satiric, a joint venture of acidic creativity coloured by a gallows humour that characterises much of Mengestu's work.[19] As Yogita Goyal notes, 'even as they parody the dream of African freedom in this macabre game, their friendship also evokes a pan-African tradition, albeit in ambiguous fashion'.[20] In his 'sober hours', Joseph is working on a cycle of poems that tries to elaborate another kind of African history, one attuned to the legacies of colonialism and imperialism. His work traces 'the history of the Congo from King Leopold to the death of Patrice Lumumba and the rise of Mobutu Sese Seko', and dwells on lines from Dante's *Inferno* which give *The Beautiful Things that Heaven Bears* its title (169). Yet, in another example of the book's caustic and unsentimental tone, the novel also appeared in the UK under the title *Children of the Revolution,* an allusion to the T-Rex song the friends are fond of singing after a few too many drinks (47). Recognising 'themselves in an anthem to the faded glory of the European counterculture of an earlier generation', the friends show how the novel as a whole moves between different modes of historical thinking about identity: the pan-africanism of the map game; the longer colonial history of Joseph's poem; and a more immediate post-1960s transatlantic political and cultural history.[21] Near the end of the novel Joseph asserts that 'All the marches in the world won't change anything anymore. We were at our best in the sixties. Africa was free. American was free. Everyone was marching for something. And now look at us', a perspective that ambiguously twins African history to the American civil rights struggle, and reflects back on the novel's broader preoccupation with black identity (220).

Alongside his exploration of these intersecting histories, Mengestu considers the scales of political geography shaping immigrant life for the three friends. Given its DC setting, it is unsurprising to find the narrative reflecting on the relationship between local and national politics. Sepha, Kenneth, and Joseph are all conscious of the presence of governmental power in the city, and, during their early years in the capitol – the late 1980s and early 1990s – their simple propinquity to the national monuments is a source of wonder and pride. The 'hyper inflated optimism' of that period has long since dissipated, however, and, looking at the 'peak of the Washington Monument', Sepha states that there is 'no mystery left in any of those building for us' (145, 146). To seriously invest hope in their symbolism seems now to be a childish fantasy. As he watches tourists crowd the gates of the White House, Sepha imagines 'all those people clamoring to get into the Oval Office, where the president sat waiting to hear their complaints and woes, their solutions and ideas. A great Santa Claus and father for adults' (76). Joseph's restaurant is frequented by politicians, and he initially believes that his 'physical proximity to power meant great things were in store for him'. Yet it becomes just another job requiring – like the map game – a kind of useless expertise, as he is 'forced to learn the names and faces' of 'all one hundred senators and close to half of the house' (168). A similar fantasy of political intimacy plays out in a scene in which Sepha looks through letters sent to Presidents Carter and Reagan by his uncle Berhane, an Ethiopian refugee who fled to America a few years before his nephew. The letters, Sepha notes, are those of a concerned citizen – though Berhane is in fact 'only a permanent resident [...] because in his heart, he will always be in Ethiopia' – but are also 'deeply personal'. 'Like any letter they are a plea to be heard. I'm not sure who else my uncle could have spoken to about such things when he first came here' (123). A committed and careful reader who regularly gets through four or five novels a week during the long hours in his quiet store, Sepha is alert to how the letters combine different forms of address to tell different kinds of history: the history of American foreign policy and Ethiopian domestic politics, most obviously, but also an intimate history of Berhane's tragic past and his slow adjustment to life in America. In the first letter, Berhane asks Carter to intervene in the 'bloody war' happening in Ethiopia – the war in which Sepha's father will be killed – appealing to the 'deep friendship between our two countries', and emphasising that it is 'imperative that the United States, along with Ethiopia's friends in Europe, come to her aid'. Sepha picks out the line about 'deep friendship' as one that would now amuse his uncle in its naive 'school-yard logic' and conception of international alliances (123–124). Subsequent letters show Berhane to be a 'quick learner', Sepha observes, because he appends pertinent clippings from the *New York Times* and *Washington Post*. But the meaning of friendship shifts in later letters. Rather than using a language of international alliances, Berhane simply reports that 'this month alone I have learned of the death of at least ten friends' (124). As Sepha sits with the letters scattered around him 'in a semicircle that begins chronologically and dissolves into carelessness', Mengestu offers another iteration of the fractured temporality of trauma and political turmoil that permeates the novel (126).

Berhane's correspondence with the President parallels another exchange of letters that begins as the narrative closes, between Sepha and Judith's eleven-year-old daughter, Naomi, with whom he develops a tender friendship. The grocery becomes a home away from home for Naomi when she and her mother first move to the neighbourhood. Her cross-cultural and intergenerational friendship with Sepha recalls Paul's unlikely relationship with the runaway

Rashid, whom Naomi resembles slightly in her precociousness and disarming humour. Initially, they are drawn together by a shared love of reading – they slowly make their way through *The Brothers Karamazov*, recalling Paul slowly flipping through Auggie's photographs – and by a similar comic sensibility. They wile away afternoons inventing a fantasy world, populated by animals, that resembles a more innocent version of the map game Sepha plays with Kenneth and Joseph. For Naomi, who is mixed race, Sepha becomes something of a substitute father, or an avuncular presence like Berhane – who we learn isn't technically Sepha's uncle – and, more broadly, their relationship is part of Mengestu's wider interest in familial relations of support and obligation between neighbours. Their correspondence begins when Judith leaves Logan Circle and Naomi goes to boarding school. Naomi ends her first letter, 'Please write back, because that's what friends are supposed to do', opening up a dialogue and setting an expectation of commitment and reciprocity that Sepha has so far studiously avoided in his life in America (215). As Stephanie Li notes, 'a future correspondence with Naomi promises a form of reading that is not an escape from life but an embrace of the vulnerabilities and visibilities required of genuine intimacy'.[22] As in my discussion of the connection between friendship and correspondence in Paul Auster's work, letters in Mengestu's novel can cultivate a kind of intimate distance.

While the portrayal of Sepha's friendship with Naomi is ultimately hopeful, the presentation of his relationship with Judith is less optimistic. Separated from her husband, Judith is a professor of American history who has arrived in Logan Circle with some of the same liberal commitments (and naivety) as Rachel in *The Fortress of Solitude*. Initially, she seems to exist far outside Sepha's orbit – he mistakes her at first for 'an agent of some city bureaucracy' – but gradually she appears to resemble him in certain ways, although their similarities ultimately draw attention to the insurmountable differences in their personal histories and material circumstances (17). Judith's purse is 'stuffed with utility bills, checks, credit cards, passport, keys to her old houses in Chicago and Virginia', recalling Sepha's own itinerancy while highlighting the different kinds of social mobility available to each (81). Judith is taking a sabbatical, and she seems caught in a state of suspension that parallels Sepha's lack of direction. She has taken a break from teaching, she tells him, because she had a premonition of herself 'twenty years in the future saying the same thing over and over to students' (54). This closely echoes Sepha's daydream: 'sometimes I like to think that if I waited ten or twenty years before opening my store, I could return to find it completely unchanged' (37). The similarity sharpens the contrast between their lived realities: for Sepha, stasis and continuity are the stuff of fantasy, for Judith, a source of anxiety. Both, however, recognise in the other a feeling of rootlessness and drifting ambition, and they soon become a source of comfort to one another. Readers are reminded of their physical closeness as next-door neighbours – a recurring joke of Judith's is to urge Sepha to 'Get home safely' – but, like the proximity of the national monuments or the President to the lives of Sepha and his immigrant friends, this proves to be a false intimacy that cannot ultimately counter the underlying power imbalance between them. Their first dinner at Judith's house is tense and awkward, Sepha anxiously trying 'to erase any sound of food being ground into bits by chewing slowly'. Judith is also nervous, and soon slips back into her academic mode, beginning to 'lecture' him 'eloquently and passionlessly' about 'Emerson and Tocqueville' (56). Like *Leviathan* and *Smoke*, *The Beautiful Things that Heaven Bears* is explicitly framed by nineteenth-century American literature and philosophy, while Judith is motived by a 'high-minded [...] belief in participatory democracy and Emersonian ideals' (197). These beliefs are elaborated in her book, *America's Repudiation of the Past*, which includes chapters on 'Tocqueville's legacy on American Poetics' and 'Nineteenth-Century American Writers search for Place', suggesting a clear dialogue between her scholarship and the wider interest in citizenship and voluntarism that defined much late twentieth-century communitarian political philosophy discussed in previous chapters (157). Sepha reads her book, as well as de Tocqueville's and Emerson's essays, though he admits that 'I can't say that I understood America any better for having done so' (158).

While it is clear that the novel's preoccupation with friendship and forms of local community is in dialogue with this familiar genealogy of American democratic thinking, it is less clear to what extent a communitarian vision of Tocquevillian voluntarism is a viable model for Sepha and his 'newly black American' friends to follow. That Judith ends up leaving Logan Circle, while Sepha has no real choice but to stay, indicates an ambivalence about the possibility of immigrants assimilating to this American conception of democratic freedom. In this regard, it is important to note that while the loose network of solidarities that emerges around Sepha's store does indeed resemble a Tocquevillian idea of local voluntary association of the kind celebrated in communitarian political philosophy, it also bears a resemblance to another model of collectivity: a *mahaber*, one of the constituent organising structures of Ethiopian civic life. In a personal essay, Mengestu describes the formation of a diasporic mahaber among a group of Ethiopian immigrants living in 'a blocklong, 12-story tower on New Hampshire Avenue in Takoma Park, Maryland' in the late 1970s and 1980s.[23] Among the residents are Mengestu's uncle and a man named Solomon, who quickly become best friends on arrival in the US. The uncle is the inspiration for Berhane in *The Beautiful Things that Heaven Bears* and, more broadly, the novel borrows from his friendship with Solomon and their experience of life in America. 'Together', Mengestu writes, 'the two did what nearly all the newly arrived Ethiopian immigrants believed was demanded of them. They worked one, often two jobs, and in the evenings, when they could afford to, they took classes. My uncle, and Solomon in particular, did so with a singular intent, one completely divorced from any version of the American dream.'[24] And, like Sepha's conversations with Kenneth and Joseph, the uncle's conversations with Solomon inevitably make their way back home. 'We were basically the same age', he tells his nephew. 'We talked about everything if it was just the two of us. When we're not in a group, then we talk more about Ethiopia. How we lost our youth. How we lost all these years, rather than enjoying our childhood and stuff like that. When we are in a group, we remember the past and joke about it.'[25] As Mengestu makes clear, this friendship functioned within a wider community of support among the residents of the apartment block, modelled imperfectly on the lives they had left behind:

> In Ethiopia, one of the organizing principles of civil society is the formation of loose social networks among friends and family to help

bear the particular costs that come with life: death, marriage, the purchase of a home, car. There weren't enough friends and family in America to recreate a version of each one of those support systems, but after almost a decade away from home, my uncle and Solomon, along with their friends on New Hampshire Avenue, created a Mahaber that, with time, would help pay for each of their weddings, their children's graduations, and 20 years later, Solomon's funeral.[26]

In *The Beautiful Things that Heaven Bears*, Sepha is part of a haphazard network that resembles this Ethiopian conception of civic life and an American idea of democratic association that, as Judith's research shows, has its roots in the nineteenth century. The hybridity of these models, and the multiplicity of identities that emerges from them, are central to Mengestu's examination of citizenship in an age of migration and globalisation. Resisting the easy sentimentality and nostalgia about either American neighbourhood community or life back in Africa, his novel offers a bittersweet and reflexive portrayal of immigrant belonging and identity rooted in friendship.

Origins, openings

A German-Nigerian psychiatrist completing his residency in Manhattan, *Open City*'s narrator Julius comes from a different background from Sepha, and moves in a different social circle and intellectual milieu. But both characters are figures of 'postcolonial alterity' somewhat adrift in America, similarly separated from their families and equally ambivalent about their immigrant identity, and about being seen as 'black' but 'without the history and community tied to American blackness'.[27] Like Sepha, Julius organises his life around a set of routines which he describes in flat, affectless prose. The most important parts of his regime are regular, long walks around New York City, which have a ruminative, dreamlike quality akin to Sepha's more occasional journeys through DC. Both narrators are keen observers of urban life for whom their adopted cities are palimpsestic, shadowed by other geographies, physical and psychic. While Sepha sees shades of Addis Ababa, Julius's mind wanders back to his hometown of Lagos as he wanders through New York and, later, Brussels. Like Sepha, Julius is a chronicler of the changes to his city, and he is keen to know and share the history of demolished buildings, built-over neighbourhoods, and redeveloped districts. Both also find in monuments a focus for their thinking about migration and belonging. Just as Sepha dwells on the significance of the Washington Monument and Lincoln Memorial, so Julius studies the Statue of Liberty and Ellis Island, 'built too late for those early Africans – who weren't immigrants in any case' and 'closed too soon to mean anything to later Africans like [...] me'. Rather, Julius considers, it is 'a symbol mostly of European refugees', and the novel is preoccupied with how narratives of African migration intersect with other histories of arrival, assimilation, and citizenship in America.[28] Both men's contemplative turn of phrase and turn of mind are portrayed as the product of traumatic pasts. Sepha thinks often of his murdered father, and Julius remembers the death of his own, his fractured childhood, and unhappy years at a military boarding school. The novel's late revelation that Julius allegedly sexually assaulted a friend, Moji, when they were both teenagers suggests that it is not just trauma but guilt that he tries and fails to leave behind in Nigeria.

Both narrators are voracious readers, but, while Sepha is content enough to trawl through his weekly library haul from his perch in the grocery, Julius's reading seems, initially at least, to lead him out into the world and to a life rich with aesthetic pleasure and cultural variety. In the novel's opening pages, we find him flicking through Barthes's *Camera Lucida* and Tahar Ben Jelloun's *The Last Friend*, before listening to Mahler's *Das Lied von der Erde*, and taking in an exhibition of John Brewster's paintings at the American Folk Art Museum (5, 17, 37). Descriptions of these encounters with interesting artworks are interspersed with descriptions of encounters with interesting people – a Japanese-American professor, an historian of Dutch colonialism – and Julius seems at first to be an accomplished 'reader' of both. Through his mentor and friend Professor Saito, he comes to appreciate 'the ability to trace out a story from what was omitted', and, as he crisscrosses Manhattan, Julius tries to render legible the city's myriad buried narratives of dispossession and trauma (9). Attuned to how historical time can seem 'elastic', his Sebaldian perspective recalls Walter Benjamin's argument in 'Theses on the Philosophy of History' – 'there is no document of civilisation which is not at the same time a document of barbarism' – which is repeatedly alluded to throughout the narrative.[29]

For early reviewers, this combination of cultural refinement and dispassionate intelligence marked Julius as a consummate cosmopolite.[30] 'From its title onwards', Pieter Vermeulen notes, '*Open City* seems to embody the cosmopolitan conviction that the cultivation of curiosity and attentiveness is the appropriate tool for fostering connections beyond ethnic, cultural, or national borders'.[31] Julius explicitly mentions Kwame Anthony Appiah's work, and the novel seems to be in dialogue with Appiah's concept of 'rooted cosmopolitanism' (186).[32] In classical cosmopolitanism, the familiar metaphors of and models for citizenship – such as friendship – are rejected in favour of a Kantian universalism. But Appiah's work highlights how this stress upon abstract global commitments fails to recognise the importance of the variegated, multiple local attachments through which people tend to situate and identify themselves. Appiah's rooted cosmopolitanism – summarised as 'universalism plus difference' – 'celebrates the fact that there are *different* local human ways of being', suggesting that 'we should learn about people in other places, take an interest in their civilisations, their arguments [...] not because that will bring us to agreement but because it will help us get used to one another'.[33] Appiah's metaphor for this kind of cosmopolitan exchange is 'conversation', a term that, as Werner Sollors notes, appears like a 'leitmotif' throughout *Open City*.[34]

Subsequent critical responses to the novel, however, have stressed how Cole 'juxtaposes the urge for harmonious cross-cultural connection with a critique of that very desire'.[35] While Claire Messud's review celebrates Julius's performance of 'a cosmopolite's detachment from his American experience', in Rebecca Clark's reading of the novel there is something 'ambivalent[ly] discomfort[ing]' about 'its detached yet somehow too-close-for-comfort narrator'.[36] As Karan Mahan notes, the narrative is characterised by 'constant misdirection', a deceptive 'movement from Julius's private problems to public questions'.[37] Often, it appears that the insights gained about culture and history from Julius's Benjaminian, Sebaldian perspective come at the expense of a wilful blindness about his own personal history, especially regarding his culpability for his alleged assault on

Moji.[38] While he cultivates a sophisticatedly cosmopolitan aesthetic finely attuned to cross-cultural affinity, his personal encounters are disquieting, and his attempts at Appiah-esque 'conversation' often go awry. This is particularly true in Julius's negotiation of his racial identity. He baulks when a taxi driver attempts to strike up conversation predicated on the fact that they are both African: 'I was not in the mood for people who tried to lay claims on me' (40). Similarly, when he runs into a black Caribbean guard from the Folk Art Museum in a downtown bar, he assumes it cannot be a coincidence, and senses a 'sexual question' behind the man's approach, cutting the conversation short (54). Later, he mistakenly assumes he shares a 'quick solidarity' with a group of young African American men he passes in the street, but is then mugged by them (212). These instances of misreading racial identity are indicative of Julius's wider disconnect from those around him, signalled near the beginning of the novel when he asks after a neighbour's wife, only to be told that she died from a heart attack some months earlier: 'I had not noticed not seeing her around' (21).

As this brief survey suggests, the critical response to *Open City* has been characterised by a debate over to what extent the novel celebrates or critiques cosmopolitanism, and to what extent Julius in particular epitomises the cosmopolitan citizen. But framing the novel in this way fails to recognise how Cole's portrayal of cosmopolitanism emerges through an exploration of its darker alternative: statelessness. The novel's evocation of cross-cultural connection and the possibility of civic identity beyond the nation state is twinned with an evocation of a different kind of transnational mobility, that of transience and displacement. As Lyndsey Stonebridge summarises, since Kant, the cosmopolitan ideal of 'a universal humanity framed by a global understanding of rights' has been 'confronted with the calamity of the radically stateless'.[39] This confrontation animates *Open City*, in which perspective frequently shifts from that of the cosmopolite to that of the refugee. For example, we hear the story of Saidu, a Liberian refugee held in a detention center in Queens, to whom Julius listens 'without interrupting'. Saidu's is a complicated story composed of a catalogue of persecutions and escapes: from his mother and sister being killed by 'Charles Taylor's men', in the Second Liberian Civil War of the late 1990s, to his fleeing to Guinea, then Bamako, Tangier, and mainland Europe, over a two-year period (64–69). Throughout, Saidu dreams of emigrating to America, because as a child he had been 'taught about the special relationship between Liberia and America, which was like the relationship between an uncle and a favorite nephew' – recalling Berhane's misplaced faith in the 'deep friendship' between Ethiopia and the US (64). Despite its detail, Julius is suspicious of the story, and wary of his own role as witness to Saidu's traumatic testimony: 'I was the listener, the compassionate African who paid attention to the details of someone else's life and struggle' (70). In his unsentimental scepticism, Julius resembles Jonas, the narrator of Mengestu's second novel, *How to Read the Air* (2010), who works in a refugee resettlement centre in Manhattan. A 'literary type' with the vague ambition of pursuing a PhD in English, Jonas is tasked with 'the job of editing out the less credible or unnecessary parts' of some of the refugees' testimonies, while 'pointing out places where some stories could be [...] magnified for greater narrative effect'.[40] Both Cole and Mengestu consequently complicate some of the clichés of the 'escape plot' that tend to dominate narratives of refugee experience.[41] Immediately after Saidu's story, we hear another, stranger story of statelessness, when Julius meets Pierre, a Haitian man, in the 'underground catacombs of Penn Station'. Pierre is a spectral figure, who speaks ambiguously of coming to America 'when things got bad [in Haiti], when so many people were killed, blacks, whites', and alludes to Dutty Boukman, one of the leaders of the Haitian Revolution in the 1790s (71–72). Other characters are haunted by more recent memories of upheaval and dispossession. Professor Saito recalls memorising poetry in an internment camp in Idaho during the Second World War, while Julius thinks of his own mother, 'born in Berlin, only a few days after the Russians had taken over the city, in early May 1945' (80).

In fact, often Julius's German heritage seems as significant to the narrative as his Nigerian upbringing. The novel dwells on European history and in particular on the 'vanished world' of the Second World War, Julius's thoughts turning repeatedly to the Holocaust and its connection with other histories of persecution (80). Riding the subway, he looks 'up at the vents' and thinks of 'the final terrible moments in the camps [...] when the Zyklon B was switched on and all the human captives breathed in their deaths, and how, while all this was happening in the early forties, my *oma* [grandmother] was on her way north to Berlin as a refugee' (229). Attending an exhibition at the International Center of Photography of Martin Munkasci's 'masterful work', Julius first studies a piece from 1931, a 'photograph of three African boys running into the surf in Liberia'. But as he moves through Munkasci's career as a photojournalist, Julius notes how the images begin to reflect 'the cool tensions of a military state', observing 'among the photographs of troops and parades at the opening of the Reichstag in 1933 [...] the image, at once expected and unexpected [...] of the new German chancellor' (154). Studying the photographs, Julius notices that he is standing beside a young Hasidic couple, and is approached by an elderly man who, 'with the slowness of someone who was entering a memory', tells him the story of his childhood, recounting how he was 'thirteen when we left Berlin in 1937 [...] and New York has been my home ever since' (153). These encounters suggest the proximity of Jewish identity and history to Julius's narrative; it is only at the very end of the exhibition that Julius observes that Munkasci 'was himself Jewish', quietly suggesting to the reader that this is significant.

On the subway and at the exhibition, Julius dwells not only on the horrors of the Holocaust but on the legacy of statelessness it engendered – represented by the elderly German refugee – linking this crisis of citizenship to other narratives of displacement, through reference to his refugee grandmother and the mention of Munkasci's photograph of African boys in Liberia, bringing to mind his earlier conversation with Saidu. These moments are indicative of how 'the whole of *Open City* could be regarded as an extended practice of bearing witness to the two historical strands of the Jewish and African diasporas it brings into conversation'.[42] Throughout the novel, Jewishness becomes important to Cole's broader exploration of the tension between the ideal of cosmopolitanism and the catastrophe of statelessness. Noting that the novel is 'bookended' with references to Mahler's music, Josh Epstein suggests that the 'Jewish Bohemian-Austrian composer' can be read as 'a double for Julius's open-bordered cosmopolitanism', arguing that 'Mahler's oft-quoted remark that he was "thrice homeless" – a

The borders of friendship 191

Bohemian in Austria, an Austrian in Germany, and a Jewish person everywhere – coincides with the thematic insistence on [...] placelessness and itinerancy' in *Open City*.[43] In the next section of this chapter, however, I will argue that Cole's novel enters into a more meaningful and sustained dialogue with another Jewish European cultural figure who also settled in New York City but who, unlike Mahler, came to America as a displaced person: Hannah Arendt. As I have suggested, *Open City* seems to direct its readers' attention to a myriad of influences and intertexts, whether it is through the cataloguing of Julius's reading lists, or his references to Freud, Barthes, and Benjamin, among many others. Indeed, it is only a slight exaggeration to say that Arendt is one of the few prominent twentieth-century intellectuals *not* referred to by name in the book. And yet *Open City* shares many of the preoccupations of Arendt's work, not least the twinning of Jewish and other minority diasporas, and the consideration of the possibilities of citizenship beyond the nation state in the wake of the Holocaust. More than Appiah's *Cosmopolitanism*, I will argue, it is Arendt's work on totalitarianism that offers a key to understanding the novel's meditation on migration and belonging. And, crucially for my discussion, Arendt's account of citizenship and statelessness in the postwar era emerges through her consideration of the politics of friendship.

Refuge, friendship

In *The Origins of Totalitarianism* (1951), Arendt sets herself the 'paradoxical task' of grappling with 'the unprecedented nature of the Nazi genocide of European Jews while simultaneously seeking the antecedent elements that help explain its possibility and marking the parallel phenomena that share its genus'.[44] Instead of searching for origins, then, Arendt outlines a 'disjunctive constellation linking anti-Semitism, imperialism, and totalitarianism', formulating a comparative approach to the history of persecution which, Michael Rothberg suggests, 'can provide resources for the rethinking of justice', and reframing discussions of citizenship.[45] Arendt argues that, after the Holocaust, we must understand 'the minority as a permanent institution' of the national imaginary, and recognise dispossession and the infringement of civil liberties as 'inherent in the structure of the nation-state since the beginning'.[46] Describing statelessness as 'the newest mass phenomenon in contemporary history', and suggesting that 'an ever-growing new people comprised of stateless persons' represents the 'most symptomatic group in contemporary politics', Arendt articulates the need for an account of citizenship and democratic politics told from the perspective of those it has failed or left behind.[47] 'When Arendt used the word "stateless" she was describing a diverse group of people', Lyndsey Stonebridge tells us, including 'refugees, political exiles, temporarily denaturalised citizens, those, like many Jews, who had been stripped of their citizenship altogether, others, like Arendt herself, who were illegal immigrants. Out of place, these people were also out of the law, and out of political and historical time.'[48] From this minoritarian perspective beyond the borders and temporal logic of a single nation, Arendt 'produces an account of the modern refugee as a symptom of a larger crisis about the meanings of citizenship and sovereignty at mid-century'.[49] To write history from this perspective, therefore, 'is to do more that to testify to the suffering of statelessness. It is also to write from within the lacuna left by the law's inability to imagine a legal cosmopolitanism capable of protecting all of humanity in the post war era'.[50]

Arendt's work is therefore not only an indictment of the ordinary brutality of the nation state but also a critique of cosmopolitan idealism. And yet she does insist that some fundamental conception of collective humanity – 'the right to have rights' – is urgently necessary in the postwar world, and, as Judith Butler notes, throughout her writing Arendt 'refers variously to modes of "belonging" and to conceptions of "polity" that are not reducible to the nation-state'.[51] And in thinking about citizenship beyond the nation state – both as a practice in her daily life, and conceptually in her political philosophy – Arendt returned repeatedly to the idea of friendship. Friendship emerges as a model of belonging and identity in Arendt's personal life in a famous letter to her prickly sometime-friend Gershom Scholem. After reading her account of the Adolf Eichmann trial in Jerusalem and her misgivings about its manipulation for Israeli national politics, Scholem accused Arendt of having 'no love for the Jewish people'.[52] 'How right you are that I have no such love', she replied, 'I have never in my life "loved" some nation or collective [...] The fact is that I love only my friends.'[53] In *Men in Dark Times* (1968), she pays tribute to her recently deceased friend Waldemar Gurian as 'a man of many friends [...] Friendship was what made him feel at home in this world and he felt at home wherever his friends were, regardless of country, language, or social bond.'[54] More formally, in her political philosophy, Arendt engaged with the Aristotelian tradition of friendship as a means of conceptualising a form of belonging that captured the 'love of friends' she practised among the group of largely Jewish European émigrés who comprised her social circle in Manhattan. Prefiguring Appiah's notion of cosmopolitan conversation, in *The Promise of Politics* (published posthumously in 2005), Arendt suggests that 'the political element in friendship is that in the truthful dialogue each of the friends can understand the truth inherent in the other's opinion. More than his friend as a person, one friend understands how and in what specific articulateness the common world appears to the other, who as a person is forever unequal or different.'[55] As such, following Aristotle, Arendt argues that the 'equalisation in friendship does not [...] mean that the friends become the same or equal to each other, but rather that they become equal partners of a common world – that they together constitute a community', closely prefiguring her more well-known conception of the 'common world', articulated in *The Human Condition*, as a place that 'gathers us together and yet prevents us falling over each other, so to speak'.[56] As Jon Nixon observes, 'totalitarianism necessitates the eradication of precisely those elements of social relationship – plurality, mutuality, and continuity – that constitute friendship', and so the dialogue of friendship Arendt elaborates – granting an understanding of the friend's 'specific articulateness' of a common and consensual community – might be a 'bulwark' against such political naivety and extremism.[57]

The idea of friendship as an alternative form of citizenship beyond the temporal and geographic strictures of the nation state recalls the depiction of Sepha's relationship with Kenneth and Joseph in *The Beautiful Things that Heaven Bears*, and, more broadly, Mengestu's fictions seems to take up Arendt's project of writing 'as a refugee'. In Cole's novel, an exploration of the politics of friendship coalesces with other Arendtian themes – namely, the resonances between the Holocaust and the history of colonialism; minoritarianism; and Jewish nationalism – when the plot moves unexpectedly to Brussels. Julius ostensibly travels to Belgium to find his refugee maternal grandmother, but he soon gets waylaid by other stories of displacement and dispossession in this second 'open city' – the term used to describe municipalities, like Brussels during the Second World War, that surrender to invading forces to avoid destruction. 'Belgium was stupid during the war', Julius is told by Dr Mailotte, a fellow-passenger aboard his flight from New York, who remembers how 'the Nazis marched in, and stayed, like parasites', and recalls 'the day the war ended for Belgium' as the happiest of her life (89, 90). Julius connects the image of Dr Mailotte 'at fifteen, in September 1944, sitting on a rampart in the Brussels sun' with that of Professor Saito 'on the same day, aged thirty-one or thirty-two, unhappy, in internment' (96). Once he lands on European soil, these histories are connected to other accounts of war and persecution, in a kind of Arendtian constellation that recalls the comparativist approach of *The Origins of Totalitarianism*. Julius admits he arrived in Brussels 'with the idea that all the Africans in the city were from the Congo. I knew the colonial relationship, I had a basic understanding of the history of the slave state there, and that had dislodged any other idea from my head' (138). He is therefore surprised to enter a club, the dance floor full with people he assumes are Congolese, and be told that 'everyone was Rwandan', contemplating that most of those dancing 'would have been teenagers during the genocide' (139). Julius soon begins to understand that the 'European reality' of 'flexible borders' means that, despite the fact that 'Belgium had not had a strong colonial relationship with any country in North Africa', much of Brussels's immigrant population is drawn from the region – including Farouq, a Moroccan immigrant who runs a bustling internet café that Julius begins to frequent (98).

Sitting at his counter with his nose in a book, Farouq resembles Sepha, though their stores are quite different places. In contrast to Logan Circle Market's quiet aisles, business is good for Farouq, his twelve computer booths alive with the 'hum' of people making calls home over Eid, to 'Colombia, Egypt, Senegal, Brazil, France, Germany' (112). 'It looked like fiction', Julius writes, 'that such a small group of people really could be making calls to such a wide spectrum of places', and the store initially seems to represent an idealised conception of cosmopolitan interconnectivity. Farouq appears to invest a sincere hope in this idea, viewing the store as 'a test case for what I believe; people can live together but still keep their own values intact [...] It happens here, on this small scale, in this shop, and I want to understand how it can happen on a bigger scale' (112–113). Farouq came to Brussels to pursue his Master's, writing his dissertation on Gaston Bachelard – whose work on the 'poetics of space' seems to influence his understanding of 'scale' – and harbouring the semi-serious ambition of becoming 'the next Edward Said' (128). An 'autodidact', his conversation is peppered with the language of postcolonial theory, as when he critiques the 'oriental element' in Tahar Ben Jelloun's fiction and questions the 'social function' of his work, after Julius expresses admiration for it (103). But, as Lyndsey Stonebridge notes, 'Arendt's and Said's is a shared refugee history', and if there is a Saidian tenor to Julius's conversations with Farouq then there is also an Arendtian inflection.[58] For example, Farouq is reading a 'secondary text' on *On the Concept of History* by Arendt's close friend Walter Benjamin – a manuscript copy of which Arendt carried in her luggage to America, when Benjamin was still unknown in the US (103).[59] Shortly after they discuss Benjamin, Farouq misquotes the former Israeli Prime Minister Golda Meir as saying 'there are no Palestinian people', a topic that clearly links to Said's personal background and research, but also recalls Arendt's critique of Jewish nationalism and dismissal of 'love' of any nation or collective (104).

A link to Arendt's work is further suggested when Farouq introduces Julius to Khalil: 'He's one of my friends, in fact I can say he's my best friend' (117). Unlike Farouq – who moves easily between the multiple languages of his customers – Khalil does not speak English, and his perspective is not so easily translated into the novel's lingua franca of cosmopolitanism. In a scene Karan Mahajan describes as the 'centrepiece of the novel', the trio sit down for what appears to be an Appiah-esque conversation – or perhaps an Arendtian dialogue – recalling the three-way conversation between friends that begins *The Beautiful Things that Heaven Bears*.[60] Khalil starts by asking Julius some general questions about the political divide between Republicans and Democrats in the US, before moving on to a blandly familiar critique of American foreign policy, which veers into a defence of Al-Qaeda. In response, Julius rather lamely calls him an 'extremist', and there is a sense that both men are, as Julius puts it, 'pretending to an outrage' neither quite feels, spouting the views expected of their respective positions – the accusatory Muslim and the offended American (120). The banality of their ideological talk recalls Arendt's infamous diagnosis of Eichmann's evil – that his first crime was his inability to think independently, betrayed in the fact that he could not defend himself without resorting to cliché.[61] But their discussion intensifies when they turn to the topic of Israel and what Khalil calls 'the Palestinian question'. Challenging Julius on the role of the Holocaust in framing the issue of Palestinian rights, Khalil complains, 'If we try to speak to the Palestinian situation, we hear six million [...] But what does this have to do with Palestinians? [...] Did the Palestinians build the concentration camps? [...] I'll tell you why the six million matter so much: it is because Jews are the chosen people. Forget the Cambodians, forget the American blacks, this is unique suffering' (122). Interrogating the Holocaust's exceptionalism and its status as a paradigmatic traumatic history, Khalil and Farouq return to some of the concerns animating Arendt's study of totalitarianism, while also recalling her misgivings about the weaponising of Holocaust trauma in the Eichmann trial. For Khalil, this discussion is linked to his own confusion over what he calls 'communitarianism in the United States', which for him includes the idea of a multicultural society based upon the competing demands of sometimes inchoate identitarian groups: 'White is a race, he said, black is a race, but Spanish is a language. Christianity is a religion, Islam is a religion, but Jewishness is an ethnicity. It makes no sense' (118). Here, Khalil gestures to the way in which the entire novel refracts the ambiguities of Julius's 'African, American' identity through the prism of Jewish identity, finding in Jewishness – as Arendt did – a figure for both the dilemma of diaspora and the possibilities of cosmopolitanism.

When Khalil leaves to take a telephone call, Julius impulsively suggests that Farouq should return with him to the US. 'There was a naive excitement about it', Julius observes, 'but if I were truly inviting him as a guest, I feared the logistics of such an invitation'. If Julius seems unsure whether what he is offering is 'truly' an act of hospitality, Farouq is certain that he does not want to accept: 'I have no desire to visit America, and certainly not as an Arab, not now' (126). Refusing the sentimental narrative trajectory of escape to the US, Farouq wishes to remain in Brussels, despite the daily difficulty of being an immigrant there. In place of Julius's 'American' hospitality, Farouq offers a competing vision of immigrant friendship, when he defends his relationship with Khalil. 'I don't view America as monolithic', he tells Julius, 'I'm not like Khalil in this way. I know that there are different people there, with different ideas […] and what is important to me is that the world realizes that we are not monolithic either, in what they call the Arab world, that we are all individuals. We disagree with each other. You just saw me in disagreement with my best friend. We are individuals' (125–126). As Julius is quick to point out, Farouq's conception of individualism chimes with US liberalism: 'I think you and America are ready for each other'. Ironically, Farouq's defence of friendship also recalls Tahar Ben Jelloun's *The Last Friend* – the novel Julius is reading at the start of *Open City*, and which Farouq dismisses as sentimentally orientalist. Ben Jelloun's novel is the story of the intense friendship of Mamed and Ali, beginning in early 1950s Tangier and chronicling their separate journeys across Europe, including Mamed's association with the French Communist Party – like Farouq and Khalil, he is a proud Marxist. It ends with Ali's statement on his friendship with Mamed, which seems to prefigure Farouq's: 'People thought we agreed on everything. In fact, what gave depth to our relationship was precisely the opposite: it was our different perspectives, our differences of opinion, freely expressed, without any kind of personal opposition between us.'[62]

If Farouq's perspective owes as much to Ben Jelloun as to Said, his evocation of friendship may also be read as an Arendtian alternative to Khalil's extremism, American individualism, and Appiah-esque cosmopolitanism. Part of Cole's argument in *Open City* is that the kind of diasporic sensibility imagined by Arendt as a Jewish intellectual who was writing after the Holocaust must now be cultivated among other 'stateless people', like Julius and Farouq.

Like Mengestu's shopkeeper Sepha, Farouq is a postcolonial subject forging an identity through necessity, piecing together a community through friendships with other immigrants and the looser connections networked through his internet café. By avoiding what Cole in an essay calls, in an allusion to Arendt, the 'banality of sentimentality', both novelists find in male friendship not an ideal model of community, nor the basis for a cosmopolitan universalism, but a refuge from the calamity of statelessness, and the traumatic histories that shape the contemporary world.[63]

Notes

1 Dinaw Mengestu, *The Beautiful Things that Heaven Bears* (New York: Riverhead Books, 2007). Subsequent references are given in the text in parentheses. In the UK, the novel was published as *Childen of the Revolution* by Vintage.
2 Sepha mentions a 'two-story organic grocery store being built' near 14th St; a WholeFoods opened there in late 2000 (75).
3 Yogita Goyal, 'We Need New Diasporas', *American Literary History*, 29:4 (2017), pp. 640–663 (641).
4 Louis Chude-Sokei, 'The Newly Black Americans: African Immigrants and Black America', *Transition*, 113:1 (2014), pp. 52–71.
5 Caren Irr, *Toward the Geopolitical Novel: U.S. Fiction in the Twenty-First Century* (New York: Columbia University Press, 2013), 50; Stephanie Li, *Pan-African American Literature: Signifying Immigrants in the 21st Century* (New Brunswick: Rutgers University Press, 2018), 84.
6 Rebecca Walkowitz, *Born Translated: The Contemporary Novel in an Age of World Literature* (New York: Columbia University Press, 2015), 115. See also Jahan Ramazani, *A Transnational Poetics* (Chicago: University of Chicago Press, 2009).
7 Felicia Lee, 'New Wave of African Writers with an Internationalist Bent', *New York Times*, 29 June 2014.
8 See Susanne Gehrmann, 'Cosmopolitanism with African Roots: Afropolitanism's Ambivalent Mobilities', *Journal of African Cultural Studies*, 28:1 (2016), pp. 61–72.
9 Aliki Varvogli, 'Urban Mobility and Race: Dinaw Mengestu's *The Beautiful Things that Heaven Bears* and Teju Cole's *Open City*', *Studies in American Fiction*, 44:2 (Fall 2017), pp. 235–257 (236).

10 Varvogli, 'Urban Mobility and Race', 235; Goyal, 'We Need New Diasporas', 642.
11 Dinaw Mengestu, 'How Novels Widen Your Vision', *The Atlantic*, 4, March 2014.
12 Teju Cole, 'A Piece in the Wall', in Cole, *Known and Strange Things: Essays* (New York: Random House, 2016), pp. 363–376 (374); 'The White Savior Industrial Complex', in *Known and Strange Things*, pp. 340–349 (344).
13 Cole, 'A Piece in the Wall', 374.
14 Li, *Pan-African American Literature*, 78.
15 Goyal, 'We Need New Diasporas', 645; Irr, *Toward the Geopolitical Novel*, 51.
16 Bruce Robbins, 'The Worlding of the American Novel', in Leonard Cassuto (ed.), *The Cambridge History of the American Novel* (Cambridge: Cambridge University Press, 2011), pp. 1096–1106 (1100).
17 Rob Nixon, 'African, American', *New York Times*, 25 March 2007.
18 Irr, *Toward the Geopolitical Novel*, 51.
19 Mengestu's second novel, *How to Read the Air*, is set in a refugee asylum centre, where 'the general mood was of overwhelming sympathy buttressed by seemingly sincere, heartfelt statements'. By contrast, Angela, with whom the narrator Jonas falls in love, 'could never talk like that [...] "Refugees," she said. "How could you not love them? Who else do you know has it worse."' Mengestu, *How to Read the Air* (London: Vintage, 2010), 21.
20 Goyal, 'We Need New Diasporas', 646.
21 Irr, *Toward the Geopolitical Novel*, 52.
22 Li, *Pan-African American Literature*, 91.
23 Dinaw Mengestu, 'Solomon's Search', *The Atlantic*, 14 May 2016.
24 Mengestu, 'Solomon's Search'.
25 Mengestu, 'Solomon's Search'.
26 Mengestu, 'Solomon's Search'.
27 Li, *Pan-African American Literature*, 57.
28 Teju Cole, *Open City* (London: Faber and Faber, 2011), 54. Further references are given in the text in parentheses.
29 Walter Benjamin, *Illuminations,* trans. Harry Zohn (New York: Schocken Books, 1968), 256. Karen Jacobs notes that 'Sebald's [...] attention to the World Wars' larger cast of surviving casualties – those émigrés, migrants, nomads, and exiles', 'prefigure[s] Cole's', while Werner Sollors explores the novel's 'Sebaldian mode'. With a different emphasis, Rebecca Clark observes that Julius presents himself

'as a self-sufficient Sebaldian musing promenading man of history-sipping free associative leisure'. See Jacobs, 'Teju Cole's Photographic Afterimages', *Image & Narrative*, 15:2 (2014), pp. 87–105 (89); Sollors, 'Cosmopolitan Curiosity in an Open City: Notes on Reading Teju Cole by way of Kwame Anthony Appiah', *New Literary History*, 49:2 (Spring 2018), pp. 227–248 (242); Clark, '"Visible only in speech": Peripatetic Parasitism, or, Becoming Bedbugs in *Open City*', *Narrative*, 26:2 (May 2018), pp. 181–200 (197). On Sebald's 'Benjaminian gaze', see Rebecca Walkowitz, *Cosmopolitan Style: Modernism Beyond the Nation* (New York: Columbia University Press, 2006), 158–159.
30 See, for example, James Wood, 'The Arrival of Enigmas', *The New Yorker*, 28 February 2011.
31 Pieter Vermeulen, 'Flights of Memory: Teju Cole's *Open City* and the Limits of Aesthetic Cosmopolitanism', *Journal of Modern Literature*, 37:1 (Fall 2013), pp. 40–57 (41).
32 See Kwame Anthony Appiah, 'Cosmopolitan Patriots', *Critical Inquiry*, 23:3 (Spring 1997), pp. 617–639.
33 Kwame Anthony Appiah, *Cosmopolitanism: Ethics in a World of Strangers* (New York: Norton, 2006), 78. Emphasis in original.
34 Sollors, 'Cosmopolitan Curiosity', 232.
35 Lily Saint, 'From a Distance: Teju Cole, World Literature, and the Limits of Cosmopolitanism', *Novel*, 51:2 (2018), pp. 322–338 (335).
36 Claire Messud, 'The Secret Sharer: Review of *Open City*, by Teju Cole', *New York Review of Books*, 14 July 2011; Clark, '"Visible only in speech"', 194.
37 Karan Mahan, 'Black Noise', *n+1*, 11, October 2011.
38 Blindness is also a leitmotif in the novel. Julius sees two blind men on the subway, and contemplates the 'many romantic ideas attached to blindness' while at an exhibition of the deaf artist John Brewster (37). Later, Farouq will discuss the work of Paul de Man, and his 'theory of an insight that can actually obscure other things, that can be a blindness. And the reverse' (127).
39 Lyndsey Stonebridge, *The Judicial Imagination: Writing after Nuremberg* (Edinburgh: Edinburgh University Press, 2011), 101.
40 Mengestu, *How to Read the Air*, 26.
41 See James Dawes, *The Novel of Human Rights* (Cambridge, MA: Harvard University Press, 2018), 44–51.
42 Jacobs, 'Teju Cole's Photographic Afterimages', 102.
43 Josh Epstein, '*Open City*'s "Abschied": Teju Cole, Gustav Mahler, and Elliptical Cosmopolitanism', *Studies in the Novel*, 51:3 (Fall 2019), pp. 412–432 (413).

44 Michael Rothberg, *Multidirectional Memory: Remembering the Holocaust in the Age of Decolinization* (Stanford: Stanford University Press, 2009), 41.
45 Rothberg, *Multidirectional Memory*, 41, 21. Rothberg usefully employs Benjamin's concept of the 'crystallised constellation' to describe Arendt's approach (44). Cole is also familiar with the concept, writing in an essay of the need to 'think constellationally' about race. Cole, 'The White Savior Industrial Complex', 344.
46 Hannah Arendt, *The Origins of Totalitarianism* [1951] (London: André Deutsch, 1986), 275.
47 Arendt, *Origins*, 277.
48 Lyndsey Stonebridge. *Placeless People: Writing, Rights, and Refugees* (Oxford: Oxford University Press, 2018), 14–15.
49 Stonebridge, *Placeless People*, 21.
50 Stonebridge, *The Judicial Imagination*, 103.
51 Judith Butler, *Parting Ways: Jewishness and the Critique of Zionism* (New York: Columbia University Press, 2012), 131.
52 See Hannah Arendt, *Eichmann in Jerusalem: A Report on the Banality of Evil* [1963] (London: Penguin, 2006).
53 Hannah Arendt, Letter to Scholem dated July 20, 1963, in Marie Luise Knott (ed.), *The Correspondence of Hannah Arendt and Gershom Scholem*, ed. Marie Luise Knott, trans. Anthony David (Chicago: University of Chicago Press, 2017), pp. 205–210 (206).
54 Hannah Arendt, *Men in Dark Times* [1968] (New York: Harcourt Brace & Company, 1983), 254.
55 Hannah Arendt, *The Promise of Politics*, ed. Jerome Kohn (New York: Schocken Books, 2005), 17–18.
56 Arendt, *Promise of Politics*, 16–17; Hannah Arendt, *The Human Condition* [1958] (Chicago: University of Chicago, 1998), 52.
57 Jon Nixon, *Hannah Arendt and the Politics of Friendship* (London: Bloomsbury, 2015), 28.
58 Stonebridge, *Placeless People*, 10.
59 See Stonebridge, *Judicial Imagination*, 102.
60 Mahan, 'Black Noise'
61 See Arendt, *Eichmann in Jerusalem*; Robert Eaglestone, *Broken Voice: Reading Post-Holocaust Literature* (Oxford: Oxford University Press, 2017), 34.
62 Tahar Ben Jelloun, *The Last Friend*, trans. Kevin Michel Capé and Hazel Rowley [French, 2004] (New York: New Press, 2006), 181.
63 Cole, 'The White Savior Industrial Complex', 340.

Conclusion

Greg Marnier, the protagonist of Benjamin Markovits's 2015 novel *You Don't Have to Live Like This*, has a pretty clear notion of what people really want:

> Small-town life, free time. People have this idea that they hate big government. But what they don't like is national government. It's a category mistake. And if you keep things local, if you pool together, if you help each other out, you can live pretty well without chasing the buck.[1]

This desire for life lived at the local level leads thirty-something 'Marny' to ditch an unpromising academic career and sign up for 'Start-from-scratch-in-America', a project begun by Robert James, an old friend from Yale with deep pockets and grand political ambitions. Robert's big idea is a 'Groupon model for gentrification', in which investors buy up and rent out vast swaths of dirt-cheap domestic and commercial real estate in Detroit, a city that has suffered from white-flight and federal underfunding since the 1960s, and which was particularly badly hit by the stock market crash of 2008, when much of the novel is set (17).[2] Backed by Goldman Sachs, 'Start-from-scratch-in-America' seems a quintessential neoliberal start-up, a 'private-public partnership' aiming to attract a young 'creative class' handpicked on Facebook to revive the Rust Belt city; Detroit witnessed many such 'regeneration' projects following the credit crunch (55).[3] Robert acknowledges that, for 'Start-from-scratch-in-America' to work, 'somebody would have to get rich off it', but he isn't motivated only by profit (48). Part of the impetus behind the project is Robert's desire to rekindle something of the feeling of 'community' he had at Yale (36). Like Norman Rush's *Subtle Bodies*, *You Don't Have to Live Like This* is a novel which takes seriously the idea that, as Marny puts it, 'college friendships can take a lot of explaining', and that their influence can last a lifetime (169).[4] Robert had always 'cared a lot about secret societies' as an undergraduate, and it is clear that 'Start-from-scratch-in-America' – planned as a series of neighbourhoods that each roughly equate to 'a midsize college campus' – is in part imagined as an updated version of collegiate life (39).

But like James Rouse, the entrepreneur behind Michael Chabon's hometown of Columbia, Maryland, Robert sees the project as part of a 'tradition' of 'small-town community' living that has its origins in 'the founding of this country', earnestly describing Marny and the other volunteers as belonging to a lineage of 'pioneers' reaching back to 'the pilgrims' and 'early settlers' (169, 53). His bookshelves are filled with old college editions of '*Democracy in America*, *The Republic*, and *Of Mice and Men*', which gives a sense not only of the political and philosophical genealogy he has in mind – and which I have discussed in previous chapters – but of the connection between the themes of political community, citizenship, and male friendship that the novel will explore (33).

Because Marny's academic specialism is 'American colonial history', Robert is keen to have his old friend on board to 'take the long view' and to interpret their project in Detroit within a broader historical context (53). In Chapter 1, I explored how Roth's American Trilogy also took the 'long view' of American democracy, connecting the politics of the 1990s to a series of earlier periods in US history. Reviewers of *You Don't Have to Live Like This* compared the novel's first-person narrative structure to *The Great Gatsby* (1925), a parallel Markovits winks at when Marny – a Yalie like Nick Carraway – describes Robert's grand mansion as 'like something from the 1920s' (31).[5] But a more immediate model might be Nathan Zuckerman's role in Roth's novels. In a review of his late novella *Everyman* (2006), Markovits notes that one of Roth's great themes is 'the growth and decay of big cities', a concern *You Don't Have to Live Like This* shares, and ventures the unpopular critical opinion that *I Married a Communist* is 'one of Roth's best novels', the strongest of 'the Zuckerman sequence', because it is most 'driven by a sharp sense, both political and personal, of what matters and what doesn't' – echoing Roth's comment that the trilogy explores 'the joining of the public and the private'.[6] Like Murray Ringold, Greg's father worked as a 'union organizer' – of journalists rather than teachers – and, given Markovits's admiration for Roth's novel of Popular Front political culture, it is not entirely surprising to find a precocious young Greg Marnier reading 'Sandburg's life of Lincoln' (3, 2).

It is the presence of another president that is more strongly felt in the novel. Obama has an important cameo appearance in *You Don't Have to Live Like This*, Markovits using the figure of the first black President to highlight issues of race and representation that the rest of the novel will explore further, just as Chabon does in *Telegraph Avenue*. After speaking at a fundraising event at Robert's house, Obama spots a basketball hoop over the garage door and organises a game of three-on-three out on the driveway. Basketball is the focus of Markovits's semi-autobiographical novel *Playing Days* (2010) – based on his experience playing professionally for a season in Germany – and sport is the subject of much of his journalism.[7] In a profile piece on the NBA All-Star legend LeBron James, Markovits reflects that 'being an athlete teaches you pretty quickly where you belong in the scale of things', but, in imagining the larger-than-life Obama hustling on the backyard basketball court, *You Don't Have to Live Like This* subtly plays with the understandings of scale.[8] Marny is charged with guarding the President and is enjoying the game before he realises that his teammate Robert is 'pissed off'. 'Maybe', he speculates, 'it was a racial thing':

> Robert played varsity basketball for Claremont High. They had one of those teams where the uniforms don't show your name. The way Robert was brought up, you played hard and you made the extra pass [...] And you didn't talk. But Obama liked to run his mouth. (189)

On the confines of the court, then, the 'racial thing' dividing Obama and white liberal Ivy League supporters like Robert becomes ambiguously accentuated, their game seeming to refract the national debate about race that Obama's election heralded.[9]

Like boxing and dancing in *The Human Stain*, or the summer-long games of 'skully' on Dean Street in *The Fortress of Solitude*, basketball becomes an evocative metaphor in *You Don't Have to Live Like This*, capturing the distinctly male and racially charged mix of rough-and-tumble intimacy and edgy competitiveness that defines personal relations in the novel not only between the hoops but out on the streets of Detroit.

Most of those moving to New Jamestown – as the neighbourhoods of the 'Start-from-scratch-in-America' enclave quickly come to be called – are white.[10] Like the mostly middle-class back-to-the-city 'pioneers' of the 1960s and 1970s portrayed in *The Fortress of Solitude*, the 'Groupon settlers' are a motley mix of 'potheads and Marxists', as well as a few 'Tea Party types' with a 'libertarian streak' (229, 127). As in Lethem's novel, the confrontation between the new arrivals and the existing black working-class population is focalised through a central interracial male friendship. Like Nathan Zuckerman, Marny is something of a 'sucker for manly intimacy'.[11] 'The thing about you', Robert tells him, 'is that you're the kind of guy who falls in love with guys, I don't mean like a gay thing, but you get ideas about them and you can't see straight' (227). Nolan Smith – a gruff would-be artist and single father who lives down the street – is one of the men Marny gets 'ideas about', although their relationship is always fraught. 'You like me', Nolan says to him, 'you're kind of scared of me, but you still think you're smarter than me because I'm black' (144). But Nolan opens up to Marny about his art and particularly his love for music, which was fostered as a kid by spending time at 'Jez's place':

> There used to be a record shop on Charlevoix, run by a white guy named Jez Lansky, who's been at the corner since the neighborhood was about a quarter Polish. Probably he'd have got robbed out of business or beaten up if people didn't like his records. But he played a lot of good music [...] Mable John and Billy Eckstine, Art Blakey and Horace Silver and Clifford Brown. Nolan's dad used to say, 'Jez is all right, you can hang out at Jez's'. (141)

Jez's place is another corner-store utopia, like the Brooklyn Cigar Company, Brokeland Records, Logan Circle Market, or Farouq's internet café. But the kinds of hangouts being started up by the white New Jamestown gentrifiers serve only to exacerbate the racial divide defining their neighbourhood. 'You didn't see many black faces at Joe Silver's coffeehouse', Marny admits, noting that 'most of the old residents kept to themselves' (151).

New Jamestown is also an experiment in Silicon Valley-style social engineering, an attempt to 'take a virtual community and make it real, give it real estate, fill it with people', as the Zuckerberg-esque software developer Nathan Zwecker puts it (153).[12] Zwecker's task is to augment the process of gentrification taking place on the streets of Detroit with an 'E-change' online platform that functions as a local auction site for goods and services, with a built-in ranking system in which users are rated for their friendliness and helpfulness, but also monitored for inappropriate behaviour. As Marny's friend Steve Zipp explains, users are marked on whether they 'show up on time, can they keep up their end of the conversation [...] Do they spend all their time checking their phones?' Marny points out that Steve checks his phone 'constantly' when they're together. 'That's because you're a real friend', Steve replies, 'I would never behave that way with a virtual friend. It kills your rating' (154–155). Like Auster, then, Markovits is interested in the indeterminacy between genuine and counterfeit friendship; and, like Chabon in his portrayal of Julie and Titus's friendship moving into the online Marvel Comics Universe, Markovits here explores how the virtual world bleeds into reality, and considers the effects on our social relations. In this regard, New Jamestown's E-change recalls Dave Eggers's portrayal of a Google-esque tech giant in *The Circle* (2013), a novel that also explores the dystopian tenor of some of Silicon Valley's grand projects of interconnectedness, and similarly points to the way 'real' friendship is distorted and devalued in an age of Facebook friends.[13]

Marny, however is something of a 'Luddite', and keeps off the E-change because his real life is 'filling out nicely' (155). He becomes one of the more unlikely success stories of New Jamestown when he begins teaching at the local school and dating Gloria, a black teacher. But Marny's attempts to enter into 'new relations with people', and especially black people, are met with scepticism from some of those around him (89). Tony, a combative Italian American and native Detroiter, warns him:

Don't expect me to say that some of my best friends are black. My best friends *aren't* black [...] I know some brothers, and like a few, too, but there's a point beyond which I don't really understand or trust them, and to be honest, the black guys I respect are the ones who feel the same about me. (63, emphasis in original)

Greg's brother Brad – a high-flying businessman who still 'dresses like a frat boy on spring break' – also questions whether the New Jamestown vision of small-town integrated community is really what people aspire to (258). 'You're kidding yourself', he says to Marny, 'if you think that Americans want to help each other out. That's not what I pay my taxes for. I pay my taxes so that other people are not my problem' (268). Brad sounds a little like Goldstine, the factory boss in *I Married a Communist*, espousing a similar conception of negative liberty, wherein the bonds of citizenship and political community are attenuated in the name of protecting personal freedom. Marny's opposing belief in positive liberty is tested when two high-profile and racialised crimes spark protests in the city; as in Logan Circle in *The Beautiful Things that Heaven Bears*, the utopian gentrification project in New Jamestown descends into dystopian violence. The second crime involves Tony and Nolan, embroiling them and Marny in a bitter legal wrangle. Marny clings to 'this idea, maybe it was a stupid idea, that Tony and Nolan could work out their differences personally, and leave the law out of it' (316). But his attempts at local democracy and the negotiation of justice between friends is quickly engulfed by a tide of court proceedings. Reflecting on his experience of the law, Marny notes that 'you realise pretty quickly that you are in the hands of massive but at the same time small-scale forces' (334). Throughout the novel Markovits explores how the scales of the national and local intersect in New Jamestown, and how easy it is to make a 'category mistake' between the two when you are trying to effect broad political change through your personal relationships.

Marny is no paragon of virtue, however, nor simply a naive liberal caught in the system. One of the defining ambiguities of the novel is whether, as Markovits notes in an interview, Marny is part of 'the problem or the solution'.[14] Like Dylan in *The Fortress of Solitude*, Greg is 'a little bit off about race', and often his attitude to black culture is not friendly but appropriative.[15] When he starts dating Gloria, for example, he begins 'reading a lot of African-American literature' and is 'a little ashamed' that he develops a 'taste for it' (222). In these moments, Markovits points to the problems of addressing race in fiction, and especially the difficulties of white authors writing black characters. He explores these tensions further in an article published shortly after *You Don't Have to Live Like This*, in which he revisits *The Adventures of Huckleberry Finn* in light of contemporary debates about 'transracial' identity.[16] Markovits approvingly quotes Norman Mailer's observation – made in 1984 on the hundredth anniversary of the publication of Twain's classic – that 'Riding the current of [*Huckleberry Finn*], we are back in that happy time when the love affair [between whites and blacks] was new and all seemed possible'.[17] This sounds a lot like Leslie Fiedler's earlier judgement of Huck and Jim's friendship, and Markovits surveys the contemporary literary scene for updated portrayals of this archetypal interracial 'love affair'. He discusses Nathan and Coleman's relationship in *The Human Stain* before noting how 'Jonathan Lethem in *The Fortress of Solitude* and Michael Chabon in *Telegraph Avenue* have not only written about black characters (from a white point of view) but adopted their voices as well'.[18] Highlighting how these authors self-consciously position themselves as part of a genealogy of American fiction reaching back to the nineteenth century, Markovits aligns his own work with this tradition.

Just as Chabon revisits his childhood in Columbia, Maryland, to write about race relations in Oakland, Markovits reflects on his very different 'experience of that love affair' growing up in Texas and being bused to a majority black school where he had 'no black friends' – a backstory he also gives to Marny (222). Markovits seems to have been particularly attuned to the question of race not only because of the demographics of his hometown but because his own ethnic identity seemed to him curiously fluid growing up. The son of a Jewish American father and a Protestant, German-born mother, Markovits reflects elsewhere that his 'Jewishness wasn't a simple matter growing up' and that, while he felt 'very Jewish in Texas', he now usually identifies as 'half-Jewish'.[19] In his *Huckleberry Finn* essay, Markovits notes that *The Human Stain* is invested in the question of whether 'the Jewish experience and the black experience are translatable into each other'. Although this issue isn't explicitly raised in *You Don't Have to Live Like This* – Marny isn't Jewish – Markovits's approach to the troubled 'love affair' between blacks and whites follows a similar pattern to that of the black–Jewish friendships discussed in previous chapters, in which male friendship becomes a prism through which to explore both the solidarities and the tensions – racialised or otherwise – underwriting American society more broadly.[20] Troubling the scales of the liberal imaginary, the interstitiality of friendship allows all of the authors discussed in this book to query how the public and the private sphere relate to and inform each another – both in reality and in our utopian political fantasies – and to probe the 'category mistakes' of the national and the local, the personal and the political, that shape and distort American life.

In the *Huckleberry Finn* essay, Markovits observes that 'the great failure of the American novel is that it has not adequately addressed the diversity of the American experience for fear of getting *the other* wrong'. One insight that Markovits seems to glean from his reading of Roth's American Trilogy is that getting other people wrong is an inevitability, that life is an extended schooling in our shared ignorance of one another, and that, if this is a source of fear that risks atomising us, it might also be a source of hope that brings us together. It can lead, for example, to the kind of open-ended, late-in-life conversation between Nathan and Murray that structures *I Married a Communist*, in which nothing is off the table, and in which each man helps the other in pulling together the pieces of the past. Or it can lead to the fraught, potentially life-changing acts of generosity that crisscross Paul Auster's fiction, in which fear and hope often intermingle in the ambiguous gifts that are the currency of friendship in his work. Or it can result in the interracial 'love affairs' at the centre of Chabon and Lethem's neighbourhood novels, where the fantasies and frustrations of integration are shown in their tangled historical context. Or it can give rise to the immigrant friendships keeping Sepha afloat in *The Beautiful Things that Heaven Bears*, or perhaps only the faltering Arendtian dialogue that can briefly be heard above the hum of computers in Farouq's internet café.

In *Subtle Bodies*, Ned remembers how he and his college buddies had hoped to 'somehow generaliz[e] their friendship' into a broader politics.[21] Over the course of this book, I have demonstrated the longevity and tenacity of that hope in US fiction and in American politics more broadly. For the authors I have discussed, male friendship continues to be a figure through which they can imagine and interrogate the forms of intersubjectivity and alliance that shape a life and a political community, to reveal that, ultimately, we are, to recall Greg's phrase, 'in the hands of massive but at the same time small-scale forces'. Beginning with portrayals of friendship between two men, these novels plot larger stories of affinity and solidarity that reach back into American history and out to a broader context. Listening to the intimate talk of friends, they bring readers into a larger conversation about what might connect and divide us as members of a community and as citizens, uncovering the imaginative and political possibilities of reordering the world with, in Ned's words, 'friendship at the core of everything'.

Notes

1 Benjamin Markovits, *You Don't Have to Live Like This* (London: Faber and Faber, 2015), 267. Subsequent references are given in the text in parentheses.
2 See Thomas Sugrue, *The Origins of the Urban Crisis: Race and Inequality in Postwar Detroit* [1996] (Princeton: Princeton University Press, 2005); Monica Davey and Mary Williams Walsh, 'For Detroit, a Crisis of Bad Decisions and Crossed Fingers', *New York Times*, 11 March 2013.
3 Marny refers to Richard Florida, the sociologist who popularised the term 'creative class' in *The Rise of the Creative Class: And How It's Transforming Work, Leisure and Everyday Life* (New York: Basic Books, 2002). On Detroit's post-2008 gentrification, see Peter Moskowitz, *How to Kill a City: Gentrification, Inequality, and the Fight for the Neighborhood* (New York: Hachette, 2017), 35–67.
4 Marny's time at Yale featured much more prominently in early drafts of the novel, which included a section on the friends' ten-year reunion. See Benjamin Markovits, 'Editorial Outtakes: Benjamin Markovits', *American Short Fiction*, 23 September 2015 [online].

5 See Francesca Wade, '"You Don't Have to Live Like This", by Benjamin Markovits', *Financial Times*, 24 July 2015.
6 Benjamin Markovits, 'A Morality Story', *Times Literary Supplement*, 5 May 2006, pp. 21–22 (21); David Remnick, 'Philip Roth at 70' [Interview], Dir. Deborah Lee, BBC4 (7 May 2003). Markovits paid tribute to Roth in 'The Great American Novelist: Philip Roth 1933–2018', *Times Literary Supplement*, 1 June 2018, p. 17.
7 Markovits briefly wrote a sports column for the *New Statesman*. See, for example, 'Benjamin Markovits Misses a Hoop', *New Statesman*, 22 May 2006. His more recent 'Essinger' novels, *A Weekend in New York* (London: Faber and Faber, 2018) and *Christmas in Austin* (London: Faber and Faber, 2019), concern a professional tennis player and his family.
8 Benjamin Markovits, 'Just Undo It: The LeBron James Profile that Nike Killed', *Deadspin*, 10, July 2014. In *Playing Days*, the narrator Ben describes training with wunder-kid Karl: 'He seemed to be moving according to a different scale'. *Playing Days* (London: Faber and Faber, 2005), 28.
9 Markovits reflects on the role of basketball in African American culture in 'The Colours of Sport', *New Left Review*, 22 (July/August 2003), pp. 151–160. He explores Obama's relationship with the game in 'A New Global Game?', *New Statesman*, 15 January 2009, p. 28.
10 Jamestown, Virginia, was the first permanent English settlement in the Americas, established in 1607.
11 Roth, *I Married a Communist*, 233.
12 In *Telegraph Avenue*, Archy resolves that is is 'time to get *real*', and starts 'selling *real* estate' (617; emphasis in original).
13 See Betsy Morais, 'Sharing Is Caring Is Sharing', *The New Yorker*, 30 October 2013.
14 Alan Bett, 'Benjamin Markovits: Class War in Rust Belt America', *The Skinny*, 12 September 2016.
15 Bett, 'Benjamin Markovits'. Elsewhere, Markovits says 'My idea was to make Marny both sympathetic and not entirely likable – he's got an honesty-kick that leaves him a little exposed on the page'. Markovits, '"Editorial Outtakes"'.
16 Benjamin Markovits, 'The Adventures of Huckleberry Finn: How to Write about Race in the US', *The Guardian*, 1 August 2015.
17 Markovits, 'The Adventures of Huckleberry Finn'. See Norman Mailer, 'Huckleberry Finn, Alive at 100', *New York Times*, 9 December 1984.
18 Markovits, 'The Adventures of Huckleberry Finn'. Markovits has reviewed two of Chabon's novels. See 'A Crack in the Ordinary', *Times*

Literary Supplement, 15 November 2002, p. 23; 'The Parrot Holds the Key', *The Telegraph*, 20 February 2005.
19 Markovits, 'The Allegiance that I Can't Quite Pledge', *New Statesman*, 17 November 2003, p. 26. In *Playing Days*, the narrator Ben shares Markovits's background, and similarly says that his 'relationship to Jewishness has never been straightforward' (64).
20 There are other Jewish characters in *You Don't Have to Live Like This*, however, including Jack Rosen, who describes his family as 'settlers' in New Jamestown, and compares his pioneering relocation from New Jersey to that of 'boys I knew from synagogue in Port Jervis' who 'moved to Katzrin', an Israeli settlement in the Golan Heights (127).
21 Norman Rush, *Subtle Bodies* (New York: Knopf, 2013), 12.

Bibliography

Agamben, Giorgio, *Potentialities: Collected Essays in Philosophy*, trans. Daniel Heller-Roazen (Stanford: Stanford University Press, 1999).

Agamben, Giorgio, *What Is an Apparatus?*, trans. David Kishik and Stefan Pedatella (Stanford: Stanford University Press, 2009).

Aldrige, Owen, *Thomas Paine's American Ideology* (Newark: University of Delaware Press, 1984).

Alexander, Edward, *Classical Liberalism and the Jewish Tradition* (New Brunswick: Transaction, 2003).

Alford, Steven 'Chance in Contemporary Narrative: The Example of Paul Auster', *Lit: Literature Interpretation Theory*, 11:1 (2000), pp 59–82.

Allen, Danielle, *Talking to Strangers: Anxieties of Citizenship since Brown v. Board of Education* (Chicago: University of Chicago Press, 2004).

Allen, Robert, *The Port Chicago Mutiny: The Story of the Largest Mass Mutiny Trial in U.S. Naval History* (Berkeley: Heyday Books, 1993).

Allen, Robert, *Brotherhood of Sleeping Car Porters: C. L. Dellums and the Fight for Fair Treatment and Civil Rights* (London: Routledge, 2015).

Alter, Robert, 'The Spritzer: Review of *Operation Shylock*', *The New Republic*, 5 April 1993, p. 31.

Altman, Janet, *Epistolarity: Approaches to a Form* (Columbus: Ohio State University Press, 1982).

Amin, Ash and Nigel Thrift, *Arts of the Political: New Openings for the Left* (Durham, NC: Duke University Press, 2013).

Anderson, Benedict, *Imagined Communities: Reflections on the Origin and Spread of Nationalism* [1983] (London: Verso, 2006).

Anderson, Terry, *The Movement and the Sixties: Protest in America from Greensboro to Wounded Knee* (New York: Oxford University Press, 1995).

Appiah, Kwame Anthony, 'Cosmopolitan Patriots', *Critical Inquiry*, 23:3 (Spring 1997), pp. 617–639.

Appiah, Kwame Anthony, *Cosmopolitanism: Ethics in a World of Strangers* (New York: Norton, 2006).
Arce, Maria Laura, *Paul Auster and the Influence of Maurice Blanchot* (Jefferson: McFarland, 2016).
Arendt, Hannah, *The Origins of Totalitarianism* [1951] (London: André Deutsch, 1986).
Arendt, Hannah, *The Human Condition* [1958] (Chicago: University of Chicago, 1998).
Arendt, Hannah, *Eichmann in Jerusalem: A Report on the Banality of Evil* [1963] (London: Penguin, 2006).
Arendt, Hannah, *Men in Dark Times* [1968] (New York: Harcourt Brace & Company, 1983).
Arendt, Hannah, *The Promise of Politics*, ed. Jerome Kohn (New York: Schocken Books, 2005).
Arendt, Hannah and Gershom Scholem, *The Correspondence of Hannah Arendt and Gershom Scholem*, ed. Marie Luise Knott, trans. Anthony David (Chicago: University of Chicago Press, 2017).
Aristotle, *Nicomachean Ethics*, trans. Roger Crisp (Cambridge: Cambridge University Press, 2000).
Ashbolt, Anthony, *A Cultural History of the Radical Sixties in the San Francisco Bay Area* (London: Pickering & Chatto, 2013).
Auster, Paul, 'Kafka's Letters' [1977], in *The Art of Hunger: Essays, Prefaces, Interviews* [1992] (New York: Penguin, 1997), pp. 134–139.
Auster, *The Invention of Solitude* (1982), in *Collected Prose*, pp. 1–150.
Auster, Paul, *The New York Trilogy* [1987] (London: Faber and Faber, 2005).
Auster, Paul, *In the Country of Last Things* (London: Faber and Faber, 1987).
Auster, Paul, *The Music of Chance* (London: Faber and Faber, 1990).
Auster, Paul, 'Auggie Wren's Christmas Story' (1990), in *Collected Screenplays*, pp. 141–147.
Auster, Paul, *Leviathan* (London: Faber and Faber, 1992).
Auster, Paul, *Mr. Vertigo* (London: Faber and Faber, 1994).
Auster, Paul, *Smoke* (1995), in *Collected Screenplays*, pp. 21–140.
Auster, Paul, *Hand to Mouth* (1997), in *Collected Prose*, pp. 151–240.
Auster, Paul, *Collected Prose* (London: Faber and Faber, 2003).
Auster, Paul, *The Brooklyn Follies* (London: Faber and Faber, 2005).
Auster, Paul, *Oracle Night* (London: Faber and Faber, 2008).
Auster, Paul, 'The Accidental Rebel', *New York Times*, 23 April 2008, A21.
Auster, Paul, *Collected Screenplays* (London: Faber and Faber, 2010).
Auster, Paul, '*Leviathan*: Drafts', Box 3, Folder 3, The Paul Auster Collection of Papers, 1987–2001 (bulk 1995–1999), The Henry W. and Albert A. Berg Collection, The New York Public Library.

Auster, Paul, '*Smoke*: Film Treatment by Paul Auster and Siri Hustvedt', Box 43, Folder 2, The Paul Auster Collection of Papers, 1987–2001 (bulk 1995–1999), The Henry W. and Albert A. Berg Collection, The New York Public Library.

Auster, Paul, 'Oracle Night Drafts', Box 23, Folder 1, The Paul Auster Collection of Papers, 1999–2006 (bulk 2000–2005), The Henry W. and Albert A. Berg Collection, The New York Public Library.

Auster, Paul and Sophie Calle, 'Gotham Handbook' (1994), in *Collected Prose*, pp. 283–292.

Auster, Paul and J. M. Coetzee, *Here and Now: Letters, 2008–2011* (London: Faber and Faber, 2013).

Auster, Paul and I. B. Siegumfeldt, *A Life in Words* (New York: Seven Stories Press, 2017).

Badwhar, Neera Kapur (ed.), *Friendship: A Philosophical Reader* (Ithaca: Cornell University Press, 1993).

Bakhtin, Mikhail, *Speech Genres and Other Late Essays*, trans. Vern McGee (Austin: University of Texas Press, 1986).

Barone, Paul (ed.), *Beyond the Red Notebook: Essays on Paul Auster* (Philadelphia: University of Pennsylvania Press, 1995).

Barone, Paul, 'Introduction: Paul Auster and the Postmodern American Novel', in Barone (ed.), *Beyond the Red Notebook: Essays on Paul Auster* (Philadelphia: University of Pennsylvania Press, 1995), pp. 1–26.

Barrett, John, 'Rethinking the Popular Front', *Rethinking Marxism*, 21:4 (2009), pp. 513–550.

Basu, Ann, *States of Trial: Manhood in Philip Roth's Post-War America* (London: Bloomsbury, 2015).

Bates, Beth Tompkins, *Pullman Porters and the Rise of Protest Politics in Black America, 1925–1945* (Chapel Hill: University of North Carolina Press, 2001).

Bauman, Zygmunt, *In Search of Politics* (Stanford: Stanford University Press, 1999).

Bauman, Zygmunt, *Liquid Modernity* (Cambridge: Polity, 2000).

Begley, Adam, 'Case of the Brooklyn Symbolist', *New York Times Magazine*, 30 August 1993, pp. 41, 52–54.

Bellah, Robert, Richard Madsen, William Sullivan, Ann Swidler, and Steven Tipton, *Habits of the Heart: Individualism and Commitment in American Life* [1985] (Berkeley: University of California Press, 2008).

Bellow, Saul, Letter to Roth dated January 1, 1998, in Benjamin Taylor (ed.), *Saul Bellow: Letters* (New York: Viking, 2010), p. 540.

Benjamin, Walter, *Illuminations*, trans. Harry Zohn (New York: Schocken Books, 1968).

Berlant, Lauren, *The Anatomy of National Fantasy: Hawthorne, Utopia, and Everyday Life* (Chicago: University of Chicago Press, 1991).

Berlant, Lauren, "'68, or Something', *Critical Inquiry*, 21:1 (1994), pp. 124–155.

Berlant, Lauren, *The Queen of America Goes to Washington City: Essays on Sex and Citizenship* (Durham, NC: Duke University Press, 1997).

Berlant, Lauren, *Cruel Optimism* (Durham, NC: Duke University Press, 2011).

Berman, Marshall, 'Dancing with America: Philip Roth, Writer on the Left', *New Labor Forum*, 9 (Winter 2001), pp. 46–56.

Berman, Morris, *The Twilight of American Culture* (New York: Norton, 2000).

Berman, Morris, *Dark Ages America: The Final Phase of Empire* (New York: Norton, 2006).

Bett, Alan, 'Benjamin Markovits: Class War in Rust Belt America', *The Skinny*, 12 September 2016.

Bhabha, Homi, *The Location of Culture* (London: Routledge, 1994).

Birkerts, Sven, 'Postmodern Picaresque', *The New Republic*, 27 March 1989, pp. 36–40.

Blades, John, 'City of Smoke and Dreams', *Chicago Tribune*, 5 November 1995.

Blanchot, Maurice, *Friendship*, trans. Elizabeth Rottenberg [1971] (Stanford: Stanford University Press, 1997).

Blanchot, Maurice, *The Unavowable Community*, trans. Pierre Joris (Barrytown: Station Hill Press, 1988).

Bloch, Ernst, 'Nonsynchronism and the Obligation to Its Dialectics', *New German Critique*, 11 (Spring 1977), pp. 22–38.

Bloch, Ernst, *The Utopian Function of Art and Literature: Selected Essays*, trans. Jack Zipes and Frank Mecklenburg (Cambridge, MA: MIT Press, 1988).

Bloom, Nicholas, *Suburban Alchemy: 1960s New Towns and the Transformation of the American Dream* (Columbus: Ohio State University Press, 2001).

Bloom, Nicholas, *Merchant of Illusion: James Rouse, America's Salesman of the Businessman's Utopia* (Columbus: Ohio State University Press, 2004).

Boddy, Kasia, *Boxing: A Cultural History* (London: Reaktion Books, 2008).

Boddy, Kasia, 'Philip Roth's Great Books: A Reading of *The Human Stain*', *Cambridge Quarterly*, 39:1 (March 2010), pp. 39–60.

Boddy, Kasia, 'Family', in Stephen Burn (ed.), *American Literature in Transition, 1990–2000* (Cambridge: Cambridge University Press, 2018), pp. 312–328.

Booth, Wayne, *The Company We Keep: An Ethics of Reading* (Chicago: University of Chicago Press, 1983).

Booth, Wayne, 'Why Banning Ethical Criticism Is a Serious Mistake', *Philosophy and Literature*, 22:2 (1998), pp. 366–393.
Boxall, Peter, *Twenty-First-Century Fiction: A Critical Introduction* (Cambridge: Cambridge University Press, 2013).
Boym, Svetlana, *The Future of Nostalgia* (New York: Basic Books, 2001).
Brauner, David, *Post-War Jewish Fiction: Ambivalence, Self-Explanation and Transatlantic Connections* (London: Palgrave, 2001).
Brauner, David, *Philip Roth* (Manchester: Manchester University Press, 2007).
Brauner, David, 'Essay Review: The Canonization of Philip Roth', *Studies in the Novel*, 39:4 (Winter 2007), pp. 481–488.
Brauner, David, 'Fifty Ways to See Your Lover: Vision and Revision in the Fiction of Amy Bloom', in Axel Stähler (ed.), *Anglophone Jewish Literature* (London: Routledge, 2007), pp. 108–120.
Brauner, David, *Contemporary American Fiction* (Edinburgh: Edinburgh University Press, 2010).
Brauner, David, 'Queering Philip Roth: Homosocial Discourse in "An Actor's Life for Me," *Letting Go*, *Sabbath's Theater*, and the "American Trilogy"', *Studies in the Novel*, 48:1 (Spring 2016), pp. 86–106.
Brauner, David, 'Performance Anxiety: Impotence, Queerness, and the 'Drama of Self-Disgust' in Philip Roth's *The Professor of Desire* and *The Humbling*', in David Gooblar and Aimee Pozorski (eds), *Roth After Eighty: Philip Roth and the American Literary Imagination* (Lanham: Lexington Books, 2016), pp. 61–78.
Bray, Alan, *The Friend* (Chicago: University of Chicago Press, 2003).
Breines, Wini, 'Community and Organization: The New Left and Michels' "Iron Law"', *Social Problems*, 27:4 (April 1980), pp. 419–429.
Breines, Wini, *Community and Organization in the New Left* (New Brunswick: Rutgers University Press, 1989).
Brooks, Daphne, '"Bring the Pain": Post-Soul Memory, Neo-Soul Affect, and Lauryn Hill in the Black Public Sphere', in Nicholas Cook and Richard Pettengill (eds), *Bringing It to the Bridge: Music as Performance* (Ann Arbor: University of Michigan Press, 2013), pp. 180–203.
Browder, Earl, *Lincoln and the Communists* (New York: Worker's Library, 1936).
Brown, James Patrick, 'The Disobedience of John William Ward: Myth, Symbol, and Political Praxis in the Vietnam Era', *American Studies*, 47:2 (Summer 2006), pp. 5–22.
Brown, Mark, *Paul Auster* (Manchester: Manchester University Press, 2007).
Bruckner, Pascal, 'Paul Auster, or The Heir Intestate', in Paul Barone (ed.), *Beyond the Red Notebook: Essays on Paul Auster* (Philadelphia: University of Pennsylvania Press, 1995), pp. 27–33.

Brühwiler, Claudia Franziska, *Political Initiation in the Novels of Philip Roth* (London: Bloomsbury, 2013).
Budick, Emily Miller, *Blacks and Jews in Literary Conversation* (Cambridge: Cambridge University Press, 1998).
Buell, Lawrence, 'Observer-Hero Narrative', *Texas Studies in Literature and Language*, 21 (1979), pp. 93–111.
Buell, Lawrence, *The Environmental Imagination: Thoreau, Nature Writing, and the Formation of American Culture* (Cambridge, MA: Harvard University Press, 1995).
Buell, Lawrence, 'In Pursuit of Ethics', *PMLA*, 114:1 (1999), pp. 7–19.
Buell, Lawrence, *The Dream of the Great American Novel* (Cambridge, MA: Harvard University Press, 2014).
Buhle, Paul, James Prickett, James Barrett, Rob Ruck, and Norman Markowitz, 'Revisiting American Communism: An Exchange', *New York Review of Books*, 15 August 1985, pp. 40–44.
Butler, Judith, *Parting Ways: Jewishness and the Critique of Zionism* (New York: Columbia University Press, 2012).
Calcagno, Antonio, *Badiou and Derrida: Politics, Events and Their Time* (London: Continuum, 2007).
Calle, Sophie, *The Address Book* [1983] (Los Angeles: Giglio Press, 2012).
Calle, Sophie, *Double Game* [1999] (London: Violette Editions, 2007).
Campbell, Julie, 'Beckett and Auster: Father and Sons and the Creativity of Misreading', in Linda Ben-Zvi and Angela Moorjani (eds), *Beckett at 100: Revolving It All* (Oxford: Oxford University Press, 2008), pp. 299–311.
Caputo, John D. and Michael J. Scanlon, *God, the Gift, and Postmodernism* (Bloomington: Indiana University Press, 1999).
Carstensen, Thorsten, 'Skepticism and Responsibility: Paul Auster's *The Book of Illusions*', *Critique: Studies in Contemporary Fiction*, 58:4 (2017), pp. 411–425.
Cassano, Graham, 'Returning to the Popular Front', *Rethinking Marxism*, 21:4 (2009), pp. 476–479.
Castiglia, Christopher, *Interior States: Institutional Consciousness and the Inner Life of Democracy in the Antebellum United States* (Durham, NC: Duke University Press, 2008).
Chabon, Michael, 'The Future Will Have to Wait', *The Long Now Foundation*, 22 January 2006.
Chabon, Michael, *The Yiddish Policemen's Union* (London: Harper Collins, 2007).
Chabon, Michael, 'Obama vs. the Phobocracy', *Washington Post*, 4 February 2008.
Chabon, Michael, 'An Article of Hope', 2008, www.michaelchabon.com/uncollected/political/obama/.

Chabon, Michael, 'Obama & the Conquest of Denver', *New York Review of Books*, 9 October 2008.
Chabon, Michael, 'Fountain City', *McSweeney's*. 36 (December 2010), pp. i–112.
Chabon, Michael, *Telegraph Avenue* (London: Fourth Estate, 2012).
Chabon, Michael, 'O. J. Simpson, Racial Utopia and the Moment that Inspired My Novel', *New York Times Magazine*, 27 September 2012.
Chandler, Aaron, 'Pursuing Unhappiness: City, Space, and Sentimentalism in Post-Cold War American Literature', PhD Thesis, University of North Carolina (2009).
Charles, Ron, 'There Goes the Neighborhood', *Christian Science Monitor*, 11 September 2003.
Cheah, Pheng and Suzanne Guerlac, 'Introduction', in Cheah and Guerlac (eds), *Derrida and the Time of the Political* (Durham, NC: Duke University Press, 2009), pp. 1–37.
Cheyette, Bryan, *Diasporas of the Mind: Jewish and Postcolonial Writing and the Nightmare of History* (New Haven: Yale University Press, 2013).
Chodat, Robert, 'Fictions Public and Private: On Philip Roth', *Contemporary Literature*, 46:4 (Winter 2005), pp. 688–719.
Chown, John, *A History of Money: From AD 800* (London: Routledge, 1994).
Chude-Sokei, Louis, 'The Newly Black Americans: African Immigrants and Black America', *Transition*, 113:1 (2014), pp. 52–71.
Clapp, Jeffrey and Emily Ridge (eds), *Security and Hospitality in Literature and Culture: Modern and Contemporary Perspectives* (London: Routledge, 2015).
Clark, Rebecca, '"Visible only in speech": Peripatetic Parasitism, or, Becoming Bedbugs in *Open City*', *Narrative*, 26:2 (May 2018), pp. 181–200.
Clarke, Jamie (ed.), *Conversations with Jonathan Lethem* (Jackson: University of Mississippi Press, 2011).
Cohen, Josh, 'Roth's Doubles', in Timothy Parrish (ed.), *The Cambridge Companion to Philip Roth* (Cambridge: Cambridge University Press, 2007), pp. 82–93.
Cohen, Robert and Reginald Zelnik (eds), *The Free Speech Movement: Reflections on Berkeley in the 1960s* (Berkeley: University of California Press, 2002).
Cohen, Samuel, *After the End of History: American Fiction in the 1990s* (Iowa City: University of Iowa Press, 2009).
Cole, Sarah, *Modernism, Male Friendship, and the First World War* (Cambridge: Cambridge University Press, 2003).
Cole, Teju, *Open City* (London: Faber and Faber, 2011).

Cole, Teju, *Known and Strange Things: Essays* (New York: Random House, 2016).
Cole, Teju, 'The White Savior Industrial Complex', in *Known and Strange Things*, pp. 340–349.
Cole, Teju, 'A Piece in the Wall', in *Known and Strange Things*, pp. 363–376.
Conn, Steven, *Americans Against the City: Anti-Urbanism in the Twentieth Century* (Oxford: Oxford University Press, 2014).
Connolly, Andy, *Philip Roth and the American Liberal Tradition* (Lanham: Lexington Books, 2017).
Cornish, Flora, Jan Haaken, Liora Moskovitz, and Sharon Jackson, 'Rethinking Prefigurative Politics', *Journal of Social and Political Psychology*, 4:1 (2016), pp. 114–127.
Corwin, Norman, *On a Note of Triumph* (New York: Simon & Schuster, 1945).
Coughlan, David, *Ghost Writing in Contemporary American Fiction* (Basingstoke: Palgrave Macmillan, 2016).
Crain, Caleb, *American Sympathy: Men, Friendship, and Literature in the New Nation* (New Haven: Yale University Press, 2001).
Crenson, Matthew and Benjamin Ginsberg, *Downsizing Democracy: How America Sidelined Its Citizens and Privatized Its Public* (Baltimore: Johns Hopkins University Press, 2002).
Crichlow, Michaeline, *Globalization and the Post-Creole Imagination: Notes on Fleeing the Plantation* (Durham, NC: Duke University Press, 2009).
Critchley, Simon, *Ethics, Politics, Subjectivity: Essays on Derrida, Levinas and Contemporary French Thought* (London: Verso, 1999).
Cucu, Sorin Radu, *The Underside of Politics: Global Fictions in the Fog of the Cold War* (New York: Fordham University Press, 2013).
Dames, Nicholas, 'The Theory Generation', *n+1*, 14 (Summer 2012).
Dames, Nicholas, 'Seventies Throwback Fiction: A Decade in Review', *n+1*, 21 (Winter 2014).
Darke, Chris, *Light Readings: Film Criticism and Screen Arts* (London: Wallflower, 2000).
Davey, Monica and Mary Williams Walsh, 'For Detroit, a Crisis of Bad Decisions and Crossed Fingers', *New York Times*, 11 March 2013, A1.
Dawes, James, *The Novel of Human Rights* (Cambridge, MA: Harvard University Press, 2018).
Decker, William, *Epistolary Practices: Letter-Writing in American Before Telecommunications* (Chapel Hill: University of North Carolina Press, 1998).
Deery, Philip, *Red Apple: Communism and McCarthyism in Cold War New York* (New York: Fordham University Press, 2014).

DeKoven, Marianne, *Utopia Limited: The Sixties and the Emergence of the Postmodern* (Durham, NC: Duke University Press, 2004).
Delanty, Gerard, *Community* (London: Routledge, 2003).
Deleuze, Gilles and Félix Guattari, *What Is Philosophy?*, trans. Hugh Tomlinson and Graham Burchell (New York: Columbia University Press, 1994).
DeLillo, Don, *Cosmopolis* (New York: Scribner, 2003).
DeMott, Benjamin, *The Trouble with Friendship: Why Americans Can't Think Straight About Race* (New Haven: Yale University Press, 1995).
Denning, Michael, *The Cultural Front: The Laboring of American Culture in the Twentieth Century* (London: Verso, 1996).
Denning, Michael, 'Afterword: Reconsidering the Significance of the Popular Front', *Rethinking Marxism*, 21:4 (2009), pp. 551–555.
Derrida, Jacques, *The Post Card: From Socrates to Freud and Beyond*, trans. Alan Bass (Chicago: University of Chicago Press, 1987).
Derrida, Jacques, *Given Time: 1. Counterfeit Money*, trans. Peggy Kamuf (Chicago: University of Chicago Press, 1992).
Derrida, Jacques, *The Gift of Death*, trans. David Wills (Chicago: University of Chicago Press, 1996).
Derrida, Jacques, *The Politics of Friendship*, trans. George Collins [French, 1994; English, 1997] (London: Verso, 2005).
Derrida, Jacques, *The Work of Mourning*, ed. Pascale-Anne Brault and Michael Naas (Chicago: University of Chicago Press, 2001).
Derrida, Jacques and Geoffrey Bennington, 'Politics and Friendship: A Discussion with Jacques Derrida', 1 December 1997, http://hydra.humanities.uci.edu/derrida/pol+fr.html.
Devere, Heather, 'Amity Update: The Academic Debate on Friendship', *AMITY: The Journal of Friendship Studies*, 1:1 (2013), pp. 5–33.
Devine, Thomas, *Henry Wallace's 1948 Presidential Campaign and the Future of Postwar Liberalism* (Chapel Hill: University of North Carolina Press, 2013).
Digeser, P. E., *Friendship Reconsidered: What It Means and How It Matters to Politics* (New York: Columbia University Press, 2016).
Dinshaw, Carolyn, Lee Edelman, Roderick A. Ferguson, Carla Freccero, Elizabeth Freeman, Judith Halberstam, Annamarie Jagose, Christopher Nealon, and Nguyen Tan Hoang, 'Theorizing Queer Temporalities: A Roundtable Discussion', *GLQ: A Journal of Lesbian and Gay Studies*, 13:2–3 (2007), pp. 177–195.
Dollinger, Marc, *Quest for Inclusion: Jews and Liberalism in Modern America* (Princeton: Princeton University Press, 2000).
Draper, Theodore, *The Roots of American Communism* (New York: Viking, 1957).

Draper, Theodore, *American Communism and Soviet Russia* [1960] (New York: Vintage, 1986).
Draper, Theodore, 'The Life of the Party', *New York Review of Books*, 13 January 1994, pp. 45–51.
Duneer, Anita, 'Brooklyn in the Making: Reading the Existential Utopian Vision in Paul Auster's *Smoke* through *The Wizard of Oz*', *Midwest Quarterly*, 50:1 (Autumn 2009), pp. 57–73.
Eaglestone, Robert, *Broken Voice: Reading Post-Holocaust Literature* (Oxford: Oxford University Press, 2017).
Edelman, Lee, *No Future: Queer Theory and the Death Drive* (Durham, NC: Duke University Press, 2004).
Eden, Kathy, *The Renaissance Rediscovery of Intimacy* (Chicago: University of Chicago Press, 2012).
Eldridge, David, *American Culture in the 1930s* (Edinburgh: Edinburgh University Press, 2008).
Emerson, Ralph Waldo, *The Essential Writings of Ralph Waldo Emerson*, ed. Brooks Atkinson (New York: Modern Library Classics, 2000).
Emerson, Ralph Waldo, 'Friendship' [1841], in *The Essential Writings of Ralph Waldo Emerson* (New York: Modern Library Classics, 2000), pp. 201–215.
Emerson, Ralph Waldo, 'Politics' [1841], in *The Essential Writings of Ralph Waldo Emerson* (New York: Modern Library Classics, 2000), pp. 378–389.
Emerson, Ralph Waldo, 'Gifts' [1844], in *The Essential Writings of Ralph Waldo Emerson* (New York: Modern Library Classics, 2000), pp. 360–364.
English, James and Ted Underwood, 'Shifting Scales: Between Literature and Social Science', *Modern Language Quarterly*, 77:3 (September 2016), pp. 277–295.
Epstein, Josh, '*Open City*'s "Abschied": Teju Cole, Gustav Mahler, and Elliptical Cosmopolitanism', *Studies in the Novel*, 51:3 (Fall 2019), pp. 412–432.
Eskin, Blake, 'Brooklyn Dodger', *Tablet*, 22 October 2003, www.tabletmag.com/jewish-arts-and-culture/books/795/brooklyn-dodger.
Esty, Jed, *Unseasonable Youth: Modernism, Colonialism, and the Fiction of Development* (Oxford: Oxford University Press, 2012).
Faderman, Lillian, *Surpassing the Love of Men: Romantic Friendship and Love Between Women, from the Renaissance to the Present* (London: Women's Press, 1981).
Fanon, Frantz, *The Wretch of the Earth*, trans. Constance Farrington [1961] (London: Penguin, 2001).
Fast, Howard, *Citizen Tom Paine* [1943] (London: Bodley Head, 1945).

Feeney, Matt, 'Michael Chabon's Oakland', *The New Yorker*, 26 September 2012.

Ferrara, Mark, *Barack Obama and the Rhetoric of Hope* (Jefferson: McFarland, 2013).

Ferry, Peter, *Masculinity in Contemporary New York Fiction* (London: Routledge, 2015).

Fiedler, Leslie, '"Come Back to the Raft Ag'in, Huck Honey!"', *Partisan Review*, 15 (June 1948), pp. 269–276.

Fiedler, Leslie, *Love and Death in the American Novel* [1960] (Champaign: Dalkey Archive Press, 2003).

Fischer, Claude, *Made in America: A Social History of American Culture and Character* (Chicago: University of Chicago Press, 2010).

Fishman, Robert, *Bourgeois Utopias: The Rise and Fall of Suburbia* (New York: Basic Books, 1987).

Fliegelman, Jay, *Prodigals and Pilgrims: The American Revolution Against Patriarchal Authority 1750–1800* (Cambridge: Cambridge University Press, 1982).

Florida, Richard, *The Rise of the Creative Class: And How It's Transforming Work, Leisure and Everyday Life* (New York: Basic Books, 2002).

Forster, E. M., *Two Cheers for Democracy* (London: Edward Arnold, 1951).

Forster, Laura, 'Radical Friendship', *History Workshop Online*, 10 June 2020.

Forsyth, Ann, *Reforming Suburbia: The Planned Communities of Irvine, Columbia, and The Woodlands* (Berkeley: University of California Press, 2005).

Foucault, Michel, *The History of Sexuality, Volume 1: An Introduction* [1976], trans. Robert Hurley (New York: Random House, 1980).

Foucault, Michel, 'Friendship as a Way of Life', in *Ethics: Subjectivity and Truth*, ed. Paul Rabinow, trans. Robert Hurley et al. (New York: New York Press, 1997), pp. 135–140.

Franzen, Jonathan, *Purity* (London: Fourth Estate, 2015).

Freedman, Jonathan, *The Temple of Culture: Assimilation and Anti-Semitism in Literary Anglo-America* (Oxford: Oxford University Press, 2000).

Freedman, Jonathan, *Klezmer America: Jewishness, Ethnicity, Modernity* (New York: Columbia University Press, 2008).

Freeman, Elizabeth, 'Packing History, Count(er)ing Generations', *New Literary History*, 31:4 (Fall 2000), pp. 727–744.

Freeman, Elizabeth, *Time Binds: Queer Temporalities, Queer Histories* (Durham, NC: Duke University Press, 2010).

Freeman, Jo, *At Berkeley in the Sixties: The Education of an Activist, 1961–1965* (Bloomington: Indiana University Press, 2004).

Freeman, John, 'Telegraph Avenue by Michael Chabon', *Boston Globe*, 1 September 2012.

Gandhi, Leela, 'Friendship and Postmodern Utopianism', *Culture Studies Review*, 9:1 (May 2003), pp. 12–22.

Gandhi, Leela, *Affective Communities: Anticolonial Thought, Fin-de-Siècle Radicalism, and the Politics of Friendship* (Durham, NC: Duke University Press, 2006).

Gates, Jr, Henry Louis, 'Critical Fanonism', *Critical Inquiry*, 17:3 (Spring 1991), pp. 457–470.

Gehrmann, Suzanne, 'Cosmopolitanism with African Roots: Afropolitanism's Ambivalent Mobilities', *Journal of African Cultural Studies*, 28:1 (2016), pp. 61–72.

Genette, Gérard, *Paratexts: Thresholds of Interpretation*, trans. Jane Lewin (Cambridge: Cambridge University Press, 1997).

Gerstle, Gary, *Working-Class Americanism: The Politics of Labor in a Textile City, 1914–1960* (Princeton: Princeton University Press, 1989).

Giddens, Anthony, *Beyond Left and Right: The Future of Radical Politics* [1994] (Cambridge: Polity, 2007).

Gilbert, James, 'New Left: Old America', *Social Text*, 9–10 (1984), pp. 244–247.

Gilroy, Paul, *The Black Atlantic: Modernity and Double Consciousness* (Cambridge, MA: Harvard University Press, 1993).

Girard, René, *Deceit, Desire, and the Novel: Self and Other in Literary Structure*, trans. Yvonne Freccero (Baltimore: Johns Hopkins University Press, 1976).

Glaser, Jennifer, *Borrowed Voices: Writing and Racial Ventriloquism in the Jewish American Imagination* (New Brunswick: Rutgers University Press, 2016).

Godbeer, Richard, *The Overflowing of Friendship: Love Between Men and the Creation of the American Republic* (Baltimore: Johns Hopkins University Press, 2009).

Godbey, Matt, 'Gentrification, Authenticity, and White Middle-Class Identity in Jonathan Lethem's *The Fortress of Solitude*', *Arizona Quarterly*, 64:1 (Spring 2008), pp. 131–151.

Goh, Irving, *The Reject: Community, Politics, and Religion after the Subject* (New York: Fordham University Press, 2014).

Golin, Steve, *The Newark Teachers Strikes: Hopes on the Line* (New Brunswick: Rutgers University Press, 2002).

Gooblar, David, *The Major Phases of Philip Roth* (London: Continuum, 2011).

Gooblar, David, 'Introduction: Roth and Women', *Philip Roth Studies*, 8:1 (Spring 2012), pp. 7–15.

Gooblar, David and Aimee Pozorski (eds), *Roth After Eighty: Philip Roth and the American Literary Imagination* (Lanham: Lexington Books, 2016).
Good, Cassandra, *Founding Friendships: Friendships Between Men and Women in the Early American Republic* (Oxford: Oxford University Press, 2015).
Goodman, David, *Radio's Civic Ambition: American Broadcasting and Democracy in the 1930s* (Oxford: Oxford University Press, 2011).
Goyal, Yogita, 'We Need New Diasporas', *American Literary History*, 29:4 (2017), pp. 640–663.
Grant, Linda, 'The Wrath of Roth', *The Guardian*, 4 October 1998.
Gray, Richard, *After the Fall: American Literature Since 9/11* (Oxford: Wiley-Blackwell, 2011).
Grayling, A. C., *Friendship* (New Haven: Yale University Press, 2013).
Greenberg, Cheryl Lynn, *Troubling the Waters: Black–Jewish Relations in the American Century* (Princeton: Princeton University Press, 2006).
Gross, Terry, '*Fresh Air* Remembers Novelist Philip Roth', 25 May 2018, www.npr.org/2018/05/25/614398904/fresh-air-remembers-novelist-philip-roth.
Gunport, Elizabeth, 'Gentrified Fiction', *n+1*, 2 November 2009.
Haddad, Samir, *Derrida and the Inheritance of Democracy* (Bloomington: Indiana University Press, 2013).
Halberstam, Jack, *In a Queer Time and Place: Transgender Bodies, Subcultural Lives* (New York: New York University Press, 2005).
Halberstam, Jack, *The Queer Art of Failure* (Durham, NC: Duke University Press, 2011).
Hale, Dorothy, 'Fiction as Restriction: Self-Binding in New Ethical Theories of the Novel', *Narrative*, 15:2 (2007), pp. 187–206.
Hale, Dorothy, 'Aesthetics and the New Ethics: Theorizing the Novel in the Twenty-First Century', *PMLA*, 124:3 (2009), pp. 896–905.
Hall, Jacquelyn Dowd, 'The Long Civil Rights Movement and the Political Uses of the Past', *The Journal of American History*, 91:4 (March 2005), pp. 1233–1263.
Hallemeier, Katherine, *J. M. Coetzee and the Limits of Cosmopolitanism* (Basingstoke: Palgrave Macmillan, 2013).
Harris, Kirsten, *Walt Whitman and British Socialism: 'The Love of Comrades'* (London: Routledge, 2016).
Hawthorne, Nathaniel, *The American Notebooks*, ed. Claude Simpson (Columbus: Ohio State University Press, 1972).
Hawthorne, Nathaniel, *Twenty Days with Julian And Little Bunny by Papa*, ed. Paul Auster (New York: NYRB Classics, 2003).
Hayes, Patrick, *Philip Roth: Fiction and Power* (Oxford: Oxford University Press, 2014).

Haynes, John Earl and Harvey Klehr, 'The Historiography of American Communism: An Unsettled Field', *Labour History Review*, 68:1 (April 2003), pp. 61–78.

Hendrix, Jenny, 'Empty Chairs at Empty Tables: Norman Rush's *Subtle Bodies*', *Los Angeles Review of Books*, 9 September 2013.

Herring, Scott, 'Material Deviance: Theorizing Queer Objecthood', *Postmodern Culture*, 21:2 (January 2011), n.p.

Hewitt, Elizabeth, *Correspondence and American Literature, 1770–1865* (Cambridge: Cambridge University Press, 2004).

Hillard, David, *The Black Panther Party: Service to the People Programs* (Albuquerque: University of New Mexico Press, 2008).

Hilmes, Michele, *Radio Voices: American Broadcasting, 1922–1952* (Minneapolis: University of Minnesota Press, 1997).

Hoberek, Andrew, "Introduction: After Postmodernism", *Twentieth Century Literature*, 53:3 (Fall 2007), pp. 233–247.

Hoberek, Andrew, 'Post-recession Realism', in Mitchum Huehls and Rachel Greenwald Smith (eds), *Neoliberalism and Contemporary Literary Culture* (Baltimore: Johns Hopkins University Press, 2017), pp. 237–253.

Hock, Stephen, 'Comix Remix; or, The Strange Case of Mr. Chabon', in Jesse Kavaldo and Bob Batchelor (eds), *Michael Chabon's America: Magical Words, Secret Worlds, and Sacred Spaces* (Lanham: Rowman & Littlefield, 2014), pp. 81–97.

Hodges, Robert, 'Deep Fellowship: Homosexuality and Male Bonding in the Life and Fiction of Joseph Conrad', *Journal of Homosexuality*, 4:4 (1979), pp. 379–393.

Holland, Mary K., *Succeeding Postmodernism: Language and Humanism in Contemporary American Literature* (London: Bloomsbury, 2013).

Hollander, Benjamin, 'The Long View Back to the Gardens: Politics as Dissident Polis in Jonathan Lethem's Dissident Gardens', *The Brooklyn Rail*, 18 December 2014.

Honig, Bonnie, *Political Theory and the Displacement of Politics* (Ithaca: Cornell University Press, 1993).

Hornung, Alfred, 'The Personal is the Fictional: Philip Roth's Return to the 1950s in *I Married a Communist*', in Gerd Hurm and Ann Marie Fallon (eds), *Rebels without a Cause? Renegotiating the American 1950s* (Bern: Peter Lang, 2007), pp. 77–95.

Horvath, Tim, '*Subtle Bodies*: An Interview with Norman Rush', *Tin House*, 25 November 2013.

Howarth, Peter, 'Rudyard Kipling Plays the Empire', in Matthew Bevis (ed.), *The Oxford Handbook of Victorian Poetry* (Oxford: Oxford University Press, 2013), pp. 605–617.

Howe, Irving and Lewis Coser, *The American Communist Party: A Critical History* [1958] (New York: Da Cape Press, 1974).

Howe, Irving, 'Philip Roth Reconsidered', *Commentary*, December 1972, pp. 69–77.

Howe, Irving, *Socialism and America* (New York: Harcourt Brace Jovanovich, 1985).

Hsu, Hsuan, *Geography and the Production of Space in Nineteenth-Century American Literature* (Cambridge: Cambridge University Press, 2010).

Huehls, Mitchum, *Qualified Hope: A Postmodern Politics of Time* (Columbus: Ohio State University Press, 2009).

Hungerford, Amy, 'On the Period Formerly Known as Contemporary', *American Literary History*, 20:1–2 (Spring/Summer 2008), pp. 410–419.

Hutcheon, Linda, *A Poetics of Postmodernism: History, Theory, Fiction* (New York: Routledge, 1988).

Hutchison, Anthony, *Writing the Republic: Liberalism and Morality in American Political Fiction* (New York: Columbia University Press, 2007).

Hutchison, Colin, *Reaganism, Thatcherism and the Social Novel* (Basingstoke: Palgrave Macmillan, 2008).

Hutson, Lorna, *The Usurer's Daughter: Male Friendship and Fictions of Women in Sixteenth-Century England* (London: Routledge, 1994).

Hutter, Horst, *Politics as Friendship: The Origins of Classical Notions of Politics in the Theory and Practice of Friendship* (Waterloo: Wilfrid Laurier University Press, 1978).

Hyde, Lewis, *The Gift: Creativity and the Artist in the Modern World* [1983] (New York: Vintage, 2007).

Iler, Dustin, 'Suicide and the Afterlife of the Cold War: Accident, Intentionality, and Periodicity in Paul Auster's *Leviathan* and Jeffrey Eugenides's *The Virgin Suicides*', *Modern Fiction Studies*, 63:4 (Winter 2017), pp. 737–758.

Immerso, Michael, *Newark's Little Italy: The Vanished First Ward* (New Brunswick: Rutgers University Press, 1997).

Irr, Caren, *Toward the Geopolitical Novel: U.S. Fiction in the Twenty-First Century* (New York: Columbia University Press, 2013).

Isserman, Maurice, *Which Side Were You On?: The American Communist Party During the Second World War* [1982] (Urbana: University of Illinois Press, 1993).

Ivanova, Velichka, 'My Own Foe from the Other Gender: (Mis)representing Women in *The Dying Animal*', *Philip Roth Studies*, 8:1 (Spring 2012), pp. 31–44.

Jackson, Holly, *American Blood: The Ends of the Family in American Literature, 1850–1900* (Oxford: Oxford University Press, 2014).

Jacobs, Jane, *The Death and Life of Great American Cities* (New York: Vintage, 1961).

Jacobs, Karen, 'Teju Cole's Photographic Afterimages', *Image & Narrative*, 15:2 (2014), pp. 87–105.

Jacobson, Howard, 'Is *American Pastoral* Philip Roth at His Best?', *The Guardian*, 11 November 2016.

James, Felicity, *Charles Lamb, Coleridge and Wordsworth: Reading Friendship in the 1790s* (Basingstoke: Palgrave Macmillan, 2008).

Jameson, Fredric, *Fables of Aggression: Wyndham Lewis, the Modernist as Fascist* (Berkeley: University of California Press, 1979).

Jameson, Fredric, *Postmodernism, or, The Cultural Logic of Late Capitalism* (Durham, NC: Duke University Press, 1991).

Jameson, Fredric, *Valences of the Dialectic* (New York: Verso, 2009).

Jardine, Lisa, *Reading Shakespeare Historically* (London: Routledge, 1996).

Jelloun, Tahar Ben, *The Last Friend*, trans. Kevin Michel Capé and Hazel Rowley [French, 2004] (New York: New Press, 2006).

Jendrysik, Mark Stephen, *Modern Jeremiahs: Contemporary Visions of American Decline* (Lanham: Lexington Books, 2008).

Jensen, Steffen and Finn Stepputat, 'Notes on Securitization and Temporality', in Martin Holbraad and Morten Axel Pederson (eds), *Times of Security: Ethnographies of Fear, Protest and the Future* (New York: Routledge, 2013), pp. 213–222.

Johnson, Christopher, 'Mauss's Gift: The Persistence of a Paradigm', *Modern and Contemporary France*, 4:3 (1996), pp. 307–317.

Johnson, Gary Chase, 'The Presence of Allegory: The Case of Philip Roth's *American Pastoral*', *Narrative*, 12:3 (October 2004), pp. 233–248.

Johnson, Sarah Anne, 'Interview with Jonathan Lethem', in Jaime Clarke (ed.), *Conversations with Jonathan Lethem* (Jackson: University of Mississippi Press, 2011), 78–99.

Jones, Alfred Haworth, *Roosevelt's Image Brokers: Poets, Playwrights, and the Use of the Lincoln Symbol* (Port Washington: Kennikat Press, 1974).

Joseph, Miranda, *Against the Romance of Community* (Minneapolis: University of Minnesota Press, 2002).

Joubert, Joseph, *The Notebooks of Joseph Joubert*, trans. Paul Auster (New York: New York Review of Books, 2005).

Jusdanis, Gregory, *A Tremendous Thing: Friendship from The Iliad to the Internet* (Ithaca: Cornell University Press, 2014).

Kakutani, Michiko, 'A Postwar Paradise Shattered From Within', *New York Times*, 15 April 1997, C11.

Kakutani, Michiko, 'Manly Giants vs. Zealots and Scheming Women', *New York Times*, 6 October 1998, C7.

Kakutani, Michiko, 'White Kid, in a Black World', *New York Times*, 16 September 2003.

Kakutani, Michiko, 'Grim View of a Nation at the End of Days', *New York Times*, 16 June 2006, E35.

Kakutani, Michiko, 'Battling Progress and Other Demons: *Telegraph Avenue* by Michael Chabon', *New York Times*, 3 September 2012.

Kaplan, Brett Ashley, "Do You Just *Love* Philip Roth?", *Studies in American Jewish Literature*, 32:2 (2013), pp. 187–191.

Kaplan, Michael, *Friendship Fictions: The Rhetoric of Citizenship in the Liberal Imaginary* (Tuscaloosa: University of Alabama Press, 2010).

Katz, Jonathan Ned, *Love Stories: Sex Between Men Before Homosexuality* (Chicago: University of Chicago Press, 2003).

Kavaldo, Jesse and Bob Batchelor (eds), *Michael Chabon's America: Magical Words, Secret Worlds, and Sacred Spaces* (Lanham: Rowman & Littlefield, 2014).

Kavaldo, Jesse, 'Real Maps of Imaginary Places; or, Michael Chabon, Shadowtail', in Jesse Kavaldo and Bob Batchelor (eds), *Michael Chabon's America: Magical Words, Secret Worlds, and Sacred Spaces* (Lanham: Rowman & Littlefield, 2014), pp. 1–17.

Kavanagh, Matt, '"Hope Unfulfilled, Not Yet Betrayed": Michael Chabon's Nostalgia for the Future', in Jesse Kavaldo and Bob Batchelor (eds), *Michael Chabon's America: Magical Words, Secret Worlds, and Sacred Spaces* (Lanham: Rowman & Littlefield, 2014), pp. 235–255.

Kaye, Harvey, *Thomas Paine and the Promise of America: A History & Biography* (New York: Hill and Wang, 2005).

Kazin, Alfred, 'What Have the '30s Done to Our Literature?', *New York Herald Tribune Books*, 31 December 1939, pp. 1–2.

Kazin, Michael, *American Dreamers: How the Left Changed a Nation* (New York: Knopf, 2011).

Keats, John, 'Letter to Charles Brown, November 30, 1820', in *Keats's Poetry and Prose*, ed. Jeffrey Cox (New York: Norton, 2009), 533.

Keith, Michael and Mary Ann Watson (eds), *Norman Corwin's One World Flight: The Lost Journal of Radio's Greatest Writer* (London: Bloomsbury, 2009).

Kellog, Carolyn, 'Review: Michael Chabon Joyfully Sets Down on "Telegraph Avenue"', *Los Angeles Times*, 9 September 2012.

Kelly, Adam, 'David Foster Wallace and the New Sincerity in American Fiction', in David Hering (ed.), *Consider David Foster Wallace: Critical Essays* (Austin: Sideshow Media Group Press, 2010), pp. 131–146.

Kelly, Adam, 'Moments of Decision in Contemporary American Fiction: Roth, Auster, Eugenides', *Critique: Studies in Contemporary Fiction*, 51:4 (2010), pp. 313–332.

Kelly, Adam, 'Beginning with Postmodernism', *Twentieth-Century Literature*, 75:3–4 (Fall/Winter 2011), pp. 391–422.

Kelly, Adam, '"Who Is Responsible?": Revisiting the Radical Years in Dana Spiotta's *Eat the Document*', in Philip Coleman and Stephen Matterson (eds), *'Forever Young'?: The Changing Images of America* (Heidelberg: Universitätsverlag Winter, 2012), pp. 219–230.

Kelly, Adam, *American Fiction in Transition: Observer-Hero Narrative, the 1990s, and Postmodernism* (London: Bloomsbury, 2013).

Kelly, Adam, 'David Foster Wallace and New Sincerity Aesthetics: A Reply to Edward Jackson and Joel Nicholson-Roberts', *Orbit: A Journal of American Literature*, 5:4 (2017), pp. 1–32.

Kimmel, Michael, 'Masculinity as Homophobia: Fear, Shame, and Silence in the Construction of Gender Identity', in Mary Gergen and Sara Davis (eds), *Toward a New Psychology of Gender* (New York: Routledge, 1997), pp. 223–245.

Kleine, Christian, *Cold War Orientalism: Asia in the Middlebrow Imagination, 1945–1961* (Berkeley: University of California Press, 2003).

Kloppenberg, James, *Reading Obama: Dreams, Hope, and the American Political Tradition* (Princeton: Princeton University Press, 2011).

Knight, Peter, 'Everything Is Connected: *Underworld*'s Secret History of Paranoia', *Modern Fiction Studies*, 45:3 (Fall 1999), pp. 811–832.

Konstan, David, *Friendship in the Classical World* (Cambridge: Cambridge University Press, 1997).

Konstantinou, Lee, 'Outerborough Destiny: Jonathan Lethem's *Dissident Gardens*', *Los Angeles Review of Books*, 8 September 2013.

Konstantinou, Lee, 'Lewis Hyde's Double Economy', *ASAP/Journal*, 1:1 (January 2016), pp. 123–149.

Konstantinou, Lee, *Cool Characters: Irony and American Fiction* (Cambridge, MA: Harvard University Press, 2016).

Krieger, Murray and Joan Krieger, *Ekphrasis: The Illusion of the Natural Sign* (Baltimore: Johns Hopkins University Press, 1992).

Lamb, Robert, *Thomas Paine and the Idea of Human Rights* (Cambridge: Cambridge University Press, 2013).

Lasch, Christopher, *The Revolt of the Elites and the Betrayal of Democracy* (New York: Norton, 1996).

Lawrence, D. H., *Studies in Classic American Literature* [1923], ed. Ezra Greenspan, Lindeth Vasey, and John Worthen (Cambridge: Cambridge University Press, 2003).

Leab, Daniel, 'How Red Was My Valley: Hollywood, the Cold War Film, and *I Married a Communist*', *Journal of Contemporary History*, 19 (1984), pp. 59–88.

Ledwidge, Mark, Kevern Verney, and Inderjeet Parmar (eds), *Barack Obama and the Myth of a Post-Racial America* (London: Routledge, 2013).

Lee, Felicia, 'New Wave of African Writers with an Internationalist Bent', *New York Times*, 29 June 2014.
Lehrer, Natasha, 'How Many Miles to Brooklyn', *Jewish Quarterly*, 51:1 (2004), pp. 14–18.
Leonard, John, 'Welcome to New Dork', *New York Review of Books*, 7 April 2005.
Lethem, Jonathan, 'Yolked in Gowanus' (2001), http://jonathanlethem.com/yolked-in-gowanus/.
Lethem, Jonathan, 'My Egyptian Cousin', *London Review of Books*, 24:24 (12 December 2002), p. 22.
Lethem, Jonathan, *The Fortress of Solitude* (London: Faber and Faber, 2003).
Lethem, Jonathan, *The Disappointment Artist: Essays* (New York: Vintage, 2005).
Lethem, Jonathan, 'The Ecstasy of Influence', in *The Ecstasy of Influence: Nonfictions, etc.* (New York: Vintage, 2012), pp. 93–120.
Lethem, Jonathan, *Dissident Gardens* (New York: Doubleday, 2013).
Lethem, Jonathan, 'Diary', *London Review of Books*, 38:24 (15 December 2016), pp. 38–39.
Lethem, Jonathan, 'Counter-Roth', in Jonathan Lethem, *More Alive and Less Lonely: On Books and Writers,* ed. Christopher Boucher (London: Melville House, 2017), pp. 41–48.
Levitas, Ruth, 'Looking for the Blue: The Necessity of Utopia', *Journal of Political Ideologies*, 12:3 (2007), pp. 289–306.
Li, Stephanie, *Pan-African American Literature: Signifying Immigrants in the 21st Century* (New Brunswick: Rutgers University Press, 2018).
Lichterman, Paul *The Search for Political Community: American Activists Reinventing Commitment* (Cambridge: Cambridge University Press, 1996).
Linder, Marc and Lawrence Zacharias, *Of Cabbages and Kings County: Agriculture and the Formation of Modern Brooklyn* (Iowa City: University of Iowa Press, 1999).
Lindman, Janet Moore, 'Histories of Friendship in Early America: An Introduction', *Journal of Social History*, 50:4 (2017), pp. 603–608.
Linke, Gabriele, 'The Public, the Private, and the Intimate: Richard Sennett's and Lauren Berlant's Cultural Criticism in Dialogue', *Biography*, 34:1 (Winter 2011), pp. 11–24.
Locke, Attica, 'Telegraph Avenue by Michael Chabon – Review', *The Guardian*, 5 September 2012.
Löffler, Philipp, *Pluralist Desires: Contemporary Historical Fiction and the End of the Cold War* (Rochester: Camden House, 2015).
Looby, Christopher, '"Innocent Homosexuality": The Fiedler Thesis in Retrospect', in Gerald Graff and James Phelan (eds), *Adventures of*

Huckleberry Finn: A Case Study in Critical Controversy (Boston: Bedford Books, 1995) pp. 535–550.

Love, Heather, *Feeling Backward: Loss and the Politics of Queer History* (Cambridge, MA: Harvard University Press, 2007).

Loviglio, Jason, *Radio's Intimate Public: Network Broadcasting and Mass-Mediated Democracy* (Minneapolis: University of Minnesota Press, 2005).

Lowenstein, Bob, 'Boxing Lessons' [Sent to Roth 28/2/97 (?)], in "Bob Lowenstein Correspondence, 1996–99", Box 20, Folder 6, Philip Roth Papers, Library of Congress, Washington, DC.

Luciano, Dana, *Arranging Grief: Sacred Time and the Body in Nineteenth-Century America* (New York: New York University Press, 2007).

Lyons, Paul, Maurice Isserman, and Theodore Draper, 'The Old Left: An Exchange', *New York Review of Books*, 23 June 1994, pp. 62–63.

MacDonald, Andrew, *Howard Fast: A Critical Companion* (Westport: Greenwood Press, 1996).

MacFaul, Tom, *Male Friendship in Shakespeare and His Contemporaries* (Cambridge: Cambridge University Press, 2007).

MacIntyre, Alasdair, *After Virtue: A Study in Moral Theory* (London: Duckworth, 1981).

Mahan, Karan, 'Black Noise', *n+1*, 11 October 2011.

Mailer, Norman, 'Huckleberry Finn, Alive at 100', *New York Times*, 9 December 1984.

Marcus, Sharon, *Between Women: Friendship, Desire, and Marriage in Victorian England* (Princeton: Princeton University Press, 2007).

Markovits, Benjamin, 'A Crack in the Ordinary', *Times Literary Supplement*, 1 November 2002, p. 23.

Markovits, Benjamin, 'The Colours of Sport', *New Left Review*, 22 (July/August, 2003), pp. 151–160.

Markovits, Benjamin, 'The Allegiance that I Can't Quite Pledge', *New Statesman*, 17 November 2003, p. 26.

Markovits, Benjamin, 'The Parrot Holds the Key', *The Telegraph*, 20 February 2005.

Markovits, Benjamin, *Playing Days* (London: Faber and Faber, 2005).

Markovits, Benjamin, 'Benjamin Markovits Misses a Hoop', *New Statesman*, 22 May 2006, p. 59.

Markovits, Benjamin, 'A Morality Story', *Times Literary Supplement*, 5 May 2006, pp. 21–22.

Markovits, Benjamin, 'A New Global Game?', *New Statesman*, 15 January 2009, p. 28.

Markovits, Benjamin, 'Just Undo It: The LeBron James Profile that Nike Killed', *Deadspin*, 10 July 2014.

Markovits, Benjamin, *You Don't Have to Live Like This* (London: Faber and Faber, 2015).

Markovits, Benjamin, 'The Adventures of Huckleberry Finn: How to Write about Race in the US', *The Guardian*, 1 August 2015.

Markovits, Benjamin, 'The Great American Novelist Philip Roth 1933–2018', *Times Literary Supplement*, 1 June 2018, p. 17.

Marling, William, 'Paul Auster and the American Romantics', *Lit: Literature Interpretation Theory*, 7:4 (1997), pp. 301–310.

Marling, William, *Gatekeepers: The Emergence of World Literature and the 1960s* (Oxford: Oxford University Press, 2016).

Marsh, Nicky, *Money, Speculation and Finance in Contemporary British Fiction* (London: Continuum, 2007).

Marshall, Sandra, 'The Community of Friends', in Emilios Christodoulidis (ed.), *Communitarianism and Citizenship* (Aldershot: Ashgate, 1998), pp. 208–219.

Mars-Jones, Adam, 'It's All in the Detail. Unfortunately ...', *The Observer*, 11 January 2004.

Martin, Brendan, *Paul Auster's Postmodernity* (London: Routledge, 2008).

Martin, Theodore, 'The Long Wait: Timely Secrets of the Contemporary Detective Novel', *Novel: A Forum on Fiction*, 45:2 (Fall 2012), pp. 165–183.

Masiero, Pia, *Philip Roth and the Zuckerman Books: The Making of a Storyworld* (Amherst: Cambria Press, 2011).

Maultsby, Portia, 'African American Musical Cultures', in Ellen Koskoff (ed.), *Music Cultures in the United States: An Introduction* (New York: Routledge, 2005), pp. 135–242.

Mauss, Marcel, *The Gift: The Form and Reason for Exchange in Archaic Societies* [1925], trans. W. D. Halls (London: Routledge, 1990).

May, Todd, *Friendship in an Age of Economics: Resisting the Forces of Neoliberalism* (Lanham: Rowman & Littlefield, 2012).

Mayo, Marjorie, *Cultures, Communities, Identities: Cultural Strategies for Participation and Empowerment* (Basingstoke: Palgrave Macmillan, 2000).

McCann, Sean, *A Pinnacle of Feeling: American Literature and Presidential Government* (Princeton: Princeton University Press, 2008).

McDonald, Brian, '"The Real American Crazy Shit": On Adamism and Democratic Individuality in *American Pastoral*', *Studies in American Jewish Literature*, 23 (2004), pp. 27–40.

McDougall, Curtis, *Gideon's Army*, 3 vols (New York: Marzani & Munsell, 1965).

McGrath, Charles, 'Zuckerman's Alter Brain: An Interview with Philip Roth', *New York Times Book Review*, 7 May 2000, p. 8.

McGurl, Mark, *The Program Era: Postwar Fiction and the Rise of Creative Writing* (Cambridge, MA: Harvard University Press, 2009).

McKinley, Jesse, 'In Berkeley, a Store's End Clouds a Street's Future', *New York Times*, 18 June 2006.
McKinley, Maggie, *Masculinity and the Paradox of Violence in American Fiction, 1950–75* (London: Bloomsbury, 2015).
McLaughlin, Robert, 'Post-Postmodern Discontent: Contemporary Fiction and the Social World', *symplokē*, 12:1/2 (2004), pp. 53–68.
Mechanic, Michael, 'Michael Chabon's Vinyl Draft', *Mother Jones*, September/October 2012.
Mengestu, Dinaw, *The Beautiful Things that Heaven Bears* (New York: Riverhead Books, 2007).
Mengestu, Dinaw, *How to Read the Air* (London: Vintage, 2010).
Mengestu, Dinaw, 'How Novels Widen Your Vision', *The Atlantic*, 4 March 2014.
Mengestu, Dinaw, 'Solomon's Search', *The Atlantic*, 14 May 2016.
Messud, Claire, 'The Secret Sharer: Review of *Open City*, by Teju Cole', *New York Review of Books*, 14 July 2011.
Michael, Magali Cornier, *New Visions of Community in Contemporary American Fiction: Tan, Kingsolver, Castillo, Morrison* (Iowa City: University of Iowa Press, 2006).
Mickenberg, Julia, *Learning from the Left: Children's Literature, the Cold War, and Radical Politics in the United States* (Oxford: Oxford University Press, 2005).
Miles, Jack, Letter to Roth dated January 1, 1997, 'Jack Miles Correspondence', Box 24, Folder 13, Philip Roth Papers, Library of Congress, Washington, DC.
Miles, Jack, Letter to Roth dated June 29, 1998, 'Jack Miles Correspondence', Box 24, Folder 13, Philip Roth Papers, Library of Congress, Washington, DC.
Miles, Jack, Letter to Roth dated October 6, 1998, 'Jack Miles Correspondence', Box 24, Folder 13, Philip Roth Papers, Library of Congress, Washington, DC.
Millard, Kenneth, *Coming of Age in Contemporary American Fiction* (Edinburgh: Edinburgh University Press, 2007).
Miller, Donald, *Lewis Mumford: A Life* (New York: Grove Press, 1989).
Miller, William, *Humiliation and Other Essays on Honor, Social Discomfort, and Violence* (Ithaca: Cornell University Press, 1993).
Monteith, Sharon, *Advancing Sisterhood?: Interracial Friendships in Contemporary Southern Fiction* (Athens: University of Georgia Press, 2000).
Moody, Alys, 'Eden of Exiles: The Ethnicities of Paul Auster's Aesthetics', *American Literary History*, 28:1 (Spring 2016), pp. 69–93.
Moore, Gerald, *Politics of the Gift: Exchanges in Poststructuralism* (Edinburgh: Edinburgh University Press, 2011).

Morais, Betsy, 'Sharing Is Caring Is Sharing', *The New Yorker*, 30 October 2013.

Moran, Elizabeth, 'Death, Determination and "the End of Ends?": Nathan Zuckerman from *My Life as a Man* to *Exit Ghost*', *Philip Roth Studies*, 11:2 (Fall 2015), pp. 5–30.

Morley, Catherine, *The Quest for Epic in Contemporary American Fiction: John Updike, Philip Roth, and Don DeLillo* (London: Routledge, 2009).

Morris, Mary, 'A Conversation with Paul Auster' [2005], in James Hutchison (ed.), *Conversations with Paul Auster* (Jackson: University Press of Mississippi, 2013), pp. 163–179.

Moskowitz, Peter, *How to Kill a City: Gentrification, Inequality, and the Fight for the Neighborhood* (New York: Hachette, 2017).

Mouffe, Chantal, 'Democratic Citizenship and the Political Community', in Mouffe (ed.), *Dimensions of Radical Democracy* (London: Verso, 1992).

Mulhall, Stephen and Adam Swift, *Liberals and Communitarians* [1992] (Oxford: Blackwell, 1996).

Mullins, Matthew, *Postmodernism in Pieces: Materializing the Social in U. S. Fiction* (Oxford: Oxford University Press, 2016).

Mumford, Lewis, *The Culture of Cities* (New York: Harcourt, Brace and Co., 1938).

Mumford, Lewis, 'Mother Jacobs' Home Remedies', *The New Yorker*, 38 (1 December 1962), pp. 148–179.

Muñoz, José Esteban, *Cruising Utopia: The Then and There of Queer Futurity* (New York: New York University Press, 2009).

Murch, Donna Jean, *Living for the City: Migration, Education, and the Rise of the Black Panther Party in Oakland, California* (Chapel Hill: University of North Carolina Press, 2010).

Murolo, Priscilla, 'History in the Fast Lane: Howard Fast and the Historical Novel', in Susan Porter Benson, Stephen Brier, and Roy Rosenzweig (eds), *Presenting the Past: Essays on History and the Public* (Philadelphia: Temple University Press, 1986), pp. 53–67.

Myers, D. G., 'Michael Chabon's Imaginary Jews', *The Sewanee Review*, 116:4 (Fall 2008), pp. 572–588.

Nancy, Jean-Luc, *The Inoperative Community*, trans. Peter Connor, Lisa Garbus, Michael Holland, and Simona Sawhney (Minneapolis: University of Minnesota Press, 1991).

Nardi, Peter, 'Friendship', in Michael Kimmel and Amy Aronson (eds), *Men and Masculinities: A Social, Cultural, and Historical Encyclopaedia* (Santa Barbara: ABC-Clio Press, 2004).

Nealon, Jeffrey, 'Work of the Detective, Work of the Writer: Paul Auster's *City of Glass*', *Modern Fiction Studies*, 42:1 (Spring 1996), pp. 90–107.

Nealon, Jeffrey, *Post-Postmodernism: or, The Cultural Logic of Just-in-Time Capitalism* (Stanford: Stanford University Press, 2012).
Nelson, Bruce, *Workers on the Waterfront: Seamen, Longshoremen, and Unionism in the 1930s* (Urbana: University of Illinois Press, 1990).
Nelson, Dana, *National Manhood: Capitalist Citizenship and the Imagined Fraternity of White Men* (Durham, NC: Duke University Press, 1998).
Nelson, Dana, 'Cooper's Leatherstocking Conversations: Identity, Friendship, and Democracy in the New Nation', in Leland Person (ed.), *A Historical Guide to James Fenimore Cooper* (Oxford: Oxford University Press, 2007), pp. 123–155.
Newton, Adam Zachary, '"I was the prosthesis": Roth and Late Style', in David Gooblar and Aimee Pozorski (eds), *Roth After Eighty: Philip Roth and the American Literary Imagination* (Lanham: Lexington Books, 2016), pp. 127–149.
Nissen, Axel, *Manly Love: Romantic Friendship in American Fiction* (Chicago: University of Chicago Press, 2009).
Nixon, Jon, *Hannah Arendt and the Politics of Friendship* (London: Bloomsbury, 2015).
Nixon, Rob, 'African, American', *New York Times*, 25 March 2007.
Nussbaum, Martha, 'Reading for Life', *Yale Journal of Law & the Humanities*, 1:1 (1989), pp. 165–180.
Nussbaum, Martha, *Love's Knowledge: Essays on Philosophy and Literature* (Oxford: Oxford University Press, 1990).
Nussbaum, Martha, 'Exactly and Responsibly: A Defence of Ethical Criticism', *Philosophy and Literature*, 22:2 (1998), pp. 343–365.
O'Heir, Andrew, 'Chabon on Race, Sex, Obama', *Salon*, 20 September 2012, www.salon.com/2012/09/20/chabon_on_race_sex_obama_i_never_wanted_to_tell_the_story_of_two_guys_in_a_record_store/.
Oldenburg, Ray, *The Great Good Place: Cafes, Coffee Shops, Community Centers, Beauty Parlours, General Stores, Bars, Hangouts, and How They Get You through the Day* (New York: Paragon House, 1989).
Olster, Stacey, *The Cambridge Introduction to Contemporary American Fiction* (Cambridge: Cambridge University Press, 2017).
Omer-Sherman, Ranen, *Diaspora and Zionism in Jewish American Literature: Lazarus, Syrkin, Reznikoff, and Roth* (Hanover: Brandeis University Press, 2002).
Osman, Suleiman, *The Invention of Brownstone Brooklyn: Gentrification and the Search for Authenticity in Postwar New York* (Oxford: Oxford University Press, 2011).
Osteen, Mark, 'Phantoms of Liberty: The Secret Lives of *Leviathan*', *Review of Contemporary Fiction*, 14:1 (Spring 1994), p. 87.
Osteen, Mark (ed.), *The Question of the Gift: Essays Across Disciplines* (New York: Routledge, 2002).

Ottanelli, Fraser, *The Communist Party of the United States: From the Depression to World War II* (New Brunswick: Rutgers University Press, 1991).
Pahl, Ray, *On Friendship* (London: Polity, 2000).
Paine, Thomas, *The Rights of Man, Part II* [1792] (Cambridge: Cambridge University Press, 2012).
Paine, Thomas, *Political Writings*, ed. Bruce Kuklick (Cambridge: Cambridge University Press, 1989).
Pakaluk, Michael, *Other Selves: Philosophers on Friendship* (Indianapolis: Hackett, 1991).
Pangle, Lorraine Smith, *Aristotle and the Philosophy of Friendship* (Cambridge: Cambridge University Press, 2002).
Papke, David Ray, *The Pullman Case: The Clash of Labor and Capital in Industrial America* (Lawrence: University Press of Kansas, 1999).
Parker, Hal, 'Review: Jonathan Lethem's *Dissident Gardens*', *The American Reader*, 1:9 (November 2013).
Parrish, Timothy, 'Becoming Black: Zuckerman's Bifurcating Self in *The Human Stain*', in Derek Parker Royal (ed.), *Philip Roth: New Perspectives on an American Author* (Westport: Praeger, 2005), pp. 209–224.
Parrish, Timothy (ed.), *The Cambridge Companion to Philip Roth* (Cambridge: Cambridge University Press, 2007).
Patterson, Troy, 'Archy and Nat's Last Stand', *Slate*, 7 September 2012.
Peacock, James, 'Faking It or Making It? Forgery, Real Lives and the True Fake in *The Brooklyn Follies*', in Stefania Ciocia and Jesús González (eds), *The Invention of Illusions: International Perspectives on Paul Auster* (Newcastle-upon-Tyne: Cambridge Scholars Press, 2011), pp. 75–96.
Peacock, James, *Jonathan Lethem* (Manchester: Manchester University Press, 2012).
Peacock, James, *Brooklyn Fictions: The Contemporary Urban Community in a Global Age* (London: Bloomsbury, 2015).
Peel, Mark, 'New Worlds of Friendship: The Early Twentieth Century', in Barbara Caine (ed.), *Friendship: A History* (London: Equinox, 2009), pp. 279–316.
Person, Leland, *Henry James and the Suspension of Masculinity* (Philadelphia: University of Pennsylvania Press, 2003).
Pierpont, Claudia Roth, *Roth Unbound: A Writer and His Books* (New York: Farrar, Straus & Giroux, 2013).
Posnock, Ross, 'How It Feels to Be a Problem: Du Bois, Fanon, and the "Impossible Life" of the Black Intellectual', *Critical Inquiry*, 23:1 (Winter 1997), pp. 323–349.
Posnock, Ross, 'Purity and Danger: On Philip Roth', *Raritan*, 21:2 (2001), pp. 85–101.
Posnock, Ross, 'Innocents at Home', *Bookforum* (Summer 2003).

Posnock, Ross, *Philip Roth's Rude Truth: The Art of Immaturity* (Princeton: Princeton University Press, 2006).

Pozorski, Aimee, *Roth and Trauma: The Problem of History in the Later Works (1995–2010)* (London: Continuum, 2011).

Pozorski, Aimee, '"An ear in search of a word": Writing and the Politics of Listening in Roth's *I Married a Communist*', in Lee Trepanned and Claudia Franziska Brühwiler (eds), *A Political Companion to Philip Roth* (Lexington: University Press of Kentucky, 2017), pp. 15–40.

Pratt, Lloyd, *Archives of American Time: Literature and Modernity in the Nineteenth Century* (Philadelphia: University of Pennsylvania Press, 2010).

Punday, Daniel, *Writing at the Limit: The Novel in the New Media Ecology* (Lincoln: University of Nebraska Press, 2012).

Putnam, Robert, *Bowling Alone: The Collapse and Revival of American Community* (New York: Simon & Schuster, 2000).

Ramazani, Jahan, *A Transnational Poetics* (Chicago: University of Chicago Press, 2009).

Rampton, David, 'Stupidity's Progress: Philip Roth and Twentieth-Century American History', in Peter Swirski (ed.), *I Sing the Body Politic: History as Prophecy in Contemporary American Literature* (Montreal: McGill-Queen's University Press, 2009), pp. 12–46.

Rawls, John, *A Theory of Justice* (Oxford: Oxford University Press, 1971).

Razlogova, Elena, *The Listener's Ear: Early Radio and the American Public* (Philadelphia: University of Pennsylvania Press, 2011).

Remnick, David, 'Into the Clear', *The New Yorker*, 8 May 2000, pp. 76–89.

Remnick, David, 'Philip Roth at 70' [Interview], Dir. Deborah Lee, BBC4 (May 2003).

Ricketts, Harry, '"Nine and sixty ways": Kipling, Ventriloquist Poet', in Howard Booth (ed.), *The Cambridge Companion to Rudyard Kipling* (Cambridge: Cambridge University Press, 2011), pp. 111–125.

Riesback, David, *Aristotle on Political Community* (Cambridge: Cambridge University Press, 2016).

Riker, Martin, 'Pen Pals', *New York Times*, 17 March 2013, BR22.

Robbins, 'The Worlding of the American Novel', in Leonard Cassuto (ed.), *The Cambridge History of the American Novel* (Cambridge: Cambridge University Press, 2011), pp. 1096–1106.

Robinson, Dean, *Black Nationalism in American Politics and Thought* (Cambridge: Cambridge University Press, 2001).

Rogin, Michael, *Ronald Reagan, the Movie: and Other Episodes in Political Demonology* (Berkeley: University of California Press, 1987).

Rohy, Valerie, *Anachronism and Its Others: Sexuality, Race, Temporality* (Albany: State University of New York Press, 2009).

Rossinow, Doug, *Visions of Progress: The Left-Liberal Tradition in America* (Philadelphia: University of Pennsylvania Press, 2008).
Roth, Marco, 'I don't want your Revolution', *London Review of Books*, 36:4 (20 February 2014), pp. 24–25.
Roth, Philip, *Portnoy's Complaint* [1969] (London: Vintage, 2005).
Roth, Philip, *Our Gang* (New York: Random House, 1971).
Roth, Philip, *My Life as a Man* (New York: Holt, Rinehart and Winston, 1974).
Roth, Philip, *Reading Myself and Others* [1975] (London: Vintage, 2000).
Roth, Philip, *The Professor of Desire* [1977] (London: Vintage, 2000).
Roth, Philip, *Zuckerman Bound: A Trilogy and Epilogue* [1985] (London: Vintage, 1998).
Roth, Philip, *The Counterlife* [1986] (London: Jonathan Cape, 1987).
Roth, Philip, *Patrimony: A True Story* (London: Jonathan Cape, 1991).
Roth, Philip, *American Pastoral* [1997] (London: Vintage, 2000).
Roth, Philip, *I Married a Communist* (London: Jonathan Cape, 1998).
Roth, Philip, *The Human Stain* (London: Vintage, 2000).
Roth, Philip, *Shop Talk* (London: Vintage, 2001).
Roth, Philip, *The Plot Against America* (London: Jonathan Cape, 2004).
Roth, Philip, *Exit Ghost* (London: Vintage, 2007).
Roth, Philip, 'Bush Is Too Horrendous to Be Forgotten', *Der Spiegel*, 8 February 2008, www.spiegel.international/de/world/spiegel-interview-with-author-philip-roth-bush-is-too-horrendous-to-be-forgotten-a-534018.html.
Roth, Philip, 'In Memory of a Friend, Teacher, and Mentor', *New York Times*, 20, April 2013, L6.
Roth, Philip, 'A Czech Education', in *Why Write?: Collected Nonfiction 1960–2013* (New York: Library of America, 2017), pp. 368–370.
Roth, Philip, '*The Counterlife*: Notes' [October 5, 1985], Box 79, Folder 2, Philip Roth Papers, Library of Congress, Washington, DC.
Rothberg, Michael, *Multidirectional Memory: Remembering the Holocaust in the Age of Decolonization* (Stanford: Stanford University Press, 2009).
Royal, Derek Parker (ed.), *Philip Roth: New Perspectives on an American Author* (Westport: Praeger, 2005).
Royal, Derek Parker, 'Pastoral Dreams and National Identity in *American Pastoral* and *I Married a Communist*', in Derek Parker Royal (ed.), *Philip Roth: New Perspectives on an American Author* (Westport: Praeger, 2005), pp. 185–208.
Royal, Derek Parker, 'Plotting the Frames of Subjectivity: Identity, Death, and Narrative in Philip Roth's *The Human Stain*', *Contemporary Literature*, 47:1 (Spring 2006), pp. 114–140.

Royal, Derek Parker, 'Introduction', in Royal (ed.), *Unfinalized Moments: Essays in the Development of Contemporary Jewish American Narrative* (West Lafayette: Purdue University Press, 2011).

Rush, Norman, *Subtle Bodies* (New York: Knopf, 2013).

Russell, Alison, 'Deconstructing *The New York Trilogy*: Paul Auster's Anti-Detective Fiction', *Critique: Studies in Contemporary Fiction*, 31:2 (1990), pp. 71–84.

Safer, Elaine, *Mocking the Age: The Later Novels of Philip Roth* (Albany: State University of New York Press, 2006).

Saint, Lily, 'From a Distance: Teju Cole, World Literature, and the Limits of Cosmopolitanism', *Novel*, 51:2 (2018), pp. 322–338.

Salvatore, Nick, *Eugene V. Debs: Citizen and Socialist* (Urbana: University of Illinois Press, 1982).

Sandel, Michael, *Liberalism and the Limits of Justice* (Cambridge: Cambridge University Press, 1982).

Schiff, James, 'A Conversation with Jonathan Lethem' in Jaime Clarke (ed.), *Conversations with Jonathan Lethem* (Jackson: University of Mississippi Press, 2011), pp. 100–115.

Schmidt, Michael, *The Novel: A Biography* (Cambridge, MA: Belknap Press, 2014).

Schrift, Alan (ed.), *The Logic of the Gift: Toward an Ethic of Generosity* (New York: Routledge, 1997).

Schwartz, Barry, *Abraham Lincoln in the Post-Heroic Era: History and Memory in Late Twentieth-Century America* (Chicago: University of Chicago Press, 2008).

Schwarzenbach, Sibyl, *On Civic Friendship: Including Women in the State* (New York: Columbia University Press, 2009).

Schweitzer, Ivy, *Perfecting Friendship: Politics and Affiliation in Early American Literature* (Chapel Hill: University of North Carolina Press, 2006).

Scorza, Jasonn, *Strong Liberalism: Habits of Mind for Democratic Citizenship* (Medford: Tufts University Press, 2008).

Scott, A. O., 'When Dylan Met Mingus', *New York Times Book Review*, 21 September 2003.

Sedgwick, Eve Kosofsky, *Between Men: English Literature and Male Homosocial Desire* (New York: Columbia University Press, 1985).

Sedgwick, Eve Kosofsky, *Epistemology of the Closet* [1990] (Berkeley: University of California Press, 2008).

Segal, Alex, 'Secrecy and the Gift: Paul Auster's *The Locked Room*', *Critique: Studies in Contemporary Fiction*, 39:3 (1998), pp. 239–257.

Self, Robert, '"To Plan Our Liberation": Black Power and the Politics of Place in Oakland, California, 1965–1977', *Journal of Urban History*, 27:6 (September 2000), pp. 759–792.

Self, Robert, *American Babylon: Race and the Struggle for Postwar Oakland* (Princeton: Princeton University Press, 2003).
Sennett, Robert, *The Fall of Public Man* [1977] (London: Penguin, 2003).
Severs, Jeffrey, *David Foster Wallace's Balancing Books: Fictions of Value* (New York: Columbia University Press, 2017).
Shechner, Mark, *Up Society's Ass, Copper: Rereading Philip Roth* (Madison: University of Wisconsin Press, 2003).
Shechner, Mark, 'Roth's American Trilogy', in Timothy Parrish (ed.), *The Cambridge Companion to Philip Roth* (Cambridge: Cambridge University Press, 2007), pp. 142–158.
Shell, Marc, *Money, Language and Thought* (Baltimore: Johns Hopkins University Press, 1982).
Sherman, Sandra, 'Book Review: Writing and the Rise of Finance: Capital Satires of the Early Eighteenth Century', *Eighteenth-Century Studies*, 31:1 (Fall 1997), pp. 144–145.
Shipe, Matthew, '*Exit Ghost* and the Politics of "Late Style"', *Philip Roth Studies*, 5:2 (Fall 2009), pp. 189–204.
Shostak, Debra, *Philip Roth: Countertexts, Counterlives* (Columbia: University of Southern Carolina Press, 2004).
Shostak, Debra, 'Roth and Gender', in Timothy Parrish (ed.), *The Cambridge Companion to Philip Roth* (Cambridge: Cambridge University Press, 2007), pp. 111–126.
Shostak, Debra (ed.), *Philip Roth: American Pastoral, The Human Stain, The Plot Against America* (London: Continuum, 2011).
Silverblatt, Michael, 'An Interview with Jonathan Lethem', in Jaime Clarke (ed.), *Conversations with Jonathan Lethem* (Jackson: University of Mississippi Press, 2011), pp. 69–77.
Simmons, Ryan, 'What Is a Terrorist? Contemporary Authorship, the Unabomber, and *Mao II*', *Modern Fiction Studies*, 45:3 (Fall 1999), pp. 675–695.
Simon, Bryant, *Everything but the Coffee: Learning about America from Starbucks* (Berkeley: University of California Press, 2009).
Simon, Sunka, *Mail-Orders: The Fiction of Letters in Postmodern Culture* (Albany: State University of New York Press, 2002).
Smith, Graham, *Friendship and the Political: Kierkegaard, Nietzsche, Schmitt* (Exeter: Imprint Academic, 2011).
Smith, Neil, *Uneven Development: Nature, Capital, and the Production of Space* [1984] (Athens: University of Georgia Press, 2003).
Smith, Vanessa, *Intimate Strangers: Friendship, Exchange and Pacific Encounters* (Cambridge: Cambridge University Press, 2010).
Smith, Zadie, 'The Difficult Gifts of David Foster Wallace', in Smith, *Changing My Mind: Occasional Essays* (London: Penguin, 2009), pp. 257–300.

Smith-Rosenberg, Caroll, 'The Female World of Love and Ritual: Relations between Women in Nineteenth-Century America', *Signs*, 1:1 (Autumn 1975), pp. 1–29.

Sollors, Werner, 'Cosmopolitan Curiosity in an Open City: Notes on Reading Teju Cole by way of Kwame Anthony Appiah', *New Literary History*, 49:2 (Spring 2018), pp. 227–248.

Solnit, Rebecca, *Hope in the Dark: Untold Histories, Wild Possibilities* (Chicago: Haymarket Books, 2004).

Solotaroff, Theodore, 'The Journey of Philip Roth', *Atlantic Monthly*, April 1969, pp. 64–72.

Solotaroff, Theodore, 'The New York Publishing World', in Bernard Rosenberg and Ernest Goldstein (eds), *Creators and Disturbers: Reminiscences by Jewish Intellectual of New York* (New York: Columbia University Press, 1982), pp. 401–419.

Soske, Jon and Joanna Walsh, 'Thinking About Race and Friendship in South Africa', in Soske and Walsh (eds), *Ties that Bind: Race and the Politics of Friendship in South Africa* (Johannesburg: Wits University Press, 2016), pp. 3–30.

Spanos, William, 'The Detective and the Boundary: Some Notes on the Postmodern Literary Imagination', *Boundary 2*, 1:1 (Autumn 1972), pp. 147–168.

Spargo, R. Clifton, 'How Telling: Irving Howe, Roth's Early Career, and the Dialectic of Impersonation in *The Anatomy Lesson*', *Philip Roth Studies*, 5:2 (Fall 2009), pp. 251–279.

Spragens, Thomas, *Civic Liberalism: Reflections on Our Democratic Ideals* (Lanham: Rowman & Littlefield, 1999).

Springer, Carsten, *A Paul Auster Sourcebook* (Frankfurt: Peter Lang, 2001).

Stein, Lorin, 'The Art of Fiction No. 177: Jonathan Lethem', in Jaime Clarke (ed.), *Conversations with Jonathan Lethem* (Jackson: University of Mississippi Press, 2011), pp. 46–68.

Stern-Gillet, Suzanne, *Aristotle's Philosophy of Friendship* (Albany: State University of New York Press, 1995).

Stockton, Kathryn Bond, *The Queer Child, or Growing Sideways in the Twentieth Century* (Durham, NC: Duke University Press, 2009).

Stonebridge, Lyndsey, *The Judicial Imagination: Writing after Nuremberg* (Edinburgh: Edinburgh University Press, 2011).

Stonebridge, Lyndsey, *Placeless People: Writing, Rights, and Refugees* (Oxford: Oxford University Press, 2018).

Sugrue, Thomas, *The Origins of the Urban Crisis: Race and Inequality in Postwar Detroit* [1996] (Princeton: Princeton University Press, 2005).

Sundquist, Eric, *Strangers in the Land: Blacks, Jews, Post-Holocaust America* (Cambridge, MA: Belknap Press, 2005).

Szalay, Michael, *Hip Figures: A Literary History of the Democratic Party* (Stanford: Stanford University Press, 2012).
Tanenbaum, Laura, 'Reading Roth's Sixties', *Studies in American Jewish Literature*, 23 (2004), pp. 41–54.
Tate, Allen, 'Tension in Poetry', *Southern Review*, 4 (January 1938), pp. 101–116.
Taussig, Gurion, *Coleridge and the Idea of Friendship, 1789–1804* (Newark: University of Delaware Press, 2002).
Thompson, Peter and Slavoj Zizek (eds), *The Privatisation of Hope: Ernst Bloch and the Future of Utopia* (Durham, NC: Duke University Press, 2013).
Thurman, Judith, 'Philip Roth E-mails on Trump', *The New Yorker*, 30 January 2017.
Thurschwell, Pamela, 'The Ghost Worlds of Modern Adolescence', in Maria del Pilar Blanco and Esther Peeren (eds), *Popular Ghosts: The Haunted Spaces of Everyday Culture* (London: Continuum, 2010), pp. 239–250.
Thurschwell, Pamela, 'Bringing Nanda Forward, or Acting Your Age in *The Awkward Age*', *Critical Quarterly*, 58:2 (2016), pp. 72–90.
Toronto, Amanda Ryan, 'Ekphrasis and the Religious Impulse in Late-Twentieth-Century American Fiction', New York University, PhD Thesis, 2009.
Trilling, Lionel, 'Manners, Morals, and the Novel', *Kenyon Review*, 10 (1948), pp. 11–27.
Uchiyama, Kanae, 'Narrating the Other between Ethics and Violence: Friendship and Politics in Paul Auster's *The Locked Room* and *Leviathan*', *English Society of Japan*, 2:7 (2004), pp. 60–78.
Van Der Zweerde, Evert, 'Friendship and the Political', *Critical Review of International Social and Political Philosophy*, 10:2 (2007), pp. 147–165.
Van Marle, Karin, 'Laughter, Refusal, Friendship: Thoughts on a "Jurisprudence of Generosity"', *Stellenbosch Law Review*, 18 (2007), pp. 194–206.
Varvogli, Aliki, *The World that Is the Book: Paul Auster's Fiction* (Liverpool: Liverpool University Press, 2001).
Varvogli, Aliki, 'Urban Mobility and Race: Dinaw Mengestu's *The Beautiful Things that Heaven Bears* and Teju Cole's *Open City*', *Studies in American Fiction*, 44:2 (Fall 2017), pp. 235–257.
Verma, Neil, *Theater of the Mind: Imagination, Aesthetics, and American Radio Drama* (Chicago: University of Chicago Press, 2012).
Vermeulen, Pieter, 'Flights of Memory: Teju Cole's *Open City* and the Limits of Aesthetic Cosmopolitanism', *Journal of Modern Literature*, 37:1 (Fall 2013), pp. 40–57.

Vernon, Mark, *The Philosophy of Friendship* (Basingstoke: Palgrave Macmillan, 2005).

Vincent, Ricky, *Party Music: The Inside Story of the Black Panthers' Band and How Black Power Transformed Soul Music* (Chicago: Lawrence Hill Books, 2013).

Wade, Francesca, '"You Don't Have to Live Like This", by Benjamin Markovits', *Financial Times*, 24 July 2015.

Wakeman, Rosemary, *Practicing Utopia: An Intellectual History of the New Town Movement* (Chicago: University of Chicago Press, 2016).

Walkowitz, Rebecca, *Cosmopolitan Style: Modernism Beyond the Nation* (New York: Columbia University Press, 2006).

Walkowitz, Rebecca, *Born Translated: The Contemporary Novel in an Age of World Literature* (New York: Columbia University Press, 2015).

Wallace, David Foster, 'John Updike, Champion Literary Phallocrat, Drops One; Is This Finally the End for Magnificent Narcissists?', *New York Observer*, 12 October 1997, p. 3.

Walter, Jess, '"Telegraph Avenue", by Michael Chabon', *SFGate*, 7 September 2012.

Walzer, Michael, 'The Pastoral Retreat of the New Left', *Dissent*, Fall 1979, pp. 406–411.

Walzer, Michael, 'Philosophy and Democracy', *Political Theory*, 9:3 (August 1981), pp. 379–399.

Walzer, Michael, 'The Communitarian Critique of Liberalism', *Political Theory*, 18:1. (February 1990), pp. 6–23.

Warner, Michael, *Publics and Counterpublics* (New York: Zone Books, 2005).

Weinstein, Cindy, *Time, Tense, and American Literature: When Is Now?* (Cambridge: Cambridge University Press, 2015).

Weller, Barry, 'The Rhetoric of Friendship in Montaigne's Essais', *New Literary History*, 9:3 (Spring 1978), pp. 503–523.

Whitfield, Stephen, *In Search of Jewish American Culture* (Hanover: Brandeis University Press, 1999).

Wiegman, Robyn, *American Anatomies: Theorizing Race and Gender* (Durham, NC: Duke University Press, 1995).

Wilcox, Amanda, *The Gift of Correspondence in Classical Rome: Friendship in Cicero's* Ad Familiares *and Seneca's* Moral Epistles (Madison: University of Wisconsin Press, 2012).

Williams, Ian, '(New) Sincerity in David Foster Wallace's "Octet"', *Critique: Studies in Contemporary Fiction*, 56:3 (2015), pp. 299–314.

Williams, Raymond, *Marxism and Literature* (Oxford: Oxford University Press, 1977).

Williams, Yohuru, *Rethinking the Black Freedom Movement* (New York: Routledge, 2016).

Wirth-Nesher, Hana, 'The Artist Tales of Philip Roth', *Prooftexts*, 3:3 (September 1983), pp. 263–272.
Wirth-Nesher, Hana, 'Defining the Indefinable: What Is Jewish Literature?', in Wirth-Nesher (ed.), *What Is Jewish Literature?* (Philadelphia: The Jewish Publication Society, 1994), pp. 3–12.
Wood, Michael, 'New Voices, New Challenges 1970–2000', in Hana Wirth-Nesher (ed.), *The Cambridge History of Jewish American Literature* (Cambridge: Cambridge University Press, 2015), pp. 144–162.
Wood, James, 'The Sentimentalist: Review of *I Married a Communist*', *The New Republic*, 12 October 1998, pp. 38–42.
Wood, James, 'Spaldeen Dreams', *The New Republic*, 13 October 2003.
Wood, James, 'The Arrival of Enigmas', *The New Yorker*, 28 February 2011.
Woods, Tom, '*The Music of Chance*: Aleatorical (Dis)harmonies Within "The City of the World"', in Paul Barone (ed.), *Beyond the Red Notebook: Essays on Paul Auster* (Philadelphia: University of Pennsylvania Press, 1995), pp. 143–162.
Zieger, Robert, *The CIO, 1935–1955* (Chapel Hill: University of North Carolina Press, 1995).
Zizek, Slavoj, 'Preface: Bloch's Ontology of Not-Yet-Being', in Peter Thompson and Slavoj Zizek (eds), *The Privatisation of Hope: Ernst Bloch and the Future of Utopia* (Durham, NC: Duke University Press, 2013), pp. xv–xx.

Index

Agamben, Giorgio 126
Appiah, Kwame Anthony 187, 191, 193, 195
Arendt, Hannah 191–198
Aristotle 7–8, 10, 11, 12, 85, 95, 193
Auster, Paul 3, 20, 21, 60
   'Auggie Wren's Christmas Story' 110
   The Brooklyn Follies 101
   Hand to Mouth 103–105
   In the Country of Last Things 122n.4
   The Invention of Solitude 104
   Leviathan 83, 88–99, 100, 102, 103, 110, 125, 183
   The Locked Room 83, 91–93, 97, 98, 100, 102, 105
   Moon Palace 105
   Mr. Vertigo 119n.105
   The Music of Chance 105–107, 110
   The New York Trilogy 91
   Oracle Night 83, 99–103, 105, 111
   Smoke 108–112, 120–124, 127, 146, 149, 157, 161, 183
Auster, Paul and J. M. Coetzee
   Here and Now 82–84, 99, 103, 111

Bellow, Saul 20, 37
Benjamin, Walter 143, 186–187, 191, 195, 201n.45
Berlant, Lauren 94, 123, 125, 126, 131, 142
Blanchot, Maurice 124, 162
Bloch, Ernst 126, 162
Booth, Wayne 86–87

Chabon, Michael 3, 20, 149, 158, 162, 204, 206
   The Amazing Adventures of Kavalier & Clay 21
   'Fountain City' 166n.40, 167n.43
   Telegraph Avenue 22, 127–147, 208
civic friendship 7–9, 10, 11, 13, 14, 17, 18, 46, 54, 95, 122, 123, 161
Coetzee, J. M. 82, 85, 87, 88, 103, 111
   see *Here and Now*
Cole, Teju 3, 175–177
   Open City 21, 22, 185–198
   'A Piece in the Wall' 199n.12
   'The White Savior Industrial Complex' 199n.12, 201n.45, 201n.63

Index

communitarianism 6, 7–9, 11, 12, 13, 17, 18, 46–48, 54, 122, 124, 127, 135, 183–184, 196
Corwin, Norman 42, 43, 55–56, 57, 58
  On a Note of Triumph 44, 54–56
cosmopolitanism 10, 22, 187–188, 190, 192, 195, 196, 197

Derrida, Jacques 9–12, 81, 85, 86–87, 92, 110
  The Politics of Friendship 9–11, 124–125

Emerson, Ralph Waldo 84–86, 87, 94, 95, 183
  'Friendship' 84–85
  'Gifts' 87
  'Politics' 94–95
ethical criticism 85–86, 87, 88, 113–114n.20

Fanon, Frantz 135, 138–139, 169n.82
Fiedler, Leslie 15–16, 18, 31, 64, 123, 163n.7, 208
Foucault, Michel 11, 12
  'Friendship as a Way of Life' 11

Howe, Irving 42, 43
Hyde, Lewis 82, 86, 87, 105

interracial male friendship 15–17, 18, 22, 64, 119n.105, 127, 130, 133, 158, 162, 175, 205, 208, 209
  Black and Jewish friendship 64, 128, 129, 136, 137, 153

Jacobs, Jane 151, 172n.124
Jelloun, Tahar Ben 186, 195, 197
  The Last Friend 186, 197

Jewish identity 20–21, 57, 63, 64, 128, 136, 141, 153, 190–191, 192, 193, 194, 196, 197, 208–209, 212n.19

Lethem, Jonathan 3, 20, 21, 86, 127
  Dissident Gardens 147–149
  The Fortress of Solitude 127, 149–162

Markovits, Benjamin 22, 202–210
  Playing Days 204, 212n.19
  You Don't Have to Live Like This, 202–208
Mengestu, Dinaw 3, 21, 175–177, 189, 193
  The Beautiful Things that Heaven Bears 22, 175–185, 193
  How to Read the Air 189, 199n.19
Mouffe, Chantal 26n.58, 122

Nancy, Jean-Luc 124, 162

Obama, Barack 144–146, 170n.96, 204, 211n.9

Paine, Thomas, 50, 51, 52–54, 56, 77n.120
postmodernism 19, 82, 86, 99, 125
  and post-postmodernism 19–20, 36, 127, 149, 162

queer theory 34–35, 156
  and friendship 13, 132
  and time 125–126, 132

Rawls, John 122
Roth, Philip 3, 20, 21, 22, 93, 203, 211n.6

Roth, Philip (*cont.*)
  American Pastoral 29, 30, 31, 32, 37, 38, 43, 45, 47, 52, 64, 76n.104, 111
  'The American Trilogy' 21, 30, 31, 32, 43, 45, 64, 89, 93, 94, 96, 99, 203, 209
  The Anatomy Lesson 35
  The Counterlife 32, 46
  Exit Ghost 66
  The Ghost Writer 32, 34, 36, 37, 52, 66
  The Human Stain, 30, 31, 32, 50, 59, 61–68, 89, 90, 205, 208
  I Married a Communist 29, 30, 31, 35–61, 63, 65, 67, 68, 90, 94, 203, 207, 209
  Letting Go 34
  My Life as a Man 33
  Operation Shylock 33
  Patrimony 29, 39
  The Plot Against America 73n.64
  Portnoy's Complaint 55
  Zuckerman Unbound 33
Rush, Norman 1–3, 4, 5, 34
  Subtle Bodies 1–2, 4–5, 12, 125, 132, 171n.117, 203, 210

Sandel, Michael 7, 8, 9, 46, 122

Trilling, Lionel 42, 57, 78n.141, 85, 86

utopianism 2, 10, 11, 15, 18, 52, 55, 94, 100–101, 111, 125, 129, 130, 134, 135, 136, 140, 143, 149, 154, 161, 178, 209
  post-utopian utopianism 124–127, 137, 144, 147, 158, 162

Walzer, Michael 136

EU authorised representative for GPSR:
Easy Access System Europe, Mustamäe tee 50,
10621 Tallinn, Estonia
gpsr.requests@easproject.com

www.ingramcontent.com/pod-product-compliance
Lightning Source LLC
Chambersburg PA
CBHW070325240426
43671CB00013BA/2364